A Good Long Drive

CHARLES N. PROTHRO TEXANA SERIES

A Good Long Drive

FIFTY YEARS OF
TEXAS COUNTRY REPORTER

Bob Phillips

University of Texas Press   *Austin*

Requests for permission to reproduce material from this work should be
sent to:
    Permissions
    University of Texas Press
    P.O. Box 7819
    Austin, TX 78713-7819
    utpress.utexas.edu/rp-form

♾ The paper used in this book meets the minimum requirements of ANSI/
NISO Z39.48-1992 (R1997) (Permanence of Paper).

LIBRARY OF CONGRESS CATALOGING-IN-PUBLICATION DATA

Names: Phillips, Bob, 1951– author.
Title: A good long drive : fifty years of Texas country reporter / Bob Phillips.
Description: First edition. | Austin : University of Texas Press, 2021.
Identifiers: LCCN 2021007073
    ISBN 978-1-4773-2401-1 (cloth)
    ISBN 978-1-4773-2402-8 (library ebook)
    ISBN 978-1-4773-2403-5 (ebook)
Subjects: LCSH: Phillips, Bob, 1951– | Texas country reporter—History. |
    Television journalists—Texas—Biography. | Nonfiction television
    programs—Texas—History.
Classification: LCC PN4874.P479 A3 2021 | DDC 070.92 [B]—dc23
LC record available at https://lccn.loc.gov/2021007073
doi:10.7560/324011

To my mom and dad, who taught me that all people are important and have a story to tell.

To Eddie Barker and the people of KDFW-TV, for giving a kid a chance.

To Ward Huey, Dave Lane, and the people of WFAA-TV, for believing in me.

And to Charles Kuralt, Tom Landry, Ann Voss Gillespie, and my brother Bill, who each had a hand in turning a boy from Old East Dallas into a good man.

Contents

Prologue

THE THREE-HOUR DRIVE FROM NACOGDOCHES TO DALLAS was long. And silent, except for the occasional "Do you think maybe . . . ?" offered by one of the four of us in the van.

My three traveling buddies—Jamie Aitken, Jason Anderson, and Larry Ellis—and I were halfway through an interview with a guy who called himself Red Eagle, a medicine man who was set to offer up his opinions and philosophies on anything we asked, when his wife brought us an urgent message from the TV station in Dallas where we worked.

"Return to the office immediately" is all it said. The call was placed by the news director's assistant.

It was September 1986 and the four of us made up the production crew for a television show that had started fourteen years earlier, almost to the day, called *4 Country Reporter*. Cell phones were still new to the market and unaffordable for those of us who lived on a salary paid by a local television station, so we just had to point our van toward Big D and drive. And wonder what the hell was going on.

"You don't think we're getting cancelled, do you?" Jason said to me.

"I don't know," I said, "but that wouldn't make sense. We had our best ratings ever in last May's book."

The "book" I referred to was the Nielsen and Arbitron television ratings, which were compiled every February, May, and November to find out how many people watched a particular TV show. There was a July book, too, but most of us ignored it, because we all knew that people don't watch as much television during the summer months when the kids are out of school and families are on vacation—the reason for the summer rerun season. And we were a family show. Good, wholesome stories with almost no negative content, just feel-good fare that was intended to make people more positive about the world we all live in. A show about being in love with Texas.

So the May book was the last one that counted, and that had been the second time we beat the number one syndicated show in America. It also happened in February 1986.

4 Country Reporter aired on KDFW-TV (in those days the CBS affiliate in Dallas–Fort Worth) at 6:30 on Saturday evening. *Wheel of Fortune* had been kicking everything in the teeth that came up against it over on KXAS-TV (the NBC affiliate) in the same time slot. It was a Monday through Friday show, but even the rerun episodes that aired on Saturday night always had incredible audience numbers. And our local show about Texas had just beaten "The Wheel" by a single share point (percentage of homes actually watching TV at the time), 23 to 22. It was the only market in America where the competition did not come out on top, and that not only made us very proud of our little show, which was cobbled together with almost no budget, but it brought some great attention to what we were doing. Even *Broadcast Magazine*, a national publication read mostly by television and advertising people, gave us a mention.

No, we just beat the competition, so cancellation can't be what this is about, I told myself over and over as we drove. But I was not convinced. I had a bad feeling. A very bad feeling.

So after we pulled into the basement garage at Channel 4, at 400 North Griffin Street in downtown Dallas, we walked to news director Wendell Harris's office in the studio on the first floor. The four of us had absolutely no idea what to expect. But Wendell had an important announcement.

"Boys," he said, "take a seat."

What came next changed my life. But at that moment, there in Wendell's office, I had no idea what was ahead for me, for my crew, or for our show.

This is the story of how a simple local TV program became a beloved Texas icon with a place in the hearts of millions of people.

It's a story about the kind of stories we tell on that show and why we think it's important to tell them, and how the show itself became a part of the story. We will tell some of those stories here, not just for their entertainment value but also to show the range of what we do and how we've been doing it for fifty years.

And it's also a story about the unlikely kid from Dallas whose life work somehow became that TV show, and how that show somehow became him.

To tell you the rest of this story, I'll first have to go all the way back to the beginning.

A Good Long Drive

Part One

ONLY THE BEGINNING

I GUESS WE ALL HAVE A FIRST MEMORY IN LIFE.
Mine is sitting naked in a galvanized tub of water at the bottom
of the stairs that went into the kitchen of our family's duplex on Bryan Parkway in Old East Dallas.

It was a rental that we paid $10 a week to occupy. My dad, my mom,
my brother, and me. I was born on June 23, 1951, at Dallas Osteopathic
Hospital, just up the street by the Sears and Roebuck store on Ross Avenue.
I figure the date of my memory of splashing in the galvanized bucket was
probably about July 1954, because that's when my family moved two doors
down to a single-family house that cost $15 more a month. The lady who
lived on the other side of the duplex kept me out of the way while the move
took place.

I was the only member of our little family who was born in Dallas. My
dad, Leon Phillips (no middle name), my mom, Sue Elma (Garvin) Phillips,
and my older brother, Billy Ray Phillips (*not* William—*Billy*), were all born
in Grayson County, north of Dallas and just south of the Red River, which
separates Texas from Oklahoma.

Daddy was born in December 1917 on a piece of land with no electricity
or indoor plumbing, near the town of Whitesboro, where Mama was born.
The family farmed about eighty acres and raised a few cows, pigs, and chickens. When my grandfather Ray Phillips died of throat cancer, Daddy was
only in the seventh grade but quit school to take over the farm. To me it
sounded like hell, but Daddy loved it and had nothing but fond memories
of those times, even the hard times, until the day he died. He spoke often of
walking behind the two mules pulling the plow that cut into the earth where
they grew their crops, and of the joys of a good harvest after all that hard

work. I think people didn't hope for as much out of life back then. They expected it to be hard, so disappointment didn't come as often as it does to those of us who were born into a world that provides everything we need. If something failed, Daddy just started all over again. That's the way life was to him. I always wished I could be more like him in that way.

When my father, mother, and brother first moved to Dallas, the tallest building downtown was the one with the flying red horse on top. Daddy took a job with a company called Safety Service Stations and pumped gas at one of their locations, at the corner of Gaston Avenue and Haskell Street. They lived in a tiny apartment on Columbia Avenue.

My dad was also extremely polite, and no matter how well or how long he knew them, he always called his customers by their last name with Mr., Mrs., or Miss in front of it. Always. When I was in college and worked part-time for my dad at the service station to make some extra money, I discovered a secret. I was filling up a customer's car at the full-service pump and noticed their last name on a piece of paper taped to the car's gas cap. I figured out my dad put it there so everyone would get truly personal service. He didn't have much of a formal education, but he knew that anyone who would pay for someone else to fill up their car in the age of self-service gas stations would never see what was taped to their gas cap.

Daddy was big on providing life lessons. He thought exposure to certain things might help me pick the right path in life as I got older, kind of a "scared straight" exercise. He hoped that if he let me see the negative, maybe I'd run toward the positive.

For example, my attitude toward drinking, smoking, and drugs goes back to when my dad's uncle, who was what people called a wino, would come through Dallas and get in touch with my dad. Daddy wouldn't let him come to our house, but would always meet him somewhere and give him a pack of tobacco and rolling papers and whatever money he could afford, usually two or three dollars.

When Daddy would take me with him to meet up with his alcoholic uncle, who sometimes was in the local jail, on the way home he would tell me to never let the influences of alcohol, tobacco, or drugs drag me down and ruin my life like his uncle had. He would warn me that "this stuff runs in the family so don't let it run in you. . . . Hear what I'm saying?"

I heard it many times and, frankly, it scared me. I wasn't a rebellious kid, so I just never tried any of it. When my friends in high school wanted to drink and smoke pot, I was always the designated driver before that was even a thing. I didn't have much of an opinion about it but knew that it wasn't for me because Daddy had warned me "it runs in the family," even though I didn't know what that meant. I was too afraid to go down that road and thought for a long time that there was some special thing my family had that made people act like Daddy's uncle, and I knew I didn't want to be like him. As a result, I missed out on a lot of the parties, and I admit that, at times, I was a bit lonely. I knew I was not cool. I'm still not cool, but now I'm okay with the path I picked.

If you were to ask people who knew him to describe my dad, most would say "nice guy" at some point in their description: a nice guy who wished he could have lived his whole life as a farmer.

Mama was born in the front bedroom of a house on Whitesboro's Center Street, which ran north from Main Street near the strip of stores that were built on raised sidewalks. I remember that, when I was a kid, the hitching posts with rings for people to tie up their horses were still there. There were six kids in Mama's family, three boys and three girls, and my grandparents, Andrew Jackson Garvin and Rosetta Webb Garvin, lived with them too. I remember hearing stories of how Grandpa hitchhiked to Sherman during the Great Depression to work on a road crew for just a dollar a day. Times were tough, and my mother never forgot, or got over, that. The memories of having nothing made her vow to always have something. She was ambitious, and, I guess, compared to how things were in her childhood years, we were doing pretty well. Even so, I remember many times riding with Daddy up to a place where he could get $10 for selling his blood. Mama could take that ten bucks and feed us for a week or more. I do not remember ever being hungry, but I knew kids who were, so I always thought we were pretty lucky. Even though we didn't have much money, Mama always found a way to make it work. I still don't know how.

There weren't many other kids in my neighborhood. It was mostly older retired folks, so I had to find a way to entertain myself. In some ways, mostly ways that affect the creative side of our brains, keeping myself occupied was probably a good thing. In other ways, mostly ways that make us social creatures, being by myself so much of the time may not have been that great for me. I was a nerd by the time I could talk and have successfully retained that characteristic throughout my life.

One of the best ways I found to keep myself busy involved the pathway that ran between the rental houses on Bryan Parkway and the mansions on Swiss Avenue. It was a rutted, unpaved road of thick North Texas clay, and the biggest mess you ever saw when it was wet. Officially, the alley was used primarily as a place to leave garbage out for pickup. Lord knows, those rich folks on Swiss Avenue did not want their garbage cans sitting in front of their beautiful homes. If you could see the houses I'm talking about, you probably wouldn't blame them. Swiss Avenue is still, to me, one of the prettiest streets in Dallas.

Whenever I could steal away from my backyard, I would venture down that alley to see what I could find. It didn't take me long to realize that people with more money often throw away some good stuff. It's amazing that I didn't grow up to become a junk dealer, but it's something I could still fall back on if everything else goes south. I am fascinated by the things Americans throw in the trash. Had I continued down the path of investigative reporting, this may have become a useful skill, but as a feature reporter, I have never used my expertise in collecting things that other people throw away.

I would go from house to house and dig through the garbage, mostly concentrating on the Swiss Avenue side of the alley because many of the older people on Bryan Parkway had lived during the Great Depression, and no one who lived through that time ever threw anything away. You may need it someday, and almost anything can be reused. I had an aunt who made us wash the aluminum foil and fold it so she could use it again, and another who tried washing paper plates.

I found all kinds of things in those garbage cans, and once my wagon was full, I would take them back to the hiding place in our garage where I kept all my treasures. Then, from time to time, I would drag them out, look at them, think about them, and, yes, even make up stories about them. On second thought, maybe my salvaging skills *have* helped my career.

Once a week a big orange dump truck with "City of Dallas Sanitation Department" on both doors would turn into the alley at the end of our street. Three men worked on the truck: one driving, one walking to the side and slightly behind, and one riding in the back.

They would stop at each house briefly while the man who was walking hoisted the old galvanized aluminum cans, full of garbage, one at a time, and with a little effort he would throw the can up to the guy riding in the back. That guy emptied the can and threw it back to the walking guy, who placed it back where it belonged, then they would move on to the next house and do it all again.

The man who rode in the back of that City of Dallas garbage truck was my very first hero. I wanted his job. You see, in the mind of a six-year-old kid who spent all his free time going through other people's garbage, the guy in the back of the truck was probably the most senior member of that three-man team: the boss. I figured he'd had to wait in line for that job to open up because I just knew that at the end of the day, the man who rode in the back would go through everything he'd emptied out of those cans and keep all the good stuff. Of course, on my block, I had already beaten him to that, so there wasn't much left.

Whenever I was introduced to someone new and they asked the proverbial question "What do you want to be when you grow up?" I would always immediately and proudly say, "I want to be a garbage man!" And, at that time, I meant it. Now, here's the good part, the part that sticks in my memory. It meant nothing to me at the time because it's one of those things in life that requires the perspective of many years on the planet, but I sure do appreciate it now.

Whenever I would say, "I want to be a garbage man!," my mom and dad would proudly say, "That's what he wants to be, all right!" as if they were truly excited about the possibility of their youngest son becoming a garbage collector. As it turned out, garbage management would have been a good choice because, as I've said for years, whoever figures out what to do with all our garbage will be a very successful and probably wealthy person. But I don't think most parents would be as supportive as mine were. In fact, some of them might be embarrassed enough to say, "Oh, he doesn't mean that, he's only six."

My mom and dad told me and my brother many times that we were lucky because we were growing up in the greatest state in the greatest country in the world, and we could become just about anything we wanted. My parents believed that the United States was the land of opportunity, and for some people it was. I even remember that when Alaska and Hawaii became the forty-ninth and fiftieth states, my dad retired the old forty-eight-star flag and said, "Maybe one of you boys will go to Alaska someday. They still have homesteading there, so you can get free land if you'll just go there and work it." Having been raised a farmer, that sounded like an incredible deal to him.

Later, as the realities of the differences in people's places in life began to set in, I started to doubt whether we could be and do anything we wanted. The good news is that after having some success in life myself, I got over it, and I'm now a big believer in the possibilities of the American Dream. It's something I want for everyone, and I still believe it can be.

My mom insisted that I grow up in such a way that I would know how to handle just about any situation. From the time I was five or six, she would go out of her way to expose me to things that most kids, at least most kids in our socioeconomic group, were not privy to. She stressed that there were different rules for different settings, and she used that as a way to explain to me why my school clothes were fine for school, but there would be times that I would need to wear a coat and tie. Most kids I knew didn't ever want to wear a coat and tie, but perhaps because my mom taught me so early, I was just fine with it.

My mother always had a job, but to make extra money, she would work at the Merchandise Mart (later the Apparel Mart) during the Women's and Children's Market held in Dallas every three months. Her boss was Milton Schulman, who owned a store called Tops and Bottoms along with some other retail clothing outlets. The quarterly market was a way to put clothing wholesalers and retailers together. Mr. Schulman had his own line of women's clothing that he sold to other retailers at the market. Mama served as both sales lady and model. She was a beautiful woman and the perfect size, so that's what she wore to work every day at the Merchandise Mart.

The market always kicked off with a huge party hosted by a local wholesaler, Nardis of Dallas. It started with a nice dinner at the Statler-Hilton Hotel on Commerce Street (kitty-corner from the Dallas Police headquarters, where Jack Ruby shot Lee Harvey Oswald). Today that Hilton Hotel has been restored to its former glory. The *Dallas Morning News*, among other businesses, now calls it home after its significant downsizing a few years back.

My dad didn't care much for things like the Nardis party, and that was just fine with Mama because she had something else in mind. Starting when I was six, I served as her escort to that event. She made a big deal out of it and talked about it for weeks before so I would know it was coming. I was to wear a coat and tie, of course, but my training didn't stop there. When we left to drive downtown, not too many blocks from where we lived in Old East Dallas, I was to open every door for her, including the car door. When we arrived, we went through a reception line, where I was expected to look people in the eye and offer a firm handshake while telling them my name.

At the table, I seated my mother before I sat down. The dinner was served in several courses, and I knew which fork was used for each one because Mama and I had practiced at the dining room table for weeks before the party. I was also expected to introduce myself and my mother to everyone at our table. All of this may seem a bit extreme for a six-year-old boy, but it would come in handy later in my life.

If you were to ask people who knew her to describe my mom, they would say things like "feisty," "temperamental," and "ambitious." She was a dedicated mother who put her kids first and never felt like enough was enough. She loved my dad, but he had been content with life on the farm. She was not. She wanted her children to have everything they would need to make it in life.

Mom and Dad met during World War II when they were both working at Camp Howze, a German POW camp and infantry training camp northwest of Gainesville, Texas. Daddy was not away fighting the war because he had lost his left arm in a traffic accident a few years earlier, so helping to build the military camp in Cook County was the best he could do to help the war effort. Mom told us that the first time she saw him, he was nailing shingles to a roof. Imagine doing that with only one hand! But my dad could do almost anything. He could even tie his shoelaces, and one time I watched him drop an engine from a '58 Buick, rebuild it, and reinstall it single-handed. Literally.

Mama thought he was extremely handsome, and it wasn't long before they drove across the river to be married in Marietta, Oklahoma, where the age of consent was only fourteen. Mom always said they had to do that because she was only seventeen, but after she died, we found out she was a year older than she thought. If the Social Security Administration is correct, their trip to Oklahoma wasn't necessary. My brother, Billy Ray, was born nine months after they were married, but it would be seven years before I came along.

When the war ended, the three of them moved to Dallas so Daddy could get a job. After his stint at Safety Service and a few years of owning and operating his own service station, he went to work for Dunlap-Swain, a company that had full-service stations all over town. When Daddy died, the *Dallas Morning News* ran an article about him, in addition to his obituary, because he was so well known as "that nice one-armed man that worked at the service station by SMU."

I guess the reason I'm telling you all of this ancient history is because it had so much to do with not only how I grew up but with who I became. I have always thought that it was the combination of being raised by a nice guy who just wanted to be a farmer and a feisty, driven woman—plus having a brother who was several years older, so it was almost like we were both raised as only children—that made me who I am. I even have to admit that being poor was probably a good thing, because I know how to do a lot of things that people with money often don't; they can simply hire someone to take care of many of the details of life. We could not do that.

I often hear people say things like "I wouldn't change a thing" and "I have no regrets." But I have always thought those are two of the biggest lies we tell ourselves; there are things we would all change if we could, and you cannot live life without regrets. But I can honestly say I wouldn't change a thing about my childhood, because it prepared me to live the unique life that I still cannot believe I have lived.

CHAPTER TWO

*F*ROM THE END OF OUR BLOCK ON BRYAN PARKWAY, you could look down the four lanes of Live Oak Street and see parts of downtown Dallas. A streetcar that ran up the middle of the parkway would take you there for a nickel. But even though we were smack-dab in the heart of Dallas, that didn't keep my parents from having some of the same critters they might have had in the rural area where they grew up. I don't remember a time when we didn't have a few rabbits living in a huge cage my dad built on the side of the house. Funny thing is, he didn't put chicken wire on the bottom, so, rabbits being rabbits, they burrowed out and ran free all over the neighborhood. But they were always inside the cage at feeding time.

We also had a pet raccoon that lived in the mulberry tree behind our house. His name was Sam, and he had a red collar. Sometimes he would climb to the top of that tree and refuse to come down, so Daddy would stretch a ladder up the side and climb up there and get him. Sam would hiss a little but eventually would climb onto Daddy's shoulder and ride to the bottom. Daddy always thought Sam might have been afraid to climb back down the tree, so he never hesitated to go after him. He was a country boy, but he had a huge heart for animals.

At some point Daddy decided living in the city wasn't the life Sam was supposed to have. He told me that we had to take him with us on our next fishing trip to Lake Texoma, not far from my parents' hometown of Whites-boro, and set him free. The plan was to take off his collar and leave the cage open so Sam could make up his own mind about if and when he would wander off into the woods on the shore of the lake, but before we could even get the collar off, Sam bolted and was gone. We fished all night but didn't see him again, so we figured he would be okay and drove home. I think we were a bit surprised at how much Sam wanted to be on his own. I was glad he was free.

A year later we went to that same spot on another all-night fishing trip. We threw a few lines into the lake but eventually got sleepy and crawled into a makeshift tent we had brought with us. The next morning, Daddy woke up early to get the fire going so he could make coffee and biscuits in the cast-iron Dutch oven, and curled up next to him in the tent was Sam. He was still wearing that red collar. I woke up and thought I was dreaming. Sam hung out until after we finished eating, probably because he knew Daddy would give him some biscuits, then we took off the red collar and he slowly walked back into the woods. I cried like a baby because now Sam seemed like so much more than just a raccoon who was afraid of heights. He was like a member of the family. We never saw Sam again.

Daddy's best friend growing up still lived in Whitesboro and ran the feed store. We would visit him on every trip to see family, and one time, just as we were leaving to head back to Dallas, he asked my mom and dad if my brother and I could each have a baby chicken. It was just before Easter, and I guess that sounded okay to them, so he went into the feed store and came back with a white box with holes poked in the lid. The box was at least a foot square, because he said he didn't want to crowd the two chicks.

When we got home, we took the box out of the back seat of the old Studebaker and took off the lid to retrieve our two baby chicks. Out came a total of seventeen baby chickens running all over our backyard. Mama was furious, but Daddy laughed because he knew it was the same kind of joke he would play on someone, given the chance.

The seventeen chicks became seventeen fully grown chickens. We had a chain-link fence around the backyard, and they pretty much stayed there, but whenever someone left the back gate open, they would go into the unpaved alley where they could easily find earthworms to eat. I remember one of them wandered into the alley and under the City of Dallas garbage truck. He ended up with his leg turned around backwards, but he didn't seem to know anything was wrong and got along just fine. We named him Hopalong and let him keep being a chicken instead of dinner.

When the mulberry tree started getting berries, the chickens thought they were in heaven. They would eat those berries until they were ready to pop, then poop purple berry juice everywhere. By this time they had figured out that they could fly just high enough to clear the four-foot fence and go hang out in Mrs. Paul's backyard next door. She had a lovely garden, and the chickens would poop all over it and her old white car until Mrs. Paul would call my mother and tell her we needed to retrieve them. My mom would have conniptions every time the chickens took a trip to Mrs. Paul's, and she would tell my dad she was going to start turning those chickens into Sunday dinner. A couple of times she made good on that promise, and being a country girl, she thought nothing of grabbing a chicken and popping its neck so she could pluck its feathers and put it in a pot for supper. I was horrified and would immediately run to the backyard to see which chicken was gone. They all had names, so I knew who was in the pot and refused to eat chicken for a while.

One day Mama was getting ready to go to her Woman's Missionary Union of Texas meeting at East Dallas Baptist Church, where we attended services every time the doors were open—or at least that's how it seemed to me. She was all dressed up for what she called Circle Meeting, where the ladies were supposed to talk about helping out the missionaries supported by the church, but the real reason they got together was to eat stuff like tuna salad served on tomato slices, peaches and cottage cheese, and some kind of strange Jell-O with carrots in it. The conversation, it seemed, was more about all the people from church who were not at the meeting. As the silent preschool kid who got to go on these outings, I learned to eat Circle Meeting food too, and to this day I love tuna on tomato slices and peaches and cottage cheese. The strange Jell-O I can do without.

Anyway, just as we were about to leave for the meeting, Mrs. Paul called to say the chickens were in the midst of another mulberry pooping trip. Mama flew out of the house and started grabbing chickens and throwing them into the back seat of our old '51 Chevy sedan. When all fifteen remaining chickens were in the car, we climbed into the front seat and drove to Daddy's service station on Cockrell Street, right in front of the old Swift meatpacking plant on the edge of downtown Dallas. We skidded into the driveway of the service station, and Mama threw open the back door and shooed the chickens out of the car. She drove off without saying a word, and we went to Circle Meeting. Daddy just stood there watching the whole thing unfold. I don't know what became of the chickens, and Mama and Daddy never said a word about the incident—at least not in front of us kids.

Daddy later had to close the service station after Swift made the decision to move its operations to Chicago. Once the plant was closed and all the employees were gone, Daddy's service station on that dead-end street had no business. That was probably my first lesson in the realities of owning your own business. Somehow you have to pay your bills.

In addition to the chickens and other farm critters we had at our house, we always had a dog. The first one I remember was named Skippy, and he followed my brother everywhere. One summer day, Billy Ray and some friends went up to the City of Dallas's Tietze Park swimming pool, and Skippy followed along. He waited outside the fence while Billy swam with his friends until a lifeguard told them they were splashing other people too much and had to get out of the pool. When Billy didn't get out of the water as quickly as the lifeguard would have liked, he went in and grabbed my brother's arm and started to pull him out. Skippy was apparently threatened by this and raced through the turnstile and into the pool, where he promptly bit the lifeguard. The City of Dallas told us we had to get rid of him, and Mama said Skippy "went to live on a farm with some real nice people in the country." I later learned that just about every other kid I knew had been told the same thing when dogs and cats and puppies and kittens suddenly disappeared from their houses. Mama and Daddy never did tell us the truth about what happened to Skippy.

There were lots of other dogs too, including a huge red Chow that we looked after while a customer of my dad's went on an extended trip. His name was Fat Man, and he was bigger than I was. I would walk that big Chow all over the neighborhood, including up and down Gaston Avenue, just two streets away. One young guy, who looked about my brother's age, loved Fat Man and would always come out to see him when I walked by his apartment. He was very nice, but looked different from anyone else I had ever seen because he was white all over, even his eyes. My mother later explained that he was an albino, a person without pigment in their skin. I eventually learned that his little brother was also an albino. They were Johnny and Edgar Winter from Beaumont, and they had just moved to Dallas so Johnny could play his blues music in some of the juke joints in Deep Ellum. I remember later buying a Johnny Winter eight-track tape just because I had met him as a kid.

We also had a little terrier named Suzy Q, but for the life of me I don't know what happened to her. One day she just wasn't there. Maybe she went to live on a farm with some nice people.

Finally, in the fifth grade, I got *my* dog, a part-Chow little girl I named Judy Denise. I have no idea where I got that name, but I liked it for some reason. Throughout my life I have always given the animals in my life people names. Animals have few if any choices in life, so a good name has always seemed important to me, kind of a sign of respect for their dignity. I had Judy until I was in high school. One day I noticed she seemed sick, so I took her to the father of a high school friend who was a veterinarian. He told me her kidneys were shutting down and she was dying. He said the humane thing to do would be to euthanize her, but I didn't have the money, and I just wasn't sure if that was the right thing to do. I learned the hard way that death for animals is nothing compared to suffering, and I vowed to never put any animal through that again.

These stories about all the animals that were part of my growing up are important because when I was eight or nine, I decided the world would love to hear about my menagerie of critters and I should write a book. I called it "All My Dogs" because, in my simple mind, I thought people would be more drawn to a dog book than they would be to a book about chickens and rabbits and raccoons, because everybody likes dogs. I would slip in those stories about the other animals after they started reading about the dogs, and they would get the whole picture whether they liked it or not.

Mama took me to Moses Five and Dime on Skillman Street, where I bought a pad and a pencil for a nickel, and I started writing. I filled up all sixteen pages. The book was never published, of course, and I have no idea what happened to my pad over the years, but that moment set something in motion inside me that wouldn't go away and still has not. I knew what I wanted to do with my life.

I was a storyteller.

CHAPTER THREE

*D*ADDY ALWAYS HAD THREE THINGS IN HIS CAR: A SET of two or three gospel songbooks, a box of dominoes, and a fishing pole.

Until I hit my teenage years, he called me Boy-Kid or Booger. As we drove here and there, often just the two of us, but sometimes with Mama too, I would sit next to him on the car's front bench seat. There were no seat belts in those days. Still, we survived.

"Pick us out a good one, Booger," he would say.

That meant it was time for me to find one of "our songs" in the gospel songbooks, so we could sing together. We did it all the time, rarely listening to the car's old AM radio. He loved the sound of gospel quartets, and our family would travel around the state to hear them, sometimes to small churches in deep East Texas where people sang from hymnals using shape notes.

Little did I know at the time that one day I would return to some of those same churches to produce a TV story on the old art of shape-note singing.

The Stamps Quartet, the Blackwood Brothers, and on and on: Daddy got to where he knew many of the musicians personally, and we would often be invited to have supper on the grounds when we visited the little churches. To me, "supper on the grounds" meant two things: the best fried chicken anywhere outside of my Aunt Lena's kitchen, and people sitting around telling stories.

Daddy was an incredible storyteller and loved to entertain people with his tales. In his repertoire he had some incredibly long jokes that would pull people in who were just waiting for the end of the story, then leave them with no punch line. He would immediately launch into a different story ("Have I told y'all the one about . . .") and pull them in again. This time the story would end with the punch line from the previous tale. As soon as they knew they'd been had, they would erupt in laughter, encouraging yet another story. I took in every word.

"People like to be snookered," Daddy would tell me, "as long as it's done with humor and it's harmless. What they don't like is to be cheated. If you start to tell a story, you gotta deliver the goods."

He was also a very accomplished practical jokester, and his pranks ran from the silly and childish—like hanging a red service station rag on a string from the back of one of his coworkers at the filling station, his version of a "kick me" sign—to the detailed ones that would take a while to pay off.

There was a man Daddy called Big John who worked at his service station at the corner of University and Hillcrest in University Park. One day Big John saw Daddy holding a horse apple and asked him what the heck he was doing with that worthless thing.

"Big John, these things aren't worthless," Daddy told him. "They pay twenty cents a pound for them down at Standard Fruit and Vegetable Company near the Farmers Market. People in California think they're exotic and eat 'em like regular apples."

"You don't say," said Big John. "I know where there's a bunch of trees just full of horse apples. I might go get some and make some money."

Daddy left it at that.

Weeks later Big John was being unusually quiet at work, so Daddy asked him if everything was okay.

"I'm fine," he said. "I'm just trying to figure out how I'm gonna get back at you."

Turns out Big John had taken the back seat out of his car and filled that space and his trunk full of horse apples, then tried to sell them at Standard Fruit and Vegetable.

"You must know Leon Phillips," the guy at the fruit and vegetable company told Big John. "He sends people in here all the time."

Daddy could wait forever for his spoofs to pay off.

The dominoes that Daddy carried in his car were for "emergency games" he would start wherever he could. He said life was too short to not make time for dominoes, so any time he found a few old guys hanging around and a table nearby, he'd get up a game.

He was a very good player, mostly Texas Moon and Forty-two, but I think he used the games more for storytelling.

"Lots of life's problems are solved around a domino table," he would say. "Presidents get elected there too," he continued, referring to the wit and wisdom that was always passed around during a game of dominoes.

Years later I would turn Daddy's statement into a question I would ask while producing the untold number of TV stories I've done on dominoes and the people who play the game.

Over and over, I've asked, "Y'all ever solve any world problems around this table? Ever get any presidents elected?"

I had no idea when I was a kid that, just like Mama was training me to handle every social situation, Daddy was training me for what would eventually become my life's work.

CHAPTER FOUR

*D*ADDY THOUGHT I SHOULD BE A SINGER. LIKE LOTS
of parents who think their kids are better at something than
they are, he thought I had a voice that could "go somewhere." I did not, but
I wanted to believe him. I wanted to make him proud of me. So I sang.

In the early years he would enroll me in singing classes at churches. These
were variations on Vacation Bible School, where the emphasis was placed on
singing gospel music, probably to keep the pipeline greased for future members of the hosting church's choir. I attended two or three but didn't care for
them. It wasn't like singing in the car with Daddy.

Then, about the time I turned eleven, my dad decided country music was
the place for me. He loved the stories told by country singers. I did too, and
would spend hours singing along with Hank Williams and Eddy Arnold.

There was a place called Panther Hall in Fort Worth (also known as Panther City), and on Saturday nights KTVT-TV (then an independent station
owned by the Gaylord family, which also owned *Farmer Stockman Magazine*)
aired a music show called *Live at Panther Hall*. Usually, a big-name country
star would play while people danced. For an independent station it was a
good use of an hour, and for the owners of Panther Hall it was a great adver-
tisement for people to come out and listen to the music, dance, and buy beer.

Up a narrow staircase from the large room where the TV show was produced and people danced was a little club called The Loft. While the big star
was playing downstairs in Panther Hall, an up-and-coming singer would
play in The Loft and then get a shot at stardom by performing one song
with the big star on the main stage.

The Loft sometimes set aside time for people who wanted to audition,
so Daddy decided we were going to drive to Fort Worth, where I would get
my big break as a country music singer. That night there was a good band

playing in The Loft, but then their singer went downstairs to play a song with Ray Price and his Cherokee Cowboys. (I found out later that he had at one time been a member of Ray Price's band.)

I knew every Ray Price song, but I had decided to sing Hank Williams's "I'm So Lonesome I Could Cry" for my audition. Hank and I had sung that song many times together in our living room, so I knew I had it down. How hard could it be? Then, when I stepped on stage, they asked me what song and what key, and I just stared at them. What key? And you mean to tell me this band was going to be playing the song for me, and I wouldn't get to sing along with Hank like I was used to? They started playing, and I started singing, and I was so lost trying to match what I was singing with what they were playing that the whole thing was a disaster. I couldn't get off that stage fast enough.

I ran back to the bar booth where Daddy was sitting and buried my face in his chest. I was crying and wanted to go, but about that time, the singer came back upstairs to The Loft and eased into the other side of our booth.

"Bobby, that's your name, right?"

"Uh-huh," was all I could manage to say with my face still buried.

"Bobby, you done real good. You just need to keep practicing. Don't give up, because the more you work at it, the better you'll get. I'm a lot older than you, and I'm still working at it."

I'll never forget those words. And I'll never forget the man who said them to me. The next day Mama drove me to Big Town Mall ("the first shopping center in Texas with air conditioned sidewalks!"), where I bought his album. It was called *And Then I Wrote*—by Willie Nelson.

Not that many years later I went to Willie Nelson's first Fourth of July picnic in Liberty Hill, Texas, as a reporter for the TV station in Dallas where I had landed a job. I was interviewing Willie backstage and said, "You and I met about eight years ago when you were playing at The Loft above Panther Hall. You came over and talked to me after I auditioned."

Willie said, "You're that little boy that sang 'I'm So Lonesome I Could Cry.'"

And not long after that, Ray Price invited me to his ranch in East Texas to do a story about how he was using water therapy to treat a horse with a broken leg, one of the first people to ever do that.

A small world indeed.

CHAPTER FIVE

WHEN I GOT TO BRYAN ADAMS HIGH SCHOOL IN THE fall of 1966, I was at first lost in the crowd. At the time it was the largest high school in the state. My class would graduate well over a thousand students in the spring of 1969, the largest graduating class in Texas history until some of the Houston-area schools eventually surpassed us. So it was hard to rise to the top of the crowd in such a sea of people.

At the beginning of our junior year, each student had to sit down with a guidance counselor and talk about what our plans were for the rest of our lives—or at least for the year after we graduated from high school. And I didn't have any. None.

First, the counselor asked about my parents. How far did they go in school? "Not very."

Then she took a look at my grades, one A with mostly Bs and a C thrown in to keep me humble, and said, "It's clear you are not college material. You need to find a trade school."

That was it. Then she called in the next student.

I was confused. Was she saying I'm stupid? I knew I wasn't in the advanced classes, but I didn't think I was someone who couldn't go on to accomplish things in life. Don't get me wrong: trade school and a blue-collar job were in my roots, and to this day I admire the people who keep life running, the kind of people who can make things with their own hands, who get up every day and get the job done. I wouldn't have been ashamed of that kind of life. My daddy wore a uniform to work at the gas station every day with his name over the shirt pocket, and I was proud of him and everything he stood for. And it bothers me still that we don't make as many things in America as we once did.

My mom had always worked because we couldn't have made it if she didn't. Besides, she simply wasn't the homemaker type. She moved from job to job a lot because she had a big mouth and was famous for saying whatever she felt, and especially in those days, the bosses, who were always male, didn't put up with that. She worked at Sears, Baylor Hospital, Blue Cross Insurance, and several other places before finally getting a job at a hotel where she was a housekeeping supervisor. And son of a gun if she didn't work her way into the executive housekeeper position and became well known in the hotel business. She opened several of the big hotels in Dallas in the 1960s, '70s, and '80s.

My first real job was washing dishes at the new Hilton Inn at Mockingbird and Central Expressway, where my mom worked. I told them I was seventeen, but truth is, I was only fifteen. I hoped they weren't going to check, and sure enough, I was hired. I also worked as a grocery bagger at a Kroger store, as a ditch digger for a landscaping company, and as a salesman at a music store called Muntz Cartridge City that sold eight-track tapes. I became the night manager at the music store while I was still a senior in high school.

No, the problem wasn't that I was afraid of hard work or put off by doing manual labor. It was just that I had this dream of being a writer, a journalist *of some kind*, a storyteller.

This school counselor was telling me that wasn't going to be possible. Shame on her. But it was actually just what I needed to hear.

CHAPTER SIX

*I*GREW UP WATCHING SHOWS LIKE *OZZIE AND HARRIET*, *Father Knows Best*, and *Leave It to Beaver*. I watched a lot of other shows too, especially westerns like *The Rifleman* and *Gunsmoke*. But the family comedy shows had the biggest impact on my life. That's because I watched and liked them, but knew we weren't like them.

It's funny how little kids' brains work and the things we notice and the things we do not. One thing I noticed was that the people in those TV shows had nice houses. They were all two-story houses, so I started thinking that anyone who lived in a two-story house was rich, like the Cleaver family, the Nelsons, and the Andersons. Their moms wore dresses while they cooked, and their dads wore suits to work. Nobody in my neighborhood lived that kind of life, but there were kids at school who did.

When we lived on Bryan Parkway, our houses backed up to the mansions on Swiss Avenue. It took two or three of the houses on Bryan Parkway to equal the width of one Swiss Avenue home. It's still that way today, though now the Bryan Parkway houses are sought after by urban pioneers who want to fix up those homes from another era. I know we paid about $55 a month to rent our house there. Today you can't buy one of those houses for much less than half a million. And to add salt to the wound, someone added a second story to our last home on Bryan Parkway—but it still doesn't look like the house where the *Leave It to Beaver* kids lived.

All this is not intended to be bellyaching or whining. It's to simply point out that I was very aware of our financial situation. But even then I felt lucky because I had the greatest mom and dad in the world, and the parents of some of the rich kids at school seemed . . . well, somehow distant, and not as involved in their kids' lives. I loved my parents dearly. To this day I can't figure out how they managed to always provide for us. But even though we never had any extra anything, and cash was a scarce commodity, our home was filled with love.

Mama and Daddy were not afraid to show their affection for each other in front of us. She called him Leedy Boy (a version of Leon, I suppose) and would regularly sit in his lap while they watched TV. They also cuddled on the couch and held hands when they walked, with my mom always on my dad's right side because he did not have a left hand for her to hold. They were as much in love as they were when they were first married, and I loved that about them.

So imagine my surprise when, right at the beginning of my first year in high school, I came home one day after school to find our front door wide open with my dad's house key still in the lock. No one was there, but in a matter of moments, they both came rushing in, screaming at each other. My mom was crying, my dad was mad, and lots of threats were thrown back and forth. The accusations, as often happens in these situations, seemed to be not only about whatever had happened to cause the current upheaval but also about things going back to before I was born.

In those brief moments, my fabulous family began to fall apart.

My brother, who was in the Air Force, was in California at the time, and I was lost. I didn't know whose story to believe, but I didn't want to believe either one. I just wanted everything to go back to the way it had been that morning when I left for school. Over the next few months my mom and dad would try to work things out, but they just couldn't get over whatever it was that happened. There were lots of fights, sometimes in the middle of the night, and one time a shotgun was fired right outside my bedroom door. Startled awake by the BOOM!, I ran into the hallway, where there was a huge hole in the ceiling. The story goes that my dad was trying to leave the house, and my mom was attempting to keep him from taking his shotgun with him. Thankfully, no one was hurt—not physically anyway.

Shortly after that, my parents told me they were separating and would be getting a divorce, a word with which I was barely familiar. My dad had to rent a room in a men's boardinghouse because they didn't have enough money to do anything else, so I was going to have to live with my mom. But I loved my parents equally and couldn't stand the idea of living with one without the other, so I told them I was going to live on my own. Surprisingly, they didn't fight me on the idea, even though I was only fifteen. I think they were so tired of fighting each other and felt so bad about what was happening that they didn't want to tell me no. While I was on a roll, I told them I was also going to buy my own car and get a hardship license. They didn't fight me on that either. Obviously, if I would be living on my own, I would have to have a job and a way to get to work.

I paid a lady down the block $125 for a grey and white 1956 Ford sedan, and I enrolled in a distributive education program at the high school that allowed me to start classes at 7 A.M. and be finished by noon so I could go to work.

So, at the age of fifteen, I left my once happy home. But instead of moving out on my own like I had threatened, I moved in with my girlfriend and her parents.

My girlfriend at the time was the most centered person I had ever known, and her parents were the most accepting people I had ever known other than my dad. They invited me to move in with them until my life settled down, and they treated me from the beginning like I was another member of their family. I had my own room, went on vacations with them, and got the same kind of parental advice they gave their daughter, including how I should always be thinking about the future.

My parents' divorce took almost three years to be finalized, and they tried several times to get back together. I was an emotional wreck from all of that, and to make matters worse, I had been taught to keep my true feelings to myself—the old "Never let 'em see you sweat" rule—so I didn't have any experience at processing feelings like the ones I was having. But my girlfriend's mom knew what was going on and would sit and talk to me at night until I fell asleep. She was my savior during those times and helped me keep my mind uncluttered by all the negative things that were going on.

That family changed my life in such a profound way that I can honestly say I would not be where I am today were it not for their good hearts and clear minds. They taught me things that I'd never even thought about, and ways to live that I didn't know were possible, especially not for me, the kid who, I had come to believe, wasn't supposed to amount to much in life.

"There are lots of ways to live a life," they said, over and over.

I found love in that second family, and because of them, my high school and college years were great. I owe so much to them. And I have always regretted how I left things. I was so immature that I did not know how to say, "Thank you for what you did for me" and, "I'm sorry I'm leaving this way. Please forgive me." I just left and never looked back, partly because I didn't know what to say, and partly because I felt so guilty about the way I left, without any explanation as to why.

The one thing they could not teach me was how to get rid of my newfound belief that love never lasts and that even the best people in the world lie to one another. My parents had, so I was sure everyone else did too. I believed that every good relationship would come to an end—and for no particular reason. I found a way to sabotage every romantic relationship I was in from the late 1960s to the early '90s. In my mind, they were all going to end just like my parents' relationship did, so it was best to just get it over with.

It took a lot of counseling in the '90s for me to finally recognize what I had been doing. That knowledge eventually set me free, but by that time I had missed the window for having kids and, I thought, for growing old with someone I love. I had vowed in 1991 that I would never again be in a permanent relationship, and I kept that promise to myself for a long time. Some people say they have no regrets, but not me. I have many.

CHAPTER SEVEN

*A*FTER THAT SCHOOL COUNSELOR PRETTY MUCH TOLD me to give up on any dreams I had, I licked my wounds and went through a period where I thought maybe she was right about me. About that same time, my brother was on his way to Vietnam. He told me in a letter that he would be working as a journalist in the Air Force, editing a newspaper called the *Defender*, an armed forces publication aimed at report-ing the news to the troops in such a way as to build morale. It was printed in both English and Vietnamese because it was also distributed to the South Vietnamese troops.

The day my brother arrived in Da Nang, South Vietnam, he had a letter waiting for him. It was from our mother, who gave him the news that she and Daddy were finally getting divorced. Welcome to Vietnam. Billy Ray, my hero, still struggles with that one. I can't say I blame him.

I eventually found out, decades later, that my big brother's job was a cover for what he was actually doing. Oh, he did edit the newspaper, but his real job involved integrating with South Vietnamese troops on some sort of mis-sions into the jungle. He now admits, at least to me, that he was not only in Vietnam but also Laos and Cambodia, where the US military denied having a presence. By now, most of us know that story was simply not true, but the strange thing is, my brother still cannot, or will not, tell me exactly what his real job was during the war. He usually changes the subject when I ask, and I think he wants to spare me the gory details. As I met more and more Viet-nam vets, I found that my brother's way of handling that war is not all that different from the way most of the others who fought there do. And I will always believe that the way we refused to welcome them home was one of the most shameful times in the history of our country.

After coming home from Vietnam, Billy Ray went to work first as a newspaper writer and columnist, then in politics. He was chief of staff for a one-term governor of Nevada before being tapped for a job in Washington, DC, as chief of staff for the Republican National Committee when Ronald Reagan was president.

He later worked for President George Herbert Walker Bush in many capacities, including as director of the Fund for America's Future, a political action committee that raised money for Bush, the then–vice president, when he was an undeclared candidate; as undersecretary of education; and as undersecretary of the Office of Personnel Management. (The media, including the *Washington Post*, kept referring to him as "William," and my brother eventually became known as just "Bill.")

After Bush lost to Clinton in 1992, Bill, who had been working on the campaign, went to Vanderbilt University as assistant vice-chancellor, but he ended up as the deputy mayor of Nashville. He has attempted to retire, but he recently came out of retirement to, once again, take the job of deputy mayor. It's in his blood. He just can't stop doing it. I'm so proud of him. If he lived in Texas, he would be a good story for our show: the guy who couldn't leave the excitement of politics behind.

But the real importance of these details goes back to that letter in which my big brother told me he was going to be a journalist in Vietnam. I had always looked up to Bill, and still do, so when he said he was going to be a journalist, it gave me just the strength and courage I needed to laugh at that misguided high school counselor. I decided my dream to be a journalist would live on.

My next stop was a visit with Ann Voss, the journalism teacher at Bryan Adams High School and sponsor of the *Cougar Chronicle*, our school newspaper. I told her I had a dream of becoming a journalist. She made it possible for me to get into her already-full journalism class and to write for the school paper.

Just months before graduation, I still had no plan for what I was going to do after high school. I had no financial support from my parents, who were continuing to struggle with their own problems. They didn't have anything to give, so I worked to pay my own way. That, along with the incredible assistance I was getting from the family that took me in, kept me afloat. Still, college did not seem like a realistic prospect.

But one day in February of 1969, Ann Voss kept me after her journalism class to ask about my plans. I told her I had none. She handed back an article I had written earlier for the school newspaper and said, "Bobby, I want you to listen carefully to me. You can do whatever you decide to do, but you have to want it. I think you have a talent for writing, and you are especially good at telling stories about people. Those are the best articles you have written, and you seem to like doing them."

Considering what I ended up doing with my life, I now have to wonder: Did this lady have a crystal ball or something?

She then outlined a plan of action for me that included applying to three different universities for admission even though I didn't have the money.

"Get in first. Worry about the money later," she said.

My meeting with Miss Voss lasted about five minutes, but it changed my life . . . again. That seemed to be a recurring theme.

I followed her plan to the letter, and to this day I don't know how it happened, but that summer I received an acceptance letter from Southern Methodist University in Dallas. I had also applied to North Texas (now UNT) and Arlington State (now UT Arlington), but the first acceptance letter came from SMU, by far the most expensive of the three since it was a private school. The acceptance was conditional. I had not taken some required high school courses, so I would first have to go to a junior college to complete those courses in math and science. If I passed those with a B or better, I was in. This bought me time to figure out the rest. I made up and adopted my new motto the day I received that acceptance letter: Bite off more than you can chew, then chew like hell.

CHAPTER EIGHT

*I*N SEPTEMBER I WALKED INTO EL CENTRO COLLEGE IN downtown Dallas. It was located in the original Sanger-Harris department store building and didn't look like any other college at that time. It was part of the fairly new Dallas County Community College District, whose goal was to provide higher education to kids who otherwise couldn't afford it. Even I was able to pay my tuition and buy my books. And I was able to enroll not only in those math and science classes I needed to get into SMU but in some other basic courses as well, including Journalism 101.

I was determined to get started right away with what I intended to eventually be my life, a life of storytelling, even though I still had no idea what form that would take. A magazine writer? A reporter for a daily newspaper? I didn't know or even care at that point. I just knew that I had taken the first step to get there and didn't plan to let anything get in my way.

In early December I walked into my journalism classroom to learn we were having a guest speaker that day. It was some guy who worked at a TV station somewhere. He looked somewhat familiar, but I couldn't place him. He was wearing a suit and tie and seemed kind of stuffy.

"This is going to be boring," I said to myself. I even thought about ducking out of class so I could use the time to study for a test I had later in my science class, a course that was kicking my butt. But I thought better of it and decided to stay and listen to what the man had to say. What followed was another life-changing moment, one of the biggest I would have. Ever. A moment I almost missed.

The speaker was Eddie Barker, the news director and evening news anchor at KRLD AM-FM-TV (later to become KDFW-TV). It was located two blocks from the college and was the CBS affiliate for Dallas–Fort Worth.

I not only learned that Eddie Barker was not the least bit stuffy, but that he had one of the most exciting lives I could imagine—a life of journalism, a life where he got to keep people informed about what was going on in their world, a life on radio and television. He was also famous for some of the stories he had covered, the biggest of them being the assassination of President John F. Kennedy, just four blocks down Elm Street from where we sat that day. In fact, Eddie was the first person to go on television and announce that President Kennedy had died, a full five minutes before CBS News anchor Walter Cronkite made his now famous announcement to the nation.

And how did Walter Cronkite know for a fact that President Kennedy did not survive? He heard it on the phone straight from his good friend in Dallas, Eddie Barker, a man he trusted.

At the end of Cronkite's 5:30 P.M. newscast, the local station played a tape of him saying, "And now stay tuned for my good friend Eddie Barker and the award-winning Channel 4 Evening News." This wasn't just a promo that Cronkite did for all the CBS affiliates around the country. He and Eddie were good friends, and the Barker family vacationed with the Cronkite family on Walter's yacht every summer. This guy was big stuff, the real deal, and he was about to become my mentor. I knew at that moment the direction I was going to go in my quest to become a journalist. Broadcasting was going to be my medium. The rest would work itself out.

When the class was over, the other twenty or so kids in the room zoomed out the door on their way to who knows where. I was the only one who stayed, and I waited patiently while the great Eddie Barker made small talk with our journalism teacher and said his good-byes.

As he approached the classroom door, I stood and said, "Excuse me, sir. I'm Bobby Phillips. Would you happen to have a business card?"

"Of course," he said, and pulled a card from his inside coat pocket. He started to hand it to me, then pulled it back slightly and asked, "What are you going to do with this?"

"I'm going to call you, sir, and ask for a job."

He smiled, handed me the card, and said, "You do just that."

I gave him thirty minutes to get back to his office.

Part Two

ACHIEVING THE DREAM. ALMOST.

CHAPTER NINE

*I*T WAS A FALL DAY IN 1983 WHEN I APPROACHED A NON-descript office building on North Stemmons Freeway in Dallas. The sign on the door said "Audience Research and Development."

I walked in, and before I could announce myself to the person sitting at the desk, she said, "Follow me, Mr. Phillips."

I stepped inside a small, dark room. It looked a little bit like what a home theater might look like today. One wall was covered with moving images of me—video that had been lifted from "air checks" of the work I had been doing since I'd been hired by KDFW-TV on January 2, 1970, while still a first-semester freshman at El Centro College. Some of it was from news stories I had produced as a reporter, but more of it was from the weekly TV show I now hosted called *4 Country Reporter*, and some of it was video of me anchoring newscasts. At the time, my life consisted of all that and much more.

The light from the video illuminated the face of the great Herman Martin Haag Jr., known as Marty.

Marty had been hired in 1973 to be the news director at WFAA-TV, the now dominant news force in the DFW market—and probably one of the best TV stations in America at the time. But before Marty walked through the door of Channel 8, there was another station, Channel 4, KDFW-TV—the flagship of A. H. Belo's broadcasting properties, and the station where I had at that point spent more than thirteen years—that was always on top in the Nielsen ratings. Marty changed that almost overnight when he brought his brand of responsive, ethical TV journalism to Texas along with a team of like-minded reporters, producers, photographers, and editors. When Marty spoke, people listened, and his word was law. By the time I walked into that room at AR&D, he was a legend, and I don't mind admitting I was a little bit frightened.

The meeting had to take place somewhere like AR&D because I couldn't walk into Channel 8 without stoking the rumor mill, and he certainly couldn't walk into Channel 4. Besides, where else could Marty project images of me on the wall, a move I suspected was part flattery, part intimidation? It worked. I felt like I was in the presence of royalty. Some would say I was.

"Sit down, Bob, and take a look at yourself," he said as we shook hands.

I stared and had no idea what to say, or even if I was supposed to say anything. Tom Wilson had prepped me a bit. "He called the meeting. Let him do the talking." So I did.

Marty then set about critiquing my work. "You do a good job at this." "You could use some work on that." The critique went on for several minutes before he asked, "What's your contract situation?"

I told him I still had time left on my current contract at KDFW-TV, then dropped the bomb that I was sure would cause him to throw me out.

"I have a one-year non-compete clause," I said, looking for a place to hide. That part of my contract meant that after leaving KDFW-TV, I couldn't go to work for another station in the Dallas–Fort Worth market for a year.

Instead, Marty said, "That's pretty standard. There are ways to work around that. Besides, I don't have anything to offer you at the moment. I'm just doing some research and thought we should meet, then stay in touch."

Over the next couple of years Marty and I did just that, usually meeting at his favorite tiny French restaurant on McKinney Avenue, where there were no prices on the menu, another intimidating thing for people like me. But he always paid the tab, and I learned to enjoy French cuisine—or at least some of it. I would have rather met at a chicken-fried steak place or a barbecue joint, but Marty said this was better, since our meetings at that point were supposed to be somewhat clandestine. We came to know a lot about one another over those lunches, and my desire to work at WFAA-TV grew stronger.

But on that day, the day of our first meeting at AR&D, he just said, "Tell me about your time at Channel 4."

"Where do I start?" I asked him.

"At the beginning."

CHAPTER TEN

W HEN EDDIE BARKER HANDED ME HIS CARD AT THE
end of my journalism class in December 1969, I was aware
that what I was calling to ask him was ludicrous. It had not yet been six
months since my eighteenth birthday, I was a first-semester college freshman, I had no marketable skills—and I was asking for a job at a major-
market TV station.

Still, I made the call. When I asked for Mr. Barker and identified myself
as the student he had just met a half hour earlier at El Centro College, the
receptionist put me on hold. When she came back on the line, she said, "Be
here at 2 P.M. tomorrow to speak to Mr. Barker." Click. Silence.

Did that just happen? Was he going to give me a job interview?

I drove to my dad's service station at University and Hillcrest and showed
him the card. He looked at it without comment, then said, "Better get a
haircut."

My hair was barely over my collar and slightly over my ears. I did not
look like the hippies my dad talked about, but I do admit that I had a lot
of hair. Still do. At the time, it swooped down over my forehead and almost
touched my eyes. It was thick and black, and, I thought, fashionable. In
other words, I looked like the kid I was.

The next day I walked into the newsroom at Channel 4 about ten minutes early. ("Ten minutes early and you're on time," Ann Voss always said.)
There was no place to sit down, so the woman at the desk in front of the
elevator door that opened into the basement newsroom told me to stand
there and wait. Mr. Barker would get to me when he could.

I had spent several minutes watching people running around the newsroom like they were in a hurry to get something important done when a
door opened to my far left and Eddie Barker rushed out, red-faced and mad

as a hornet, screaming, "Damn it to hell! Who let the ribbon run out on the AP wire machine?"

Then he approached the person who was closest—a young guy, maybe in his twenties—and shouted, "That's your job! You're fired!" Then he stormed off to an office on my right.

The lady at the desk said, "I think you can go in now."

Go in? Couldn't we let him cool off first? Maybe it would be better if I came back another day?

I walked in scared to death.

Much to my surprise, Eddie stood up from his desk and smiled. It was like his meltdown never happened. I started to remind him of my name when he interrupted me. "Bobby. I remember. Sit down."

The conversation was incredibly short. He asked a few questions about my life and goals. I told him I knew I wanted to be a journalist but hadn't known what kind until I heard him speak to my class the day before. Now I knew for sure that I wanted to work in broadcasting. I wanted to be like him.

He asked about my current skills, and I answered as honestly as I could.

"None," I said. "I have no idea what I'm doing, but I want to learn. In the meantime, I'll sweep the studio floor if you'll give me a broom and a chance."

He looked at me and stared for what seemed like forever.

Then he said, "I can't add another person until next year, which is only a couple weeks from now. We pay two bucks an hour for beginning employees [minimum wage]. Come back to work on Friday, January 2nd, and be prepared to work all weekend. You need to wear a coat and tie to work every day. Anything else?"

"No, sir! Thank you, sir!"

"Oh, and Bobby, get a haircut."

CHAPTER ELEVEN

O N JANUARY 2, I REPORTED TO WORK AS INSTRUCTED.
I had no idea what I would be doing but didn't care. I was
working at a major TV station, and I was only eighteen years old. At that
point I would have picked up my boss's dry cleaning or washed his car. I had
my foot in the door. It was a start.

The assignments editor, Buster McGregor, a journalism warhorse with
little tolerance for monkey business, was my boss. He told me to sit in a
room and listen to the police and fire scanners, and let him know if anything
was going on. There was a Dallas police officer named Murray Jackson sitting in the same room because he did the traffic reports on KRLD radio. It
was an incredible education sitting in that room listening to all the predic-
aments people get themselves into and hearing the backstories from Officer
Jackson. I immediately loved my job.

I was so important to the operation at Channel 4 that I was trusted on
my very first day with one of the most important jobs in the newsroom—or
so I thought.

Buster came in shortly before the 6 P.M. newscast and said, "Hey, kid,
it's your job to pick up dinner for the night shift. Head up to Henderson's
Chicken and get this." He handed me a list of what I was supposed to pick
up and some cash. "And bring back the change."

I felt proud that I got to do this task, and I found what would become
some of my favorite fried chicken at the same time. The good news was that
the people at the TV station sent me there for food a lot.

But remember me telling you how ambitious my mother was? It rubbed
off on me, I guess, because less than a month into my new job, I was ready
for another challenge. And I got it.

There was a news photographer named Sandy Sanderson who had come to work at the station to help them convert from black-and-white to color news film. He had been a movie newsreel guy in Los Angeles for years, and there was nothing about shooting film that Sandy did not know.

One day Buster walked into the scanner room and said, "Sandy is too old to drive the news units, and we can't afford to be without him. Since you're the new guy, your job will be to drive him whenever he needs to go out on a story."

That sounded great. Yes, I was now someone's driver, but I was also getting a chance to go out on real news stories and see how this was done.

The first day Sandy and I climbed into Unit 2 together with me behind the wheel and Sandy in the passenger seat, he asked, "Do you have any interest in being a news photographer?"

I told him I absolutely did and had done still photography work for the student newspaper. He said it was the same thing except news film was moving pictures, not still pictures.

Then he said, "If you're serious about this, I'll make you a deal. You get me where I need to go and do what I say, and I'll teach you everything I can."

I agreed. Then he told me to drive us to a barbecue joint where he could get a chopped beef sandwich and a beer. I asked if we shouldn't get to the story. He responded, "Like I said, do what I tell you. The story will still be there when we get there."

Sandy then introduced me to the original Sonny Bryan's Barbecue on Inwood Road near Parkland Hospital. After that, he spent every spare moment teaching me how to shoot news film. I picked it up quickly and loved everything about it. The science, the art, the craft. It was a dream come true for me. I even started wondering if perhaps this was what I wanted to do, instead of reporting.

Less than two months after starting my job at Channel 4, I was promoted to the position of news photographer.

CHAPTER TWELVE

*F*ROM THE MOMENT I BECAME THE STATION'S NEWS
photographer, it was a constant whirlwind of shooting fires
and wrecks, school board and city council meetings, and interviews with city
and county officials—and people no one knew. I started to realize that the
news of the day touches all kinds of people leading all kinds of lives. And
I developed a sense that what I was doing was somehow important, that
people depended on it. I may have been only eighteen, but I took the job
very seriously. And the best thing about it was it didn't even feel like work. It
felt like something I would do even if I were not getting paid my two bucks
an hour.

News photography was something I would do for the next sixteen or
more years, though in the early 1980s the TV station sold all the film equipment and made us convert to videotape. I didn't care much for video because
the equipment was heavy and bulky, and not user-friendly, but I had no
choice, so I converted too. By that time I had a film camera of my own
and managed to keep shooting film for some side jobs I picked up here and
there.

One Sunday morning I walked into an empty newsroom to hear the
scanners going off and lots of people talking. Something was going on. I was
the first one in the newsroom on Sundays because we didn't have a newscast
until 5:30 P.M. Because I was the new guy, I drew the short straw and had to
be there early in case something needed to be filmed. Lots of times the news
photographers would go out by themselves to pick up images that could
be used in an anchor reader or as part of a package a reporter was putting
together.

I quickly figured out that they were looking for someone who was missing at a nearby lake. Two young boys had gone out in a rowboat and had

not come back. I looked at the schedule to make sure there was nothing on it that I was supposed to shoot, then headed to the lake. When I arrived, a couple of guys from the local fire department were about to go out looking for the missing boys. (Several others were already searching.) I talked my way onto their boat, and we started scanning the shoreline. After only a few minutes, we happened upon the boys, both clinging to a tree that was only about twenty yards from dry ground. They had been horsing around and flipped the boat, which floated off upside down. They were too scared to try to make it to the shore, so they had just held on to the tree, hoping someone would come along.

The boys were in good spirits, weren't hurt at all, and acted like it was no big deal. They apparently had only been out there for a little while and were mostly worried about what their mom was going to say when they returned home. I suspected they weren't supposed to have been in that boat alone.

I captured all of that on film. When we got back to shore, I asked the boys if they would be willing to answer a couple of questions on camera. They were excited about the idea, so I pointed the camera toward them and held the microphone out while I filmed. This was about to be my first inter-view as a professional broadcast journalist!

The boys started talking and wanted to make sure everyone knew they weren't scared. Then I asked what time they flipped their boat, and they said something like, "Must have been about seven this morning, right after we got in it."

Now, here it was, my first follow-up question as a big-time, major-market TV journalist. Ready? Wait for it. . . .

"Hmmm, 7 o'clock, huh?"

Seriously. All I could think of to say was that stupid response. It was a very short interview. And it would later end up on the air.

I was about to pack up and leave when I thought, "If I had a reporter with me on this story, they would want to do a standup." That's the part where the reporter gets their face on camera saying something brilliant.

So I put my Auricon 16mm film camera with a 12 × 120 Angenieux zoom lens onto a tripod, set it for a wide shot with the lake in the background, started the camera, and ran around in front of it saying something brilliant into the ElectroVoice 635A stick mike. Or so I thought. And at the end of my brilliant words, whatever they were, I said, "Bob Phillips, Channel 4 News, Cedar Creek Lake."

Since I had noticed that no one else in the newsroom had a name like "Bobby," I'd decided that if I ever got on camera, I'd have to shorten it to "Bob" so people would take me seriously. And that's what I did. It must not have occurred to me that no one would take an eighteen-year-old seriously no matter what name he used.

That was the very moment when Bobby Leon Phillips became just Bob Phillips. Since that time, only my family and some of my closest friends have called me Bobby.

When I got back to the station, I was still the only one in the newsroom, so I decided to try my hand at writing a script for my little story. Later, after the film had been processed, I went into the room used for editing. In those days the narration was on a cart that looked kind of like an eight-track tape, so I did that too.

That day the person who would produce and anchor the 5:30 P.M. newscast was a gruff old guy named Roy Nichols, a seasoned journalist who had more knowledge about television in his little finger than I would have in three lifetimes. I didn't know him well, but he was grumbling that we didn't have much new stuff to put on the air, so he'd have to use a lot of repeat material from the 10 o'clock news the night before. I wasn't sure that the story I had done was a story at all since the rescue was short-lived and it all turned out okay, but I took a chance. It was then, and only then, that I told him what I'd done with the story at the lake early that morning.

To my surprise, he said, "Show it to me." So I did. And to my greater surprise, he said, "We need to fix a couple things, but I think I'll use it." He then had me watch while he did some re-editing and explained to me why he was making changes. I learned more from people like Roy Nichols, and there were lots of them in that newsroom, than I learned in most of my college courses. In fact, I ended up placing out of some of my journalism and broadcasting classes because the professors teaching them realized that I was already doing professionally what they were about to teach. I owe that to those incredible journalists who taught me so much at KDFW.

So here it was, a Sunday evening in March 1970, and even though I had been at the station less than three months, I was about to go on the air, in what was then the eleventh-largest market in the country, with a bootleg news package I had done just to see if I could.

CHAPTER THIRTEEN

*T*HAT DAY I WALKED INTO EDDIE BARKER'S NEWSROOM FOR my job interview and witnessed him firing a guy for letting the ribbon run out on a wire machine, I was scared to death. But not so scared that I didn't take the job.

During my employment, Eddie fired me four times that I remember, and it could be more. But I quickly learned that he wasn't firing me, just warning me that he took the news business very seriously and wanted everyone else to do the same. That, combined with an explosive temper, led to the screaming. I also discovered that he usually "fired" the first person he saw when something like that happened, even if that person had nothing to do with the problem.

Assistant news director Bill Ceverha, a man I came to respect and love during our time working together, would quietly follow behind Eddie after one of his fits and tell the "fired" person to just stay out of Eddie's way the rest of the day, and he promised it would all be forgotten by the next day. It always was.

Except for one time. One employee's desk was the first one Eddie would see when he pounded out of his office looking for a victim, so that guy was "fired" more than anyone else. Eddie also had a habit of kicking the three-foot-tall trash cans placed around the newsroom. The cans were extra tall because newsrooms in those days were filled with papers from the wire machines, which were discarded after they were read. Every trash can in the newsroom was dented from years of Eddie kicking them.

As it turned out, the employee who sat just outside Eddie's office was planning to go to work for another station in another city, but not without one last hurrah with Eddie Barker. So he waited patiently for Eddie to have another tantrum and leave his office in search of a victim. This time, when

Eddie screamed and kicked the trash can, it didn't budge. It sat right there by the man's desk like it was made of steel. Seems he had secretly filled the can with bricks, then put wire copy paper on top to cover them up.

When Eddie kicked the can and it didn't go anywhere, he turned all shades of red and purple. But the guy's fun wasn't over yet. He said, "Damn it, Barker, I've had enough of this!" and then pulled a pistol, aimed it straight at Eddie, and fired. It was, of course, a starter pistol, and while it made a horrendous noise, that's all it did. The best part is that Eddie regained his composure and said quietly, "This time you *are* fired." The guy got his stuff and walked out, never to be heard from again.

Even those times Eddie "fired" me, I knew not to take it personally. Turns out he became one of my biggest champions in life. He not only gave a poor kid from Old East Dallas a chance to achieve his dream, he went out of his way to help me when he could. He even asked me to shoot some film one evening at a dinner at the Dallas Press Club, and told me I was welcome to stay and eat, something we rarely had time to do in the fast-paced world of TV news. I sat at the same table with Eddie and his wife, along with Bill Ceverha and a few others from the station.

Two or three weeks later the station had to lay off some people, and Eddie had to trim several jobs. I was the last one hired, so I knew I was out the door when I caught wind of the layoffs, but when the pink slips arrived, I didn't get one. I knew better than to question it and just laid low and wondered. Many years later, as I sat at Eddie's bedside two days before he died, I asked why he kept me, why I hadn't been fired in that layoff.

"Remember when I invited you to sit with us at that Dallas Press Club dinner?" he asked. "You knew which fork to use, even though I knew you were a poor kid from Old East Dallas. I knew you had potential."

Thank you, Mama.

Not long after my job interview, Eddie asked about my plans for completing college. He knew I was attending a junior college, since that's where we'd met, but he wanted to make sure I was going to at least finish my bachelor's degree. I told him I had a conditional acceptance at SMU but couldn't afford it, so I would have to figure out something else.

A few days later Eddie gave me a name and phone number and told me to call for an appointment. It was the number of a financial aid counselor at SMU, where Eddie occasionally taught journalism classes. I made the appointment, and when I walked out a couple hours later, I had a financial aid package made up of loans, grants, and scholarships that would allow me to attend SMU and not worry about the money until two years after graduation.

I told everyone who asked that I figured SMU had some policy about letting in at least one local poor kid every year. Truth is, I think I received special treatment because of Eddie Barker. He was highly thought of in the community, knew all the right people, and to have him vouch for you went a long way. I am convinced that had it not been for Eddie's help, I would never have attended SMU, where I not only finished my Bachelor of Arts degree but hung around long enough to get my Master of Liberal Arts degree too.

Eddie Barker and Bill Ceverha did many other things for me. Bill would throw freelance work my way whenever he could, and when you're making two bucks an hour, every bit helps. When the now famous tennis match between Rod Laver and Ken Rosewall was played in Dallas in 1972, he referred me to the World Championship Tennis people as the guy who could shoot the matches for them. I knew nothing about tennis but got help from the sports director at Channel 4, and I was present for the match that had everything: a huge title, comebacks by both players, heavy money, and a game filled with tension. Rosewall won the match 4-6, 6-0, 6-3, 6-7(3), 7-6(5), and took home a $50,000 check presented by Neil Armstrong, a gold ring, a giant trophy, and a Lincoln Continental. It's been said that this was the match that "made" tennis in the United States, and I not only got to be there, I made some good money doing it.

The summer after I was hired to work at Channel 4, Buster McGregor, the assignments editor, asked me if I'd like to travel with the Dallas Cowboys and shoot their games. That sounded to me like a silly question. Who wouldn't want that job? But he said some guys didn't want to make the commitment because it took them away from their families too much. He thought that since I was nineteen and single, I wouldn't mind doing it. I tried to act like it wasn't the dream job for me.

I traveled with the Cowboys for the next thirteen years, flying on the team plane, staying at the team hotel, sometimes eating meals with the players. I was there for Super Bowl VI, when Dallas beat Miami at Tulane Stadium in New Orleans (before the Super Dome was built); Super Bowl X, when they lost to the Pittsburgh Steelers; and Super Bowl XII, when the Cowboys beat the Denver Broncos. Sometimes I was called on to shoot for NFL Films, and at one point I was offered a job to do that full-time. By then, though, I was thoroughly attached to another project at the TV station, the one that would turn out to be my life's work, so I didn't even consider the offer. Instead, Reuben Porras, a guy who sometimes worked as my film loader when shooting for NFL Films, landed that job and went on to become an Emmy Award–winning superstar cinematographer. He died a few years ago while shooting a piece with the acclaimed sports journalist Bob Costas.

Of all the people I met in my career, Cowboys coach Tom Landry was among the most meaningful. My dad considered Landry a god and told me to listen to everything the man said. That was hard to do because he never said a word to me. I was just some kid shooting the games. I stayed quiet and under the radar as much as possible because I loved shooting the Cowboys games and didn't want to do anything to mess it up. Silence and keeping my nose to the grindstone, I thought, was my best plan.

That all changed at Super Bowl VI. It was media day, when the journalists get a chance to interview the players from both teams. I was shooting for sports director Dick Risenhoover, and we had just finished interviews with Miami quarterback Bob Griese and Miami kicker Garo Yepremian (who would score the Dolphin's only points of the game) when I heard a strange noise in my camera.

I was shooting with one of the station's new CP-16 cameras, a lighter, more agile alternative to the big Auricon boat anchors we had previously carried around. It had an onboard battery for power instead of a heavy battery pack the photographer wore over his shoulder, and the whole system weighed less than half of what we shouldered using the old system. But that rattling noise was not good.

I dropped to the turf in the stadium where we were shooting and opened the loading door of my camera, knowing that the film would be ruined by the light, but also knowing that the film I cared about was already on the take-up reel in the film magazine resting on top of the camera. To my surprise, I saw film bunched up inside and panicked. I just knew this was going to be the end of my short career. I thought I was going to cry and couldn't imagine what was wrong with the camera, but I had already learned that, in this business, blaming the equipment was not acceptable.

I must have been saying something out loud because at that moment Coach Landry dropped to one knee beside me and said, "Bob, take a deep breath. You'll figure this out."

I looked at him and did exactly what Daddy told me to do. "Listen to everything the man says." I took a breath, wondered how in the world this great and powerful NFL coach even knew my name, and tried to relax. Coach quickly moved on to handle whatever was on his plate besides me, but that moment was the beginning of a lifelong friendship. I could go on and on about all that Coach Landry did for me—in fact, I could probably write a book about it—but suffice it to say that his counsel and direction were guiding lights in my life for years to come. Coach did the same thing for many people. He was much more than an NFL coach. He was an expert at turning boys into men and played a substantial role in doing that for me.

In the spring of 1997, I was doing a commercial for a senior housing development, Sun City, in Georgetown, Texas. I was their spokesperson, and I had invited Coach to do some TV spots with me. The great Bob Lily, the first player drafted by the Dallas Cowboys, lived at Sun City, and he also did some spots with me. On the day Coach Landry and I were shooting some scenes out on the golf course, my dad, who had just been diagnosed with leukemia, was coming down from Dallas to watch from the sidelines. We knew Daddy only had a few months left, and I thought seeing the great Tom Landry in person, a man he idolized, would lift his spirits.

I told Coach so he would know who the man sitting behind the cameras was, and he said, "Let me know when he gets here." When the car pulled up with my dad inside, I pointed it out to Coach, and he got out of the golf cart we were in and said to the director, "Let's all take a ten-minute break." He then went straight to the car, helped my dad out, then escorted him inside the clubhouse and ordered an iced tea for each of them. This was the only time I ever saw my dad speechless. I think he was having trouble believing what was happening.

Later, when we broke for lunch, Coach told the catering people to set up a table for two where he and my dad would eat. We all backed off and gave Daddy this moment alone with his hero. I can't say that I have ever admired anyone more than I did Tom Landry on that day. He was my hero too, and always will be.

At the end of the day Coach Landry told me my dad was a fine man and that he always wondered where I came from. Now he knew.

Daddy died in July of that year.

CHAPTER FOURTEEN

*D*URING MY SIXTEEN-PLUS YEARS AT KDFW-TV, I DID a little bit of everything. I started as a "gopher" (go for this, go for that), quickly became a news photographer, added reporter to my title within three months of starting my job there, and eventually was a news producer, assignments editor, and news anchor. I never left one position to move on to another. I just added the new one to the list. I enjoyed it all, and working there gave me opportunities I hadn't even dreamed of. For the most part, my job never seemed like work.

One special ongoing assignment I had at Channel 4 was working with the legendary Judy Jordan, the first female anchor in the DFW market. Judy covered the arts and entertainment beat back then and interviewed lots of big stars. Many of the interviews took place late at night, after concerts and events. Since I was the youngest person in the newsroom and didn't need sleep, I guess they figured I wouldn't mind that kind of schedule. I got to hang out with legendary bluesman B. B. King and had dinner at the old Railhead on Greenville and Park Lane with the members of Chicago. This was huge for a kid my age, and I learned a lot about social news reporting from Judy.

I even got to spend a week with her in Hawaii, where we were covering the first KVIL radio trip, which set the model for the radio station trips that are still done today. In those days, Braniff Airways was flying its 747, painted bright orange and nicknamed Fat Albert, to Hawaii every day, even though the plane was sometimes almost empty. Legendary DJ Ron Chapman, whom I had listened to and admired my whole life, told Braniff he could fill up that plane—and he did. In fact, he took more than three hundred people to Honolulu, where they stayed at the brand new Sheraton Waikiki Hotel, and the cost was under $300 per person. It was the first time I had ever been on an airplane. I thought all flights would be like that one.

Since I was the cameraman for the trip, I had to race ahead of the group so I could be in front of the Sheraton when the buses pulled up and the hotel was officially opened. That meant I was the first registered guest at the Sheraton Waikiki, and that meant I got to stay in the penthouse suite. When the Sheraton celebrated its twentieth anniversary, they invited me back for a free week in that penthouse suite. Those were great days.

Most normal days at work were filled with the usual news stuff: fires, wrecks, city council and school board meetings—the things that fill up a newscast when there's no big story going on, like the tornadoes and hurricanes on the Texas Gulf Coast and other natural disasters that I covered (along with a fair share of man-made calamities).

As I gained more experience, I started to cover bigger stories. I spent a good part of my summer in 1972 covering the Democratic and Republican national conventions, both held in Miami that year. That was the same summer as the burglary at the Watergate Hotel, which, of course, would become a huge story, but not before I got to cover Richard Nixon's second inauguration in January 1973. Years later, in 1984, I produced the station's coverage of the Republican National Convention when it was held in Dallas. I was behind the scenes working for Channel 4, and my brother, who was chief of staff of the RNC at the time, was onstage sitting next to Ronald Reagan while Nixon stood at the podium and gave his acceptance speech.

If I had spent my entire career as a photographer or reporter—or, in my case, a combination of both—I would have enjoyed a great life, the one I set out to have all the way back in my high school years. But there was something else.

I often thought of the words of my high school journalism teacher, Ann Voss, who noticed that I seemed to enjoy doing stories about people and their lives, and thought that was what I should be doing.

There was a reporter on the CBS network at that time who was doing the closest thing to what Ann Voss was talking about. I watched everything he did and admired his work. He was the best storyteller I had ever heard, even better than my dad. His stories had purpose and meaning and hope. He had been a "real" reporter, had even served as a war correspondent in Vietnam, but his forte, it seemed, was telling the American Story, about the everyday men and women who keep the country running.

His name was Charles Kuralt.

On the Road with Charles Kuralt was the result of some brainstorming that took place between Charles and CBS News anchor Walter Cronkite, commonly called "Uncle Walter" because of his ability to communicate to America that no matter how bad things were at the time, "Everything's going to be all right." And he did that without ever saying the words. He was a constant, a touchstone for the American people, the most trusted man in the country. Plenty of people believed the old adage "Walter said it, I believe it, and that's that."

But Cronkite was also a realist who somehow had his fingers on the pulse of his audience. In the late 1960s, he was acutely aware of the tumultuous decade that America had just been through, and of how important the medium of television had become to the world. It started with the assassination of President Kennedy and continued through the ramping up of the Vietnam War, war protests, the great division that had developed between the Baby Boomers and their parents, the assassinations of Martin Luther King and Bobby Kennedy, and the race riots in every major city in the country. At the end of a newscast, Cronkite would wonder if his audience was worn out from hearing all the bad news and felt like killing the messenger.

Cronkite suggested to Charles Kuralt that perhaps they should consider finishing up every week with a final story, the last one on the CBS Evening News each Friday, filled with good news so that just maybe America could go into the weekend with positive thoughts instead of thinking about blood and guts and doom and gloom.

On the Road with Charles Kuralt was born.

As a TV journalist who was full of the energy and hope that go with being young, I watched Kuralt's *On the Road* series with the belief that there was room for more of what he was doing, and that I was just the guy to do it.

"We can do the same thing," I thought, "except ours will be in Texas."

The more I thought about it, the more promising my idea seemed—at least in my mind.

I think I was probably like a little kid who wants something and constantly pulls on his dad's pants leg asking if he can have it. "Let me! Let me! Let me!" I don't know how many times I approached Bill Ceverha and Eddie Barker with my half-baked idea, but I feel like it was a lot. Had Eddie shut me down with a firm no, I might not have kept going back to him with the idea, but I got the "Let me think about it" answer instead. To me that meant "maybe." I kept asking.

The thing that finally pushed my idea into a real discussion was a visit by a man named Frank Magid, a former social psychology professor who headed up a market research company he had founded in the late 1950s, Frank N. Magid Associates. *Time* magazine called him "the local television news doctor."

Frank had no idea who I was, of course, but he was an advocate of changing the face of local news by convincing TV stations to abandon the old single-anchor format and introduce what we now refer to as "happy talk," the light banter between anchors. He was a proponent of morning news shows becoming more than just a repeat of the stories that had aired on the 10 o'clock news the night before, by including social news and stories about both celebrities and ordinary people plus a sprinkling of stories about the economy, education, beauty secrets, and personal finance. His research, he claimed, proved that viewers were tired of the same old, same old television news.

And (trumpets sound here) he was a huge believer in the power of human-interest stories, the very thing I had been begging to do at Channel 4.

Frank told the bosses at KDFW-TV that they were missing out on reaching a new audience by not doing more human-interest stories, and he pointed out that the station was uniquely positioned to gain viewers by doing just that because of the geographic makeup of the DFW market. Most of the viewers might live in Dallas and Fort Worth, he told them, but lots of viewers lived in the mid-cities area between the two, and lots more viewers lived in the little towns within a hundred-mile radius. He told them the only time those viewers saw anything on Channel 4's newscast specifically about the town they lived in, it was when something happened there—and most of the time that something was bad.

Frank told the bosses to send reporters out into the little towns and out-of-the-way places within the Channel 4 viewing area and do "good news" stories. Talk to the people on the streets, get their opinions, ask them what they think about what's going on in the world. The man-on-the-street interview was a staple of every newscast in those days, but they were almost always conducted on the streets of downtown Dallas and Fort Worth. Frank argued that people in small towns have opinions too and should be asked to share their thoughts. But probably the most important reason Frank gave the bosses for doing this was "Some of those people also have ratings diaries"— the book that some viewers were asked to fill out in the days before ratings were calculated electronically.

Those bosses at Channel 4 took Frank Magid's advice and, in the summer of 1972, decided to not only include human-interest stories in their news, but to produce a weekly half-hour show that would be filled with that kind of reporting. It would also include man-on-the-street interviews with people in the smaller towns within the Channel 4 viewing area.

Finally, they were going to act on my idea. But I would not be the one doing it.

Part Three

THE FIRST YEARS OF FIFTY

CHAPTER FIFTEEN

SUPER BOWL VI, MY FIRST SUPER BOWL, WAS PLAYED ON January 16, 1972. Channel 4's sports director, Dick Risenhoover, flew commercial and left town early because he was stopping somewhere else first and would join me in New Orleans shortly after the team arrived. I flew on the Dallas Cowboys charter, a Braniff Airways plane that the team always used. Same pilots, same flight attendants, same everything every time.

After Dick left the station to catch his flight, Eddie Barker introduced me to a new employee named Norm Hitzges. I asked what he would be doing, and Eddie enthusiastically said, "He's our new assistant sports director." I welcomed Norm and told him we would be working together quite a bit since I traveled with the Dallas Cowboys. Norm would go on to become a Dallas sports legend and still is today. I've never met anyone who knows sports quite like Norm, and I am one of his many admirers and friends. He's a media legend, at least in Dallas–Fort Worth.

When Dick and I met up at the team hotel, just across the highway from the New Orleans airport, I asked how he liked his new assistant sports director. His reaction wasn't what I expected.

"What?" he almost screamed. "I don't know anything about an assistant sports director! What are you talking about?"

I told him about meeting Norm and apologized for breaking the news to him because I thought surely he had approved the hire.

I later confirmed that nobody had told the sports director he was getting a new employee, much less an assistant SD. The timing, with Dick out of the office for more than a week to cover the Super Bowl, seemed pretty strange too, but what did I know?

I couldn't imagine why someone would hire an assistant director without telling the director, but I was only twenty-one at the time and knew I had a lot more to learn, so I didn't give it much thought—until something similar happened to me. I would come to know that this is just the way things in business are sometimes done.

In August of that year, after I had just returned from covering the national conventions in Miami, I saw a new employee walking around the newsroom. I asked Buster McGregor who the new guy was, and he just said, "That's John MacLean. He was at a San Antonio station and was hired to work here while you were gone."

John had a deep, soothing, somewhat rural-sounding voice and speech pattern, and a look that was memorable: mutton-chop sideburns, a full head of curly hair, and wire-rimmed teardrop glasses. You couldn't help but like him. He was a nice guy.

Later that day I overheard some of the photographers talking about the new show the station would be airing soon.

I asked what they were talking about, and they told me it was a weekly program with human-interest stories and some man-on-the-street interviews filmed in the smaller towns in the viewing area. And they said the new guy, John MacLean, would be hosting it.

All the air was sucked out of the room. I almost blacked out. My head was spinning. Nothing made sense, and I couldn't believe what I was hearing. I was pretty sure no one else knew I had been tormenting the boss to do this show for months because I always kept things like that quiet, so I knew they weren't making this up just to see my reaction. I learned early on that a newsroom is a very competitive place, and you can't trust anyone, so it was always best to keep things to yourself.

It was late in the day by then, and I knew I couldn't go into Eddie's office and ask about it without being emotional. My shift was over, so I quietly slipped out the back door and went home. I agonized about it all night, with my mood swinging from devastated to angry to just blank. I wondered what I had done wrong to have this happen. I wondered if I was losing my job for some reason. My mind raced, and I got no sleep that night.

I wasn't supposed to go to work the next day until 3 p.m. because it was my turn to work the 3–11 shift, but I got up early and was waiting by Eddie's office when he walked in the back door. Only a few people were there that early, and Eddie invited me in and told me to shut the door.

I sat down and started to speak, but he interrupted me. "Let me tell you what's going on." He said he knew I would be upset and had intended to tell me before I heard it from someone else, but an important meeting the day before had kept him out of the newsroom most of the day. Then he said the words that rang in my ears for days after.

"Bob, you're not ready for this. You're only twenty-one and you're still in college. This is a full-time commitment and when your classes start again, you'll be back to working afternoons and evenings, and this show will require more than that. You might even have to give up shooting the Cowboys games."

I just looked at him, because I had no response. He was right. I knew it, he knew it, the whole world knew it. I wasn't ready, and my school schedule wouldn't allow me to give 100 percent to the new show. It was basically my idea, but I wasn't going to be the face of the show when it went on the air.

Eddie told me he did want me to work on the show—producing, shooting, and editing, whatever was needed. I would still have to do my news shifts and travel with the Cowboys, but he wanted me to be involved. He acknowledged that I had proposed the idea before Frank Magid presented it, and that he and I would always know that, but it wasn't going to be my show.

Since I wasn't due to go on the clock until midafternoon, I left the station and just drove around for a while, thinking about the turn of events and coming to terms with it. I ended up going by the place my mother worked. By then she had left the Hilton Inn and was the executive housekeeper at the Holiday Inn Central, a famous 1950s-style hotel on Central Expressway that was well known for, among other things, its long hallway art gallery where many portraits by Dallas artist Dmitri Vail were hung. Mr. Vail even had his own table in the hotel restaurant, a circular booth with a red phone and a sign that said "Reserved for Dmitri Vail."

I remember going into my mother's office and crying on her shoulder. This was my safe place, where I could let my emotions go, and I did. She told me all the things that mothers say at a time like that and said my day would come, but it was hard to believe at that moment.

I then met my dad for lunch at the Bonanza Steak House on Mockingbird Lane. It had become a tradition for us to eat there when I worked the late shift, and today was one of those days.

He knew pretty quickly that something was wrong but waited for me to bring it up. When I told him why I was upset, he said what dads say at a time like that. He told me the truth.

"Eddie is right. You can't do that and finish school, and you're probably not ready for this. Eddie is a good man and you need to trust him on this."

I knew he was right but still had to protest.

"You don't even know him," I said. "How do you know he's a good man?"

He then told me something I should have known almost three years earlier, when I was hired for the job, something neither my dad nor Eddie had ever mentioned . . . until that day.

"Eddie's been a customer of mine for years," Daddy told me. "I've known him for a long time. He lives in the second house behind my service station on University Drive."

My head swirled like it was in a bowl being beaten with a KitchenAid mixer. "Did you have anything to do with me being hired in the first place?"

"Not a thing. Eddie never mentioned interviewing you or hiring you or working with you. Not one time since the day you met him. He keeps that separate. Like I said, Eddie is a good man."

CHAPTER SIXTEEN

4 COUNTRY REPORTER WENT ON THE AIR ON OCTOBER 7, 1972. The time slot was 6:30 Saturday night, immediately after the 6 P.M. newscast.

A lot of decisions have to be made before a new TV show can go on the air. Those decisions were made in the short amount of time between August and October, most of them last-minute.

In 1972 this stuff was much simpler than it would be today. Nowadays it usually takes months or years to get a show on the air because everyone has to sit around and talk it to death. Now we talk about the graphics package, the music, the pacing, the mood, the shooting style, and on and on. We might even produce a rough-cut pilot episode and show it to some focus groups to get feedback. Back then we just did it.

Many of the decisions we had to make were pretty much made for us by Kerry Richards, a very talented young director who worked closely with the station's promotions department. Long before the show was planned, after Frank Magid first suggested that the station pay more attention to the small towns in its ADA (area of dominant influence, the name for the viewing area back then), Kerry produced a lengthy promotional piece to run on Channel 4 several times a day. It was primarily beauty shots, mostly of the rural areas in the ADA, and it had no narration, just music and an announcement at the end to go along with a graphic on the screen that said, "This is 4 Country!"

The audience had never seen anything like it. Most promos were fast-paced action shots with the faces of the station's reporters and anchors rushing here and there looking like they were doing something important. This promo was a breath of fresh air, and the audience responded to it. The tagline "This is 4 Country!" became the station's slogan, and Kerry quickly produced other promos. The new show itself was still on the distant horizon.

But when it came time to put it on the air, Kerry stepped up and said, "Why don't you just call it *The 4 Country Reporter?*" After some discussion, it was decided to drop "The" and just call it *4 Country Reporter*, plain and simple. "This is 4 Country, and the guy who hosts the show travels around looking for stories, so he's the 4 Country reporter."

Then, just as the final editing was being done for the first episode, Kerry had either a lucky moment, or a genius moment, or a moment of divine intervention. We needed music to open the show, and he said, "I know just the piece."

He went into a room we used to produce sound and emerged a while later with a cut from an album called *Pops Goes West*, by Arthur Fiedler and the Boston Pops Orchestra. There was some grumbling about using "orchestra anything," and some people were asking why the hell would we use something from a Boston orchestra instead of a Texas piece of music, but there wasn't time for a real protest, and when Kerry played the song, everyone agreed that it had to be the music we used. Besides, who says we have to use the same piece every week? We can change it when we want to, right?

That piece of music became the show's signature, and it turned out that its roots were in Texas. It's called "Hill Country Theme," and it's a rousing piece written by a movie theme composer named Glen Paxton. It had been commissioned by the ABC network for a special program they produced when Lyndon Johnson was president, called *LBJ's Hill Country*. It had words too, written by Cindy Walker of Mexia, Texas, a member of the Country Music Hall of Fame for the many songs she had penned, but we didn't use them, at least not in the early years of the show.

A few years after we first used "Hill Country Theme," I ran across an obscure album by Willie Nelson called *Texas in My Soul*. It was obscure because Willie had changed record labels after recording it, and somewhere along the way the master recording had been destroyed. One of the pieces on *Texas in My Soul* is "Hill Country Theme," sung, of course, by Willie Nelson. We used it for one of the many musical features we did on the show over the years, and you would have thought it was the Second Coming. Viewers let us know immediately they wanted to hear more of Willie singing the song, so we would trot it out once or twice a year to give them what they wanted.

In the days before email and social media, TV stations depended on three things to know what the audience was thinking: phone calls, which provided instant feedback; good old-fashioned snail mail, letters and postcards delivered by the US Postal Service; and finally, the ratings service, but that took months. After the first airing of *4 Country Reporter*, the phones lit up. In the early seventies, KDFW-TV still had a receptionist who sat by the front door and answered the phones, even nights and weekends. All calls in those days came through the main switchboard before being forwarded to the person or department the caller was trying to reach.

Several of us who had worked on putting the first show together were at the station that evening in October when the show aired, and before it was even over, the receptionist signaled an employee walking through the lobby to look at the switchboard. Every line was lit up, and she was answering calls as quickly as she could. We later found out that most of the callers were simply showing support for what we were doing and said they wanted to see more shows like that. The calls continued into the night. On the Tuesday after the first show, a bag of letters and postcards arrived at the station, most of them echoing the sentiments expressed by the callers, and some of them suggesting other stories we might look into.

The decision had been made by public opinion: the show would continue. By Christmas we would know what the ratings for the month of November were, but the fact that viewers liked the show enough to write and call was all the station needed. It's interesting to look back on those times and think about how slowly the Nielsen ratings came in. Today the ratings are almost instant, and decisions are sometimes made about the future of a TV show immediately after its first episode airs. But in 1972, this was the best we could do.

For the next several months *4 Country Reporter* continued to produce more human-interest stories, some better than others, as the show tried to find its niche. There were stories on farmers, bakers, boot and spur makers. Stories about old-fashioned hardware stores where they carried items you didn't see much anymore. A few of the stories were meant to be humorous, while others had a more serious tone, yet never as serious as the hard news stories people were used to seeing. No two stories were exactly alike, and a true formula for the show had yet to develop as those who worked on it kept trying new ideas to see which ones worked.

The one thing we all knew was this: people saw the show as a respite from the news, a place where they could escape the real world, or at least the real world as it was presented on the news. It was important that it stay that way, but hardcore journalists consider the kind of stories presented on *4 Country Reporter* unnecessary and they usually call them "fluff"—and the news bosses were determined to mark the show with their brand.

The order came down prior to the first episode of the show that it would contain at least one segment of news-related material. This would be done in the man-on-the-street format, and it was easy for them to justify because it was precisely what the consultant Frank Magid had recommended: "Go out and see what people in the small towns in your ADA think about what's going on in the world." The news gods needed no more justification than that.

To make matters worse, I thought, the man-on-the-street interviews came smack-dab in the middle of each episode. The show started with scenes from the Texas back roads with the theme music playing, then went into the first story. After a commercial break, the viewers would see the *4 Country* van pulling off the back roads and heading back into downtown Dallas. The van was an old Ford Econoline with an aftermarket air-conditioning unit on top (we had named it Esmerelda for no particular reason). Then the show host, sitting on a stool and wearing a coat and tie, would introduce the man-on-the-street topic of the week (Watergate, Vietnam, who should be president, blah-blah-blah), followed by the interviews, which were followed by a tease of the story that would be coming up in the last segment of the show. The final video, set to music as we were going into the next commercial break, was of the Dallas skyline getting smaller and smaller in the van's big rearview mirrors.

I thought this was a mistake, but, again, what did I know? I was twenty-one and still in college. My experience in the business was short compared to others'. All I knew was that Charles Kuralt on CBS did not travel all over America asking people what their opinions were on Watergate and Vietnam, or who the president should be. I thought they were missing the point of the show to include that stuff, and even suggested that those man-on-the-street interviews be shot in small towns, while the human-interest feature stories were being filmed, and then included in newscasts, not in *4 Country Reporter*. But even though a few shows into the first season it was easy to see that people in small towns were just as divided on the issues as people in big cities were, the newsy stuff would continue for a while.

By the time the November 1972 ratings period (better known as "sweeps") was over, eight episodes of *4 Country Reporter* had aired, with the last four of those episodes counted in the numbers we would see in the upcoming ratings report. We had to wait until December 22 that year to get the book, but when it arrived, it was truly a Christmas present. The ratings for the new show were through the roof.

It was looking like *4 Country Reporter* was here to stay.

CHAPTER SEVENTEEN

*I*THINK EVERY PHOTOGRAPHER IN THE CHANNEL 4 NEWS-room worked on the show at one time or another during the first few years. A few photographers preferred the fast pace of shooting and editing news stories, while others were attracted to the longer-format, slower pieces produced for a thirty-minute show. The first few months, I worked on the show every chance I got, which was a lot. Looking back, I sometimes think the assignments editor, Buster McGregor, was being nice to me by not throwing as many news stories my way, freeing me up to work on the show. I was probably a pain in Buster's side sometimes, but we had a lot of mutual respect.

But as the months went on, it seemed a couple of the news photographers got to spend most of their time shooting and editing *4 Country*. Mike Phillips (no relation as far as he and I know) started working almost full-time on the show, and he and John, the host, seemed to work well together. I, on the other hand, did not fit well with John. We were about as different as night and day and had little to talk about, so it was probably difficult for him to spend an entire day with me working on a story. I know that working with him all day was hard for me, but I learned early on that in the TV news business, you are going to be paired with people who are not to your liking, and the best thing to do is concentrate on getting the job done.

I always remember a piece of advice Buster gave me early on: "At the end of the day, these people are not going to be your best friends, so just keep it professional."

I kept my hand in the show as much as was practical but didn't go out of my way to be on every story, and I started spending less and less time on it. Instead, I started producing human-interest stories for the newscasts. They could only be a maximum of about two minutes long, but I got to do more of what I wanted to do. Besides, after the success of *4 Country Reporter*, sprinkling more human-interest pieces into the newscasts was an easy sell.

I graduated from SMU in May 1973 and was immediately given a full-time reporting job. Since I had been doing a lot of one-man-band stories, what the promotion meant to me was that now reporting was my primary job and photography was my secondary job instead of the other way around. I still shot many of my own stories, but now I was expected to take whatever general assignments stories Buster told me to do. Reporters were also expected to show up every day with a story in mind in case it was a slow news day, and I was pretty good at coming up with those.

One thing I was attracted to early on was social news reporting, especially if it got me out of boring city council and school board meetings. I had subscriptions to magazines like *Cosmopolitan* and *Glamour*, where I would find stories about women's health that I could easily convert to a TV news story by finding the local angle. I kept my ear to the ground and did a lot of stories on trends like aerobics, an exercise philosophy invented by Dallasite Dr. Ken Cooper. I also got a chance to cover a few political stories and found that sometimes interesting but often boring.

The next several months went along without drastic changes, and *4 Country Reporter* became firmly entrenched in the Channel 4 schedule and continued to do well in the ratings. I had to admit that John MacLean did a good job with it. I would watch every week and see things I liked and things I would change if I could, but overall, I liked the direction in which the show was going. If only they could get rid of those damn man-on-the-street interviews.

Then, out of the blue, the guys that ran the station decided that if one *4 Country Reporter* show was such a success, there should be two *4 Country Reporter* shows. But, again on the advice of the consultant, the second show would be aimed at a younger audience. This is where it gets messy because, once again, I was bypassed for the show. Well, sort of. They asked a reporter who had been there longer and was a couple of years older to do the new version of the show, and even I admitted that was the right thing to do. At first he said yes, but then he reconsidered and said it wasn't what he wanted to do with his career, and then there was some back and forth. If I'm remembering correctly, I think he participated in the pilot and maybe even an episode or two, but eventually he begged off, and I got the call.

Just as it did with the original *4 Country Reporter* show, the station didn't spend a lot of time coming up with a name. It, too, would be *4 Country Reporter*, but because it would be aimed at a younger audience (loosely identified as anyone still in their teens or maybe early twenties), the name, as uncreative as it could be, was going to be *Young 4 Country*. Wow.

Here's the good news. At that time the top-ranked show on American television was *The Waltons*, on the CBS network. The bosses at KDFW-TV decided *Young 4 Country* would air at 6:30 P.M. on Thursdays, leading into *The Waltons*, which was a huge show for family viewing. This meant we would get the benefit of any early tune-ins, with the audience getting a glimpse of the end of our show while they waited for *The Waltons*. Taken together, the two shows would amount to an hour and a half of TV shows promoting American family values.

It worked. It took almost no time at all for *Young 4 Country* to achieve the same kind of ratings the original show was getting on Saturday nights, and some weeks our ratings were better. It was kind of funny how we went about doing this, because both shows shared the same vehicle and that took a lot of planning. When things got tight, we would either borrow one of the news cars or use our personal cars, but Esmerelda, the *4 Country* van, had started to develop an identity of her own so we wanted to have her with us as much as possible. We worked it out.

The two shows coexisted for a while, both enjoying excellent ratings, both developing audience loyalty, until late one night when the walls came tumbling down. In a matter of minutes, what had been would be no more.

CHAPTER EIGHTEEN

*J*OHN MACLEAN HAD DEVELOPED QUITE A FOLLOWING among the early viewers of *4 Country Reporter*. He had an easy-going style, a good smile, and a look that could be either back-roads savvy or GQ cool. This was the early 1970s, and it was hard to tell if he was a city guy who looked a little bit hippie or a country boy who didn't quite give in to the big-city look. This was a good place to be if you were hosting a show like *4 Country Reporter*, because the audience is made up of all kinds of people, and the best-case scenario is for each viewer to think you're just like them.

It was no secret in the newsroom that I wanted the job John had. After all, I had come up with the idea for the show long before Frank Magid legitimized it with his audience statistics. But no matter how big my imagination was or how high my dreams soared, I was also a realist and knew I hadn't been in the business long enough to do something just because I wanted to do it. I accepted that. And I still believed I had a great job, far better than I had imagined when I was growing up. I was okay with it . . . at least for a while.

When the *Young 4 Country* job came along, I was grateful, and even though some of the guys in the newsroom called it *Baby 4 Country* or *4 Country with Training Wheels*, I laughed along with them. I enjoyed working on the show, and that's all that mattered to me at the time.

It was also no secret that John and I were about as opposite as two people can be. I've always been a nerd. The life lessons my dad gave me early on stuck with me, so I was never part of the cool crowd and was in no way a party animal.

John, on the other hand, was the kind of person everyone wanted at their party, the kind of guy that other guys wanted to have a drink with after work. We lived in opposite worlds.

I don't know exactly what happened, and I'm not confident enough with hearsay to repeat it here, but what I read later is that one night the Dallas Vice Squad served a search warrant on John's apartment and arrested him. He was charged with something to do with drugs. I honestly never knew the exact charges and always figured it was none of my business. I knew enough to stay out of it.

The TV station almost immediately suspended John and sent him home. This was a public relations problem; you don't want one of your on-air personalities to have a drug charge hanging over their head. But I always thought it was strange that lots of TV people had been charged with DWI over the years and most of them just kept on doing their jobs. If drugs were involved, it was a completely different matter, and I don't think that has changed much almost fifty years later.

Of course, I endured a few people in the newsroom who made cracks like, "Hey, Phillips, are you the one who narc'd on John?" I'm sure some people thought it made perfect sense that the guy who openly coveted John's job had turned him in to the cops. But here's how naïve I was about that world: I did not know if John, or anyone else for that matter, used drugs, or sold drugs, or manufactured drugs, or what. I didn't even know what kind of drugs people used other than the pot that everyone seemed to be smoking in those days. I just wasn't clued in to that stuff enough to narc on them. And it's simply not something I would ever do.

Eventually, months later, I was told that John had entered into some kind of plea bargain and most of the charges against him were dropped. But apparently there was still at least one charge, because the same day the plea was entered, KDFW-TV terminated his employment. End of story. Except not for John. He adamantly denied all charges against him and even wrote a screenplay about what had happened. Friends who knew him said he spent many years trying to get someone to make the movie, but that never happened. I personally never heard from or saw John again, and have no idea how life turned out for him, but I wish him all the best. He was always nice to me, and I am grateful to this day for the work he did to make *4 Country Reporter* a success from the beginning. He blazed a trail for me.

Right after John was arrested, the guy who was initially supposed to do *Young 4 Country*, Jeff Rosser, was moved into the driver's seat on *4 Country Reporter*. Jeff was a great-looking guy, blonde with dimples and a fabulous smile. He was very sharp and knew what he wanted to do with his life, and it was not driving around in an old van producing stories about ordinary people doing extraordinary things. Jeff was a thinker, and the kind of guy you immediately knew could go wherever he wanted. But he took the job and did great things with it because "the show must go on." The audience was used to John, but quickly warmed up to Jeff.

Then Jeff announced that he was leaving the station to become assistant news director at a station in Tulsa, Oklahoma. He wanted to be in management, and he pursued that dream. Years later he returned to KDFW-TV as vice president and general manager. He was running the station where he had started his career as an intern. I have always admired Jeff for knowing what he wanted and going after it. And I was grateful that he kept the show going until I could take it over.

There was some jockeying around with the host position on *4 Country* until the station hired a guy named Joe to be the new full-time host. I think he came from a market in Georgia. He looked kind of like Jeff and had a true southern—not Texas—drawl. Eddie Barker and Bill Ceverha had left by then, and the people who were running both the station and the newsroom were not Texans. In fact, they were from California, and Connecticut, and places about as opposite from Texas as you could get, so to them a drawl was a drawl. The only qualification you had to have to host the show, it seems, was that you talked slowly.

But the new host bombed. The phones lit up, the letters poured in, and my recollection is that Joe lasted about a month, maybe less. It was a disaster.

Then, on a Thursday evening, immediately after *Young 4 Country* aired and just as *The Waltons* was starting, I got the call. Wayne Thomas, the news director, said, "How would you like to host *4 Country?*"

He didn't have to ask twice.

CHAPTER NINETEEN

W E TRIED TO KEEP BOTH *4 Country* SHOWS GOING FOR a while, but that didn't last long. One day I was told *Young 4 Country* was going away, and I was to "roll" those stories into the original show. I said I would—then I just kind of "forgot." I never thought they were serious about doing that. It was just a good line to use in a press release. The station had to have a reason for cancelling the show about young people. But they didn't. I sensed that was the case and was fine with it.

I'd been wanting the show for years, starting in 1971 with me pulling at Eddie Barker's pants leg begging, "Let me! Let me! Let me!" And finally the show I had dreamed up was mine. Of course, it wasn't exactly the show I had dreamed up. Everyone puts their own spin on things and brings their own strengths to any project. Even with different hosts, the show was still the one John had put on the air. Everyone else just kind of filled in the blanks and kept doing what he had been doing.

By this point, Channel 4's news ratings had dropped, and the station "down the street," WFAA-TV, was kicking our butts. The great Marty Haag had arrived at WFAA around the same time that we put *4 Country Reporter* on the air, and he was turning Channel 8 into the TV journalism mecca of America. Every serious journalist wanted to work there, and it was becoming like the college team that wins lots of national championships—all the best athletes want to play ball there. WFAA had their pick of talent and assembled a staff made up of the cream of the crop.

I noticed that *4 Country Reporter* was no longer "top of mind" for the bosses at Channel 4 because they were fighting for their lives in the news ratings. That meant less scrutiny of me, and the first thing I did was drop the in-studio segment from the middle of the show, the part where the host suddenly appeared in a coat and tie instead of the jean jackets or denim shirts that we wore in those days for the other parts of the show. I never once appeared on *4 Country Reporter* in a coat and tie, hosting from the studio.

The news director said I could not, under any circumstances, drop the man-on-the-street interviews, so we compromised. I did the hosting part for that segment the same way we did all the others: from the *4 Country* van and wearing boots and jeans like I did in everyday life.

I also changed the invitation line at the top of the show. John would tell the audience what was coming up on that night's show, then say, "Let's go listen to the people of *4 Country*." My line was, "Why don't you hop in and travel with me?" It was just a different approach, and to my way of thinking, the line seemed more inclusive and less newsy sounding. It was as if I were saying, "That seat over there is for you, so get in and ride along with me." I cannot tell you how many letters and, later, emails we have gotten over the years that said something like, "I feel like I'm riding along with you." That was the idea, an idea that worked like I'd hoped. We still get those emails daily.

For a while I continued asking people, "What do you think about Watergate? About Vietnam?"—or whatever was going on at the time—until one day when we were shooting the man-on-the-street segment in Forney, a little town just a few miles to the east of Dallas. I still hated the news aspect of the show. In my mind, that was never part of the equation. This was supposed to be people's respite from news, a few minutes that they could just kick back and enjoy.

That day in Forney I told the photographer who was working with me to just go along with what I was going to do. Then we walked up to two guys having a conversation over the bed of a pickup truck. You see guys posed like that a lot, especially in small towns and especially around feed stores, hardware stores, farm stores, and the like. These two were no doubt solving world problems.

I said, "Excuse me, fellas, but could either one of you gentlemen set me straight on something? I'm wondering . . . Does a cow stand up with her front legs or back legs first?"

Without skipping a beat, the guy on the right side of the truck said, "Back legs."

Then the guy at the rear of the truck looked at his friend and said, "Since when?"

The friend fired back, "Since the dawn of time, that's since when!"

Then they went at it, each of them sure they were right, and each one arguing the point without backing down. Finally, they both just stopped talking and shook their heads like they were completely disgusted by their friend, who clearly did not know this essential information. It was great.

Powerful television. Totally meaningless fun. And it was not at all newsy. I have no idea how that question got into my brain. I just blurted it out.

We ended that segment with a shot of a cow that could barely be seen lying in a field of bluebonnets. Then she stood up. We said nothing, and let the picture speak for itself. End of segment. Commercial break.

I figured that after the show aired on Saturday, I would be called on the carpet for dropping the news question I was supposed to ask. But on Monday, the news director passed me in the hall and said, "Great show this week. You should do more middle segments like that. I laughed my ass off."

And that was that. We continued with the man-on-the-street interviews for a while, but news questions were now a thing of the past. Just like that.

Instead we went to the town of Fate and asked people what they thought about destiny.

We went to the town of Comfort and asked people if they were comfortable in their lives there.

When we finally traded in our old van, we had a "Name the New Van" show. We took the new *4 Country* vehicle home to, where else, Van, Texas. There we talked to people who knew the van when it was younger, before it hit the big time on TV. A high school coach remembered the van was quite a sprinter on the track team. And we had a mechanic crawl underneath to determine if the van was male or female. (Remember, the original van was named Esmerelda.) He came rolling out from under the new van on a mechanic's creeper and yelled, "It's a boy!"

"Are you sure?" I asked.

"Oh, definitely!"

Of all the names submitted by the audience, the one that was finally chosen was "Jerod Armadillo DeFooch." It made no sense. But not everything needs to make sense. Some things are just fun. It was perfect.

When we did ridiculously silly television, people loved it. We provided lighthearted moments in very serious times. And it was just the thing to allow me to transition *4 Country Reporter* into the show I originally had in mind. I had gotten lucky . . . again.

CHAPTER TWENTY

*H*AVING SUCCESSFULLY CHANGED THE SHOW FORMAT to get rid of the hard news aspects, it was time for us to concentrate more on the reason I wanted to do this show in the first place—storytelling. I simply wanted to tell the stories of ordinary people. We had been doing that from day one, but not exclusively. Now that would be our bread and butter.

My dad always told me that "everybody has a story." I believed that then and still do. Our job is to find out what that story is and tell it in such a way that other people want to hear it.

WHEN WE FIRST STARTED OUT, PEOPLE DIDN'T KNOW US. There were times that we would show up in a small town, and people either looked at us like we were up to something or shied away from us. In big cities, people were used to seeing TV cameras on the street, but not in the smaller towns.

One time we were in East Texas during a particularly beautiful sunset. A huge orange ball was setting behind a line of pine trees with a pasture full of Hereford cows grazing in the foreground. Since we were always on the lookout for beauty shots that we could work into the show to establish a mood, we pulled over quickly to the side of the road and set up the camera on a tripod to roll some film. The photographer and I were both standing outside the barbed-wire fence when we heard a voice. "What are you boys doing to my cows?"

I turned around, startled, and there stood a man in overalls pointing a shotgun at us. He was smiling so I thought maybe he was joking, but I was still scared that he was not. I wasn't sure I had heard him correctly, so I said, "I'm sorry, sir. What did you say?"

He repeated his question. *Yep, I thought that's what he said.* Now I was getting the idea that this was no joke. I started talking very fast, explaining that we were just two working guys from Dallas who were shooting beautiful scenes of the East Texas countryside for a TV show and that his cows were absolutely gorgeous and we didn't think he would mind if we took a picture of them. I probably went on longer than that in hopes that he would put the gun down. And he did.

He smiled even bigger, obviously flattered that I was aware of how beautiful his cows were, and said, "Oh, that's all right. Sure, you can take their picture. I just saw that contraption you were pointing at 'em and thought you might be trying to beam 'em up to your mother ship."

Seriously. I can't make this stuff up. He later told us the gun was not loaded.

After the show had been on for a while, people started recognizing us, or at least they recognized the van with the name of the show plastered on it.

A few years after the "mother ship" incident, we were out very early to grab a shot of the sun coming up over a field. We weren't but a few miles from the spot where the man pointed the shotgun at us when the sky started to turn red, meaning the sun would be up in a few minutes. It was just light enough that we could see several acres running next to the road where there was some cotton growing, and we decided that would need to be the spot or we were going to miss the sunrise.

We let ourselves through an unlocked gate and went out a ways to set up and get the sunrise shot, trying not to disturb anything. We left our van out on the roadside because we weren't about to drive over someone's cotton, so we all squatted down to admire our beautiful shot as the sun rose over the horizon.

About that time, one of the guys said, "Uh-oh," and we all turned to see a combine heading toward us with its headlights on, making the machine look like an evil creature marching across the earth to swallow us up. I flashed back to the shotgun scene and wondered how much trouble we were in.

The combine pulled right up to us, and the farmer swung open the door and jumped out. He took a look at us and said, "Oh, it's you. I was afraid it was some kids out here tearing things up. When's this gonna be on *4 Country?*"

My, how things had changed.

There were lots of bizarre encounters and interesting interviews over the years, like the time I topped Medina Mountain on Highway 16 going toward Kerrville and encountered an ostrich. She was running fast toward me but in the other lane. That ostrich was going somewhere. Just around the next curve, as I drove the switchbacks on that piece of road, was a guy wearing a clown suit and riding a tiny bicycle. He was carrying a lasso and going after that ostrich as fast he could go.

But one of my favorite encounters was with Jay Gentry of Lake Creek. Jay owned a little grocery store south of Paris, Texas. The sign that at one time had hung over the entry had blown down years ago and never found its way back up. His shelves were stocked with mostly canned goods, things like Vienna sausages and Beanee Weenees, and just about all of those cans were covered in dust. We learned why when we looked at the expiration dates and found that some of them had been there for ten or twenty years. He did sell a few newer items like bread and cans of Coke and Dr Pepper, and packages of nuts and crackers brought there by the Tom's deliveryman.

It seemed that the most popular product in Jay's store was conversation. Several men were gathered around, most of them sitting on a box or a stool, and they talked about whatever came up. We had already learned that we couldn't go wrong with a story about an old store, especially if there were people there who were willing to talk.

I pulled out a couple of the go-to questions I had learned from my dad, such as, "Say, are you guys about to get that trouble straightened out in your church?" Daddy said every church he ever heard of had some kind of problem and that asking like you knew about it often brought on a great conversation. And, of course, I asked if they solved any world problems in that little store. And, of course, they said they did.

One of the old guys kind of whispered to me, "Ask Jay about television."

I whispered back, "Why? What's that about?"

"Jay has never seen television. Never."

We set up to do a one-on-one interview with Jay Gentry, with the two of us standing near the front door. He told us about his little store and how long it had been there, and that it was the heart and soul of the little community, where people liked to gather, and he liked for them to do just that.

When we had exhausted other topics, I said, "Hey, Mr. Gentry, I notice you don't have a television in here."

"Nawwww," he said. "I don't watch television."

"You don't watch television? You mean you've never seen our TV show?"

"Nope," he replied. "I've never seen it in my life."

Then he paused and said, "I've never seen television at all. I've had folks tell me about it, but it sounded like a waste of time to me."

"You've never seen it? Never? That means you didn't get to see the men landing on the moon, doesn't it?"

"Nope," he said. "You never will make me believe they landed on there. I don't believe in stuff like that."

"You don't believe that men landed on the moon? What do you think all that was?"

"Well, it was just a fake," he said.

And that was that. Except at that point Mr. Gentry glanced up at the clock hanging over the front door to his store and said, "Oh, it's five o'clock."

And without saying another word, he grabbed a fishing pole and walked out. Our camera followed him as he crossed the road in front of the store and kept walking across a field.

One of the old guys in the store said, "He does that every day at this time, rain or shine. There's a pond back there with some nice bass."

The interview was over. Fishing took priority. I remember thinking, "Now there's a man who has his priorities straight and his life figured out."

A few months later we were on our way back to Paris to do a story about a grave marker in the town cemetery. We had heard that one particular gravestone had a statue of Jesus on it—and that Jesus was wearing cowboy boots. We couldn't miss that, because we were certain cowboy boots didn't exist at the time that Jesus walked the earth.

Since the road to Paris took us right by Jay Gentry's store, we decided to stop and say hello.

After we exchanged the usual pleasantries, Mr. Gentry said, "I hitchhiked up to Paris to watch that show of yours. I've got a friend that lives in a nursing home up there. I saw the story you did on this place."

I couldn't help but think how strange it must have been that the very first time Jay Gentry saw television, HE was on it.

I asked him what he thought about the show.

"Oh, not too much," he said. "I don't think I've been missing out on anything."

What a delightful, honest man.

CHAPTER TWENTY-ONE

*H*OLDING ON TO THE PAST" HAS BEEN A RECURRING theme for us. We seem to be attracted to people who are either living in the past, longing for the past, or dealing with their past in some way.

Another favorite story relating to this theme was the time we met Opal Hunt. Like Jay Gentry, Opal had a little grocery store. It had belonged to her father, and she grew up in it when it was the center of Bradshaw, Texas, about halfway between Tuscola and Winters on Highway 83 south of Abilene. When Opal was a little girl, she would play in the store, and she worked there when she was old enough. Over time, Bradshaw had pretty much dried up and blown away. But Opal stayed right there in her daddy's store. She said she wasn't going anywhere.

It was a cold, wintry day when producer/photographer Brian Hawkins (or BH, as we call him) and I stopped by. Opal was wrapped up in a heavy sweater, with a scarf around her head, and was sitting by an old potbelly stove. It was the only heat she had. Like Jay Gentry's store, the few items on Opal's shelves were covered in dust. There were some items I was sure were not even made anymore. I asked if anything was for sale.

"Just sodie pop," she said.

I asked why she stayed.

"Ohhhhh, these are my memories, Bob. I wouldn't take anything for them."

I stayed the whole day with Opal. I sat on a peach crate while she rocked in her chair and told story after story about the glory days of Bradshaw, Texas, and about her family, especially her dad. The more she talked, the more I realized this place wasn't just full of Opal's memories. It was a shrine to her father, a man she worshipped. He was the type of man that Opal realized wasn't made anymore. There would be no more like him.

We stopped by to see Opal from time to time when we were in the area, and I watched her getting older as the store deteriorated around her. Still, she sat in that rocking chair.

Then the day came when Opal moved to a nursing home in nearby Winters, Texas. And not long after that, we got word that everything left in the Bradshaw store would be auctioned off. It made me sick to my stomach to think about it, and I wondered if Opal was aware that her memories were about to belong to the highest bidders. I hoped she did not know.

One day I stopped by the nursing home to say hello, and the first thing Opal said was that "They're having an auction, gonna sell everything in my store." I tried to tell her it didn't matter, that it was now just stuff, and asked how she liked having real heat and running water. My question did not distract her from the problem at hand.

"I just wish I could have my rocking chair," Opal told me.

BH has no tolerance for a world where the things and the people that used to be important, the things and people that got us all where we are today, have no value. He refuses to stand by and allow someone who can't stand up for themselves to be treated badly. And he was not about to let some junk dealer walk out of that store with Opal Hunt's chair. I could almost see his brain working as he figured out a plan.

I don't know how he did it. I swear I do not. And I probably don't want to know. Well, I do, but it's probably best that I don't. But BH called me and said, "C'mon. I got the rocking chair. We're going to Uvalde."

Like Bradshaw, Uvalde is located on Highway 83, but it's an almost four-hour drive south, at the intersection with Highway 90, almost due west of San Antonio.

Uvalde is the home of a man named Robert Hensarling, and he was another of our favorite stories. Robert had been a Uvalde police officer who made mesquite rocking chairs at night and on the weekend, and the chairs he made were unlike any we had ever seen before. They were, and are, works of art. I have one, and I cringe anytime someone visits our home and sits in it. I would just as soon have it on display like it's in an art gallery.

I don't know if our story had anything to do with this, but after it aired, Robert quit being a Uvalde police officer so he could just work on his chairs.

And now BH and I were headed out of West Texas to South Texas and Robert Hensarling's shop.

Opal Hunt's chair, it seemed, had seen better days and was not safe to sit in, so of course we could not let her have it in that condition. We pulled up to Robert's shop and told him the story.

"Let me have it for a few days," he said. "I'll fix it. Opal's gonna have her chair."

We delivered the chair to Opal at the nursing home in Winters on her 101st birthday. The people who took care of her weren't sure how much she would remember, but they told her, "Bob and Brian are coming to visit you."

We went in to say hello, and I said, "Opal, I've got a birthday present for you." Then I went out the door and came back in carrying the rocking chair.

Opal collapsed, sobbing.

"I thought it was gone," she said over and over.

She cried, I cried, BH cried, and everyone in the nursing home cried. She sat in her chair again, just like she did the day we met. There was no potbelly stove, and the old store was gone, but Opal had that chair, the conduit to her memories of growing up, to her memories of her father.

When I left, Opal was holding court in her chair, telling stories about the Bradshaw store to anyone who would listen. She was smiling and laughing.

I never saw Opal Hunt again.

CHAPTER TWENTY-TWO

SOMETHING THAT STILL AMAZES ME ABOUT THE STORIES we tell on the show is how close we often get to the subjects. It doesn't happen every time, probably not even most of the time, but there are certain stories, certain people, that just find their way under your skin and then travel all the way to your brain, your heart, your soul.

For me, Milton Watts was one of those people.

Milton grew up in Marion County on a farm and ranch. You've probably noticed that I often combine those two things, farms and ranches, when I talk about them. That's because most families did a little bit of both in the old days. Many still do. They grow their own food. Some of it comes from the ground, some of it from animals they raise. For some people, it's a matter of survival.

Milton's family always had a herd of cows on the land his father bought in 1923, and they also grew some fruits and vegetables. In tough times, they were still going to eat. That's what Milton had planned for his life too. But for Milton, that wasn't going to happen.

On December 11, 1959, the US Army Corps of Engineers completed construction of Ferrell's Bridge Dam on Big Cypress Bayou. The dam was needed for flood control and water storage, not to mention the fish and game preservation that would come as a by-product.

In a matter of a few months, the Watts land had been flooded, and it eventually became Lake O' the Pines in deep East Texas.

I first heard about Milton in 1982, when I received a letter from a man who said he delivered Coca-Cola products to Milton's store at Island View Landing on Lake O' the Pines. He said Milton had written hundreds of poems, some of them six or seven pages long, and that he could stand in front of you and recite most of them from memory.

"The man is a poet," he said. "But when you first meet him, you won't think so."

I had to go see for myself, but I admit I wasn't expecting what I found. First, I figured a guy who ran a bait shop and grocery on the edge of a lake probably wrote rhymes, not poetry. But since I know nothing about poetry, it didn't matter to me what he wrote. It sounded like a fun story, and he sounded like a fun guy.

Second, when I first saw Milton Watts standing on the edge of the lake, helping some city kid with his fishing pole, I thought this guy was straight out of a movie. He had the look of an authentic backwoods entrepreneur, the kind of guy who never met a stranger, the kind of guy who had his fingers in every pie. I was right about that part. He was wearing a felt gambler's hat that had grown permanently fixed to his head at just the right tilt. His long-sleeved shirt was kind of tight, with the sleeves rolled up a couple of times, and two or three top buttons undone in front. He looked like a guy who could hold his own and came to get the job done. He did not look like a poet.

I could quickly see that whether or not he was a poet, this man was a lot more than a rancher-farmer–fish camp owner. He was also something of a backwoods philosopher, and when he talked, his voice was easy, but the feelings deceptively deep. You have to watch out when you're talking to Milton because he can hypnotize you with his stories, make you slow down when you don't think you can, make you consider the quiet, important things in life.

Looking back on it, I now realize Milton did not look like *my idea* of what a poet would look like. Even after all this time traveling the back roads, I know I am still guilty of conjuring up mental images of people after hearing something about them, especially after talking to them on the phone. Time and time again I have been wrong.

Milton showed us around his place and told us the story about the dam and the lake. Standing at the end of a pier that hung out over the water, he told me about his dad.

"He was the type of man who could raise ten or fifteen bales of cotton with a mule," he lamented. "And yet he wasn't able to afford a pair of overalls with what he made. I get kind of emotional telling this, and sometimes I get choked up and I can hardly talk about it because I want people to *remember* men like him, and I want people to *respect* men like him."

Milton's words went deep into my soul. He and I were instantly and forever connected . . . just like that. I know why, and so do you. He wasn't just talking about his dad, he was talking about my dad too. And his words expressed what I had not been able to put into words. I just had the feelings.

Milton said them out loud for all to hear. My respect for this man will last my whole life.

Milton told me he turned to poetry when most of the family land was underwater and he had been left on the water's edge to make a living selling bait and Cokes to city slickers.

"I wanted to be a farmer and a rancher," he told me. "I planned to put a big piece of beef on people's tables. That was important to me."

When reality set in, Milton turned to telling his story and those of others around him. He became a student of poetry and mastered the skill to the point that he found himself giving lectures at colleges and universities, and matching wits with degreed English professors who were fascinated by his understanding of how the classic poets worked.

Dr. Jerry Hopkins of Marshall, Texas, a historian and retired university professor, said this about Milton Watts: "Home-spun wisdom and common-sense observations about everyday life. He has that rare gift of poetic expression and enthusiasm that captures and captivates. You will find his poems descriptive and interesting, sometimes rough, even at times crude, but they are a product of his East Texas experience and environment."

Milton just puts it like this:

> By nature I'm a gentle man, conservative, square,
>   perhaps at times however I am a bit prone to swear.
> Over-emotional Irish ancestors like emotions to me did bequeath.
> I'm something of a weeper, a wailer, a gnasher of teeth.

In person, Milton seemed to like ending his poetry sessions with what sounded to me like instructions for his tombstone:

> Greedily I feasted on life. Sometimes I fasted.
> Life is now gone. The epitaph: it was good while it lasted.

His book is called *Poet o' the Pines: The Accumulated Works of Milton Watts.* I highly recommend that you read it. It's the story of this true Texan's backwoods life, sprinkled with a bit about the history and culture of the part of East Texas where he grew up. It's important.

I visited with Milton many times after our first meeting, and he appeared on the show several times. He is a Texas treasure and will forever be my friend.

CHAPTER TWENTY-THREE

W HEN *4 COUNTRY REPORTER* FIRST STARTED AIRING
on KDFW-TV, it was the golden-haired boy. By the time
the show turned ten or so, it had become the red-headed stepchild.

The show itself was getting better and better, and the ratings were too.
The commercial spots were always sold out. But management had become
preoccupied with other, more important things. I was never allowed to forget that we didn't do "real news." We were considered the fluff guys, and had
our stories been used in a real newscast, they would have just been filler. It
was a constant fight to keep the show on the air, but I kept fighting. And,
to be fair, we were one half-hour program every week, and the TV station
management had 24/7 to worry about. We were still supported and still on
the air, and that's what mattered.

But there were other problems too. The problem was that management
and I no longer got along. I had become a thorn in their sides. They had a
successful show, but it was headed up by a guy who didn't play by their rules.
That was nobody's fault; we just didn't see eye to eye. Don't get me wrong,
there was no open animosity, just a difference in philosophies about the
show. It happens routinely in our business.

Channel 4 had been through a few changes in the news director position.
Eddie Barker had left back in the mid-seventies and was replaced by a man
named Wayne Thomas. Wayne and I had a mutual respect and got along
fine, and he was a big fan of *4 Country Reporter*. He's the one who offered
me the hosting job after trying "the three Js" (John, Jeff, and Joe). For the
next several years, things were stable. Then came a few more management
changes, and in 1984, Wendell Harris moved from the *Times-Mirror*–owned
station in Austin to the newly acquired *Times-Mirror*–owned station in Dallas: KDFW-TV.

Wendell was an interesting man. He had been on an almost identical career path to mine at a *Times-Mirror* station in Birmingham, Alabama, where he had been a reporter, anchor, and assignments editor. Then he decided to go the management route and became a news director. People who knew him at Channel 13 in Birmingham said he had been a good reporter and knew his way around a newsroom. We never got to see that side of him in Dallas because he rarely left his office. It was a glass cubicle that overlooked the studio where Channel 4 was now broadcasting its news programs.

On his third day at KDFW, Wendell summoned me to his office for what I was told would be a get-acquainted talk.

It's important to know that by this time I had carved an office for *4 Country Reporter* out of a storage room down a long hallway near the engineers' garage, on the exact opposite side of the building from the newsroom. KDFW had never given our show its own space to work in, and we were supposed to just squat where we could. The problem was that in those days the show was recorded on what was called quad tape—huge, heavy reels of two-inch-wide videotape. As producer of the show, I had to keep track of those tapes. There was no place to store them safely anywhere in the station, or at least that's what I was told. I decided I would have to take matters into my own hands.

One Saturday I went to the station and walked around until I found a long, narrow storage closet that was mostly filled with empty boxes. It had a long cabinet on one side that was perfect for keeping track of the show tapes, and an old metal desk in one corner. I moved the boxes out, swept and mopped the floor, and claimed it. By the time Wendell Harris arrived, I had already been there for more than a year.

When I walked into Wendell's office, right there in the glass cube where everyone in the newsroom could see, he didn't stand up, didn't shake my hand, didn't even look at me for a long time.

His first words to me were, "I don't know *who* you are or even *where* you are or *what you do* most of the time. I've been here three days and this is the first time I have ever seen you. [We had been on the road shooting the show.] All I know is that you are a line item on my news budget and I don't like it. I hear you produce and host a popular show here, and my boss tells me I can't cancel it, but you will do nothing without my permission from now on. Are we clear?"

I said, "Yes, sir" and left his office. Nothing else was said.

After leaving Wendell's office, I wrote down exactly what he had said so I could read his words later and try to figure out what he meant. I was stunned. I had no idea how to react. I didn't know how to proceed at that point. Up until then, I had tried to produce the show without getting in the way of the news folks. They had a job to do, and so did I. I always thought it was best for me to do nothing to bring attention and scrutiny to our show, though sometimes I found myself fighting for it.

After rereading his words and thinking about them, I still didn't like what Wendell had said. But I remember thinking that if I were in his position, I would probably feel the same way, so the next day I dropped a calendar off at the newsroom secretary's desk. It was filled out with exactly what we were doing every day for the rest of that week and the next. Fran, the secretary, said she would give it to Wendell and let me know if he needed anything else. I heard nothing back, so I continued dropping off those calendars with all the information I could think of: what stories we would be shooting for the show, where they were, phone numbers where we could be reached; the fact that we would be editing all night every Thursday because we weren't allowed to take up valuable news editing time and space (and did much of the editing over the weekend); the fact that I would be in the control room directing the final posting of the show every Friday from 1 P.M. to 4 P.M.; and, finally, the fact that I regularly worked a minimum of twelve hours a day.

I didn't hear another word about my schedule or where we were or anything from Wendell Harris . . . until he called me in a few weeks later and asked if it was true that I was interviewing for a job at WFAA-TV.

CHAPTER TWENTY-FOUR

*I*N THE FALL OF 1984, AS I SAT AT THE STEMMONS FREE-
way offices of Audience Research and Development talking
with news director Marty Haag about my future, I remember asking myself,
"Why me?"

At that point I had close to fourteen years of experience in the local news
business. I had received my Bachelor of Fine Arts degree from Southern
Methodist University in 1973 and my master's degree from SMU in 1977.
I had covered some major stories, but nothing that made me a big deal,
certainly not a household name. I was the backup anchor on the morning
and noon news shows when longtime anchor Walter Evans was off work.
He had been at Channel 4 so long he had at least twelve weeks of vacation
a year, so that meant I had to go to work at 3 A.M. for a period of time, plus
do my other work. To put it bluntly, I was not a star. I was just one of many
beat reporters, and had it not been for my other role as host of *4 Country
Reporter*, not too many people would have known my name. In short, the
way I saw it, there was nothing special about me. So I asked Marty.

"Your Q Score is through the roof," he said.

My what? I had never even heard of a Q score before that moment, so
I didn't know what to say. I think I just stared.

"For whatever reason, you have a high rate of recognition among people
in this market and they like you," he continued.

Okay. So that's it? That's hardly an endorsement of my work. In fact,
I thought he was almost saying it . . . *reluctantly*. I later found out that that
was just Marty Haag. He didn't get too excited about stuff. Everything was
very matter-of-fact with him. I think it was part of his unbiased look at the
world.

Nothing was settled between Marty and me that day. Like he said, he was just opening up the conversation for the future.

I found it interesting that Channel 8 had tried numerous times to introduce their own local shows in the Saturday 6:30 P.M. time slot, and that even though they were now the uncontested news leader in the DFW market, the shows they put up against *4 Country Reporter* never did well in the ratings and never lasted. To me, they seemed formulaic. In fact, each time they tried a different show against ours, we were seriously worried at first, simply because they were the big guys in town, and we thought they could crush us if they wanted to. But it only took a few episodes to realize we had nothing to worry about. It almost looked like they were stuck in a rut, because they repeatedly trotted out the same anchor guy to do various versions of what seemed like the same old show to compete with *4 Country*.

In the end, our ratings continued to be great, with *4 Country* coming in during February 1986 at a 13 rating/23 share, while *Six-Thirty*, the latest Channel 8 attempt, came in with a 2.8 rating/5 share. Maybe that had something to do with why Marty and I had a secret meeting at AR&D, and why he had blown-up video on the wall with images of me.

Marty did eventually offer me a job at Channel 8. He wanted me to host *PM Magazine*, which was created by the Group W-owned station in San Francisco. It was later expanded to stations all over the country after the Federal Communications Commission enacted its Prime Time Access Rule, requiring the top fifty US TV markets to fill the time between 6:30 P.M. and 7 P.M. with locally produced programming. The *PM Magazine* formula was great for helping stations comply with the FCC restrictions, because each market used their own local talent to introduce not only local feature stories but also stories produced by other *PM Magazine* crews across the country. Kelli Lee (Kelli Phillips, after we married) would eventually become co-host of *Texas Country Reporter*. She was the co-host of the San Antonio version of that show at KENS-TV when she was just eighteen years old, about a year or two after I would have been host of the Dallas version of the show—had I accepted the job.

The DFW version of *PM Magazine* was one of the most successful anywhere, hosted by Leeza Gibbons, who went on to become a huge national TV personality, and Bill Ratliff, who became the face of WFLA-TV in Tampa for almost thirty years. Ratliff had already left WFAA-TV for Florida when Marty offered the *PM* slot to me.

I turned it down for two reasons. First, it was a bit too much "happy talk" for my taste, and the stories were mostly lighthearted. They were well done but usually had no soul. Each segment had a predetermined length, whether it was merited or not. The other reason, the reason I gave Marty, was that

I had heard WFAA was considering dropping *PM Magazine* after the current season. Group W had raised its fees for the local stations while decreasing the amount of local advertising time in each episode, making it difficult for local stations to make money on the program.

PM Magazine lasted nationally until about 1990, but less than a year after Marty offered the host position to me, WFAA-TV dropped the program. It moved to KDFW, where I was still working at the time. At KDFW, the show had a greatly reduced budget from what it had at WFAA and died a slow, painful death. The ratings weren't good, and Wendell Harris told me I had to do a special segment on *4 Country Reporter* about the host of *PM Magazine*. He wanted to capitalize on our show's ratings to help kickstart the other show. That was about as far off in terms of the format of our show as it could get. I protested, but my protests were useless. Luckily, I never had to do that piece because my show was cancelled before I could get around to it. Darn the luck.

CHAPTER TWENTY-FIVE

*I*N SEPTEMBER OF 1986, AS JAMIE, JASON, LARRY, AND I sat in Wendell Harris's office after being summoned back to Dallas for some important news, we had no idea what to expect. He told us to sit down while he shared some important news with us.

"Boys, *4 Country* has outlived its usefulness," he said. "You've done your last episode. It is cancelled as of this minute, though repeat episodes will continue to air until our new show is ready."

The words rang in my ears, and Jamie, Jason, and Larry appeared to be in shock. But I wasn't really surprised because I knew how bad the tension had become between Wendell and me, especially recently.

Somehow word had gotten out that I had been meeting for the last couple of years with Marty Haag from WFAA-TV, the crosstown rival. There was speculation about it in local newspaper columns in the *Dallas Morning News*, the *Dallas Times-Herald*, and the *Fort Worth Star-Telegram*.

A couple of months earlier, when Wendell had asked me if it was true that I had interviewed for a position at WFAA, I told the truth.

"No, I have not."

And I hadn't. There was no position available that I wanted. I had turned down the offer to be the host of *PM Magazine*, a position I did not seek, long before Wendell asked me about interviewing at Channel 8. Since that time, Marty and I had met a few times for lunch, just staying in touch. I had never set foot inside WFAA-TV at that point.

To some, my answer to the question "Have you been interviewing for a job at WFAA?" might seem incomplete. But I could justify it because I had not interviewed for a specific job. In my heart, I knew I was interested in moving to WFAA-TV, because I thought it was a way I could keep doing the kind of work I enjoyed without moving to another market where I would have to start all over again. But a desire is very different from an interview.

I did have one brief, chance encounter with the WFAA-TV general manager, Dave Lane, and the sales manager, Buff Parham. Although Marty and I usually met at his favorite French restaurant on McKinney Avenue, one time we went instead to the S&D Oyster Company, also on McKinney. Just as we were finishing lunch, Dave and Buff came in the front door. They headed to our table and said hello. We made small talk, and I distinctly remember Dave asking Marty, "You guys getting anything figured out?"

Dave then turned to me and said, "I love your show. You do a great job with it," and told me about seeing a guy he knew from his hometown of Fairfield, Texas, who had been featured on *4 Country* recently.

Before we parted, Marty said, "Don't take this the wrong way, but I wish Channel 4 would just cancel your show."

I knew what he meant by that. *4 Country Reporter* had a large, extremely loyal audience. Marty and the others at Channel 8 did not want to be the bad guys by stealing me—or the show. If I left of my own accord, it would probably look to the audience like a money or power grab. People don't care what your reasons are, just what you do. None of us wanted to be the bad guy.

When Wendell told us our show was cancelled, he let it sink in for a minute. He then looked at the other three guys and said, "We are starting a new show called *Sports Scene* that will air at 6:30 on Saturday nights, and you three will be working on that."

He then looked at me. "And you, Bob, are going back to general assignments reporting. You could use some more time on the street."

At that point I was five months shy of my sixteenth anniversary of going on the air at that very station and was the senior reporter in the newsroom, though I had been doing less news reporting lately. But Wendell thought I needed more time on the street. I was okay with that, because I knew that my immediate plan upon hearing that *4 Country* was cancelled was to move to WFAA . . . if I could.

The next day I reported to the assignments desk and asked if they had anything for me. They said, "Not yet. Give us a little time to go through the day's stories."

A few minutes later my phone rang. (I had moved from my storage room office to a desk in the newsroom the afternoon before.) The call was from an old friend at the Dallas Police Department.

"I don't know if this is anything," he said, "but one of our officers was arresting a guy, and the guy bit the officer. Then he told our officer he has AIDS. The DA is considering filing attempted capital murder charges on him."

I was back at the assignments desk in a flash and told them what I had found out. AIDS was still fairly new to the world, and people were scared to death of it. If the attempted capital murder charges held up, it would be the first time in the United States that this had happened. A photographer and I left and interviewed the officer, a police spokesperson, and an assistant district attorney.

That night my story was picked up by the network and aired on the *CBS Evening News* with Dan Rather. It was my first day back to full-time reporting. Wendell never acknowledged that my first story after he cancelled *4 Country Reporter* made the network news, but others in the newsroom were aware, and there were lots of high-fives that evening, including from the assistant news director, Steve Hammel, who told me the irony of the moment did not escape him. The guy who bit the officer, by the way, did not have AIDS. It was just a threat in the heat of the moment.

In spite of everything that had occurred, the management of KDFW-TV apparently still felt that I had value. My contract had expired more than a year before and we had been in negotiations since then, so they could have easily fired me when they cancelled the show. Not only did they not do that, two days after they cancelled the show I was called into Wendell's office and presented with an offer.

"Maybe you and I got off on the wrong foot," he said. "I don't dislike you or your show. The reason for canceling it is that the parent company has an opportunity to bring in a major sponsorship from a beer company, and they couldn't do that on *4 Country*. It will mean a lot of money to the station."

I appreciated getting this information because it had been killing me to think they had cancelled my show for no reason. Apparently, they had one, and it was a legitimate business decision.

"I can't extend an actual offer at this time," he continued, "but here's what we have in mind."

"We" had to mean Times-Mirror Broadcasting president John McCrory. He had been the general manager at Channel 4 when *4 Country* started and, at least at one time, considered the show to be "his baby."

Everyone knew that no one at KDFW-TV, including Bill Baker, the news director and GM, made any serious decisions without John's approval. He was a very hands-on boss.

"Steve Bosh probably won't be staying when his contract is up in a few months," Wendell said. "There will be some anchor changes, and we want to consider you for the 5 or the 6 and 10."

I wasn't buying it. And even if I considered this to be a serious suggestion, it wasn't an actual offer. Nor did I want to be a full-time news anchor. Instead, after almost sixteen years, I felt it was time for me to leave.

I told Wendell I was flattered, but the truth was I had greater opportunities elsewhere.

CHAPTER TWENTY-SIX

*T*HE DAY AFTER *4 COUNTRY REPORTER* WAS CANCELLED, Ed Bark, the *Dallas Morning News* TV critic and a well-respected voice in the community, wrote an article about the fate of the beloved show. It appeared on the front page of the metro section. Like WFAA-TV, the *Dallas Morning News* was owned by A. H. Belo Corporation; in fact, the two sat across a shared driveway from one another. At KDFW-TV we had been told that Ed Bark was the voice of Channel 8, and to take anything he wrote with a grain of salt. We were also told that anyone caught talking to him would be fired.

This WFAA-TV conspiracy theory was also the reason that employees at Channel 4 were no longer allowed to enter their work in the Katie Awards competition, an event produced by the Dallas Press Club every year. According to KDFW management, it was controlled by WFAA. I doubt that anyone believed that. I know I didn't.

Ed Bark's article ended with something like "maybe WFAA will step up and save the day." Similar articles by Bob Brock of the *Dallas Times-Herald* and Art Chapman of the *Fort Worth Star-Telegram* appeared the same day.

At that time most of downtown Dallas was on the 744 and 748 telephone exchanges. So many calls from angry viewers poured into KDFW-TV's switchboard that other people were having trouble getting through to the banks, law offices, and other businesses in downtown Dallas that were also on the 744 and 748 exchanges. The same thing was happening over at WFAA-TV, with anxious viewers demanding to know if Channel 8 would be picking up *4 Country Reporter*.

But before word got out to the public, the news of our show's cancellation had made it over to WFAA. I took a call from Marty Haag within a few hours of hearing the news myself.

Marty said, "I think it's time for you to come over and talk."

"At the station?" I asked.

"Sure, why not? I'm okay with it if you are."

Marty set the meeting for later that week because "a couple of key players can't be here until then."

I arranged to go to work late that Friday morning, and at 10 A.M., Marty met me at the front door of WFAA-TV and led the way to an office in the front of the station. In the office sat the general manager, Dave Lane; the sales manager, Buff Parham; and the program director, Bill Cox. The next hour was filled with lots of questions and answers. There was an urgency to get to where everyone was trying to go.

At the end of the meeting, everyone but Dave and I left the room. Dave asked if my crew from Channel 4 would want to come with me if they decided to pick up the show. I told him I would find out over the weekend and let him know on Monday.

The next evening Jamie Aitken, Larry Ellis, Jason Anderson, and I gathered at my house in Old East Dallas, and I recounted my meeting with Dave Lane and company at Channel 8. We were each aware that TV shows aren't always successful when they move from one network or station to another. We also agreed that it was worth taking the chance.

On Monday, after my call to Dave, another meeting was set, and another after that, with the same crowd gathered as before.

By this time I had been contacted by Ed Bark, Bob Brock, and all the other media beat columnists and reporters in the Dallas area, who wanted me to comment on what was going to happen to our show. Their newspapers were receiving huge numbers of letters to the editor asking why the show had been cancelled and what was going to happen to it. I decided the best course was to be honest and admit that I was trying to move the show to Channel 8. Even though I was still an employee of Channel 4, I didn't want to be in the position of deceiving the public, the very people who had made my show a success. It would make things uncomfortable while I was working at KDFW, but at least I wasn't hiding anything. I could live with that. But could they?

Some of the letters to the editor published by local newspapers gave me the courage to speak out publicly about the show's cancellation.

Virginia Oldham of Dallas wrote to the *Dallas Morning News*, "There is only one *4 Country* with Bob Phillips—probably the most sane program on TV. My family desperately needs *4 Country*."

Lynda Everheart of Grand Prairie told them, "Bob Phillips not only seemed to care for the people we saw on the screen, he kindled an interest in the way things were done in our past and where to go for a small bit of beauty and peace remaining in the world."

It took a few weeks, but when we finally got to the point where it was decision time—Was our show moving to Channel 8 or not?—we knew there were logistical questions that had to be answered. Some of them were very simple.

"What are we going to call this show?" Dave asked. "We can't exactly call it *4 Country Reporter.*"

Buff Parham was the one who said, "No, but we sure as hell can call it *8 Country Reporter* and keep the equity that's been built up in the name."

I found out later that Ward Huey—the president of Belo Broadcasting and vice chairman of Belo's board of directors, a legend in the broadcasting business—thought Buff's idea for the name was a good one. As it turned out, he was a huge fan of our show and became one of my greatest champions. I'm sure Ward played no small part in what was happening in the room that day.

It was time to put the plan in motion, so Dave picked up the phone and called KDFW-TV.

"This is Dave Lane at WFAA," he said. "Is Bill Baker available?"

In the next two or three minutes, Dave laid out the planned course of action for Bill, KDFW-TV's general manager.

"We are hiring Bob to come over here and do his show, and we plan to call it '8-Country Reporter.' Bob says he wants to bring his crew with him, and they want to come."

I couldn't hear what was being said on the other end of the line, but Dave's response was, "Bill, you guys cancelled the show, and I'm sure you know the viewers are upset about it. You have a chance to turn this around and look like heroes. We both do."

Dave put the phone down and said, "He'll call back in five minutes."

In less than the promised five minutes, he did. Bill agreed to all of Dave's terms. They would even make a joint announcement about the two stations working together to save the beloved program. That never happened.

Bill's parting words were: "Tell Bob he and his guys have thirty minutes to clear their personal things out of our building."

Part Four

A NEW BEGINNING

CHAPTER TWENTY-SEVEN

*H*ERMAN "TRAIN" GATES WAS STANDING IN FRONT OF his shop on a corner in a residential neighborhood in Carthage, Texas. We had heard about a man who worked at one of the schools in this East Texas town, a man who was a hero to the kids there. That's because . . . well, here's what I said in the story I wrote back then:

> Herman Gates is kind of a hero to the Carthage kids. That's because, when chains slip and spokes break and tires blow, Herman Gates is always there, with a quick fix and a smile. The kids have even given him a nickname.
>
> "They call me Train," he says.
>
> "They call you Train?" I ask. "Why is that?"
>
> "Because I imitate a locomotive," he replies.
>
> "A locomotive?" I ask. "Let's hear that."
>
> "Train" Gates then cupped his hand over his mouth and let out a sound that was . . . well, exactly like a train whistle.
>
> "That's the reason they call me Train," he says.
>
> But it's writing poetry that warms the heart of Herman "Train" Gates. He calls them his little speeches, but poems is what they are. Poems about life, and love, and people.
>
> "I've even got one on myself," Train says. "I know it, by memory, my first one and all of 'em like it!"

> Now some folks call me Shorty, and others call me Slim
> My brother calls me Buddy, and Mama calls me Jim
> My cousin calls me Wayne, my white friends call me Train.
> I don't care what they call me, even though it isn't sweet,
> Just so long as my wife calls me when it's time for me to eat!

Those were the highlights of the first story we ever produced for the new *8 Country Reporter*. That first show also contained a whimsical piece on the Lickskillet Store, an old retail establishment that had the state line between Texas and Louisiana running right down the middle of it. There were two phones—one on the east wall, one on the west—and it was a long-distance call between them. Our "serious" piece for that first show was about a place called Ramage Farms, an old homestead that was now being run by the second or third generation of the Ramage family. It was a thought-provoking piece that made you wonder about the future of the family farm while making a statement about the American family itself.

A few days earlier we had walked out of KDFW-TV after the phone conversation between Channel 8 GM Dave Lane and Channel 4 GM Bill Baker.

As promised, we were given thirty minutes to get our personal things and leave the building. Even though I had been there almost sixteen years and had practically lived at that station, I was expected to walk out with one cardboard box. They say you shouldn't take your personal stuff to work. I'm here to attest to that. Don't do it.

The guard at the front door was assigned to accompany us as we got our stuff and left. When no one else was around, the guard apologized for the treatment, but I told him that I might do the same thing if I were Channel 4 management. The fact is, we were leaving to join the competition and shouldn't be lingering in our old offices or stirring up discontent with the employees. And we had no discontent to stir. This was simple survival.

I noticed that the tapes containing the last couple seasons of *4 Country*, the ones that were in my old storage room office, had been removed. I don't know where they took them, but years later I found out that they were erased and used again for other projects. And the film reels in the basement that contained the first ten seasons of the show were loaded up into a van and taken to the city dump. All of the other taped episodes were discarded too. But I don't think this was a malicious move. The station had new management, and they simply weren't clued in to the history of what had happened with our show. Why would they be? In television years, it was ancient history. As far as they knew, they were just doing some remodeling of an old building and had to make room for other things. Our old tapes were in the way. I do wish someone had let us know. We would gladly have picked up the tapes. But I don't think anyone thought to do that either. Again, ancient history.

For the most part, the first fourteen years of *4 Country Reporter* do not exist. I say "for the most part" because a few of the engineers grabbed a keepsake clip or two and later gave them to me. It was a symbolic gesture from some guys who worked hard to make that show a success—and who became a group of *Texas Country Reporter* devotees.

I left Channel 4 with nothing but warm feelings for the station and the people who had given an eighteen-year-old kid a break and nurtured me to the point where I had my own TV show. I still have fond memories of those days and admire what KDFW-TV was and is: one of the greatest TV stations in the country.

Because we left KDFW with nothing, we had to rebuild everything from scratch, but for the team we worked with at WFAA, that was no big deal. Those folks could move mountains, and we knew we were working with the best of the best. At Channel 4, we were on our own to get the job done. At Channel 8, other employees welcomed us and offered to help if they could. That was especially surprising to us because WFAA had recently gone through a 10 percent staff reduction following an efficiency study, so we naturally thought there could be some resentment from employees whose friends had been laid off. It didn't happen. The people there welcomed us warmly.

After we moved over to WFAA, we spent just one day getting settled and setting up the stories for our first show, then hit the road. We used camera equipment provided to us by the production department, and the best time for us to shoot stories without getting in anyone else's way was on the weekends. For that first show, we left on Friday morning, shot three stories—along with all the interstitials (beauty shots, stand-ups, and extra shots needed for editing)—and rolled back into the station late Sunday night. We spent the next three days writing the scripts for those stories and setting up future episodes of the show, and edited all day Wednesday and all that night. At 1 P.M. on Thursday we went into Control Room A and mixed the first show, which would air the next night at 6:30 P.M., one day earlier than the time slot we had at Channel 4. We were replacing the second half-hour of WFAA's 6 P.M. newscast.

Early Monday morning, after the airing of the first *8 Country Reporter*, I was walking down a long corridor that ran from the Channel 8 newsroom toward the back door of the station when I encountered Bert Shipp, the assignments editor for WFAA-TV news. Bert was an old warhorse TV journalist, one of those guys who was there when the building cornerstone was laid. He knew more about TV news, and more about the Dallas–Fort Worth market, than any other person alive. Bert was there with a camera when President John F. Kennedy's motorcade passed down Elm Street in downtown Dallas, moments before he was assassinated near the now infamous Texas School Book Depository. He was a no-nonsense guy who was stingy with a compliment. Most people called him "Hoss." I was both incredibly impressed by him and scared to death of him because Bert always told it like it was.

"Well, well, Phillips," he said as he approached me. "Caught ya' show Friday night. You [and I'll have to clean this part up by paraphrasing] kind of used every bullet in your arsenal, didn't ya'." That last part was a statement—definitely not a question.

"We'll see if you can do it again this week."

And that was that. The first episode of *8 Country Reporter* had just received the highest accolade it could achieve, at least as far as I was concerned. Bert Shipp liked it. This was going to work.

The letters and phone calls from the viewers confirmed what Bert had said. So did the November 1986 ratings book. The ratings did not match what we had at Channel 4, but we didn't expect that so early in the transition. And they were still very respectable. Since Bert was the first to say he liked it, and he was a god in the business, I believed we were on the right track.

CHAPTER TWENTY-EIGHT

W HEN WFAA-TV'S GENERAL MANAGER DAVE LANE offered to save *4 Country Reporter* by moving the show from KDFW, where it was born, to his station across town, the offer did not come without a few caveats. No one was sure that a show that had been so successful at a crosstown rival station would still be successful after changing its address.

Articles by Ed Bark, the *Dallas Morning News* TV critic, certainly helped us make that transition. He was highly complimentary of our work and ran an article on Saturday morning, before the first episode at Channel 8, reminding viewers to tune in.

WFAA also gave us some on-air promotional support.

When superstar sports anchor Dale Hansen—whom I worked with at KDFW and WFAA, and consider a friend—had left KDFW a few years earlier to go to work at WFAA, the promo showed Dale walking out the front door of Channel 4, hailing a taxi, and taking the short ride over to Channel 8, all the while telling the cab driver where he was going and why.

When I made the switch from *4 Country Reporter* to *8 Country Reporter*, the promo showed me walking out the front door of KDFW (*THAT was an uncomfortable moment*), hailing a cab, and telling the cab driver where I was going and why. The taxi pulled up to WFAA's building, and as I got out and walked away, the camera cut to a tight shot of the taxi driver, the first time viewers saw his face. At that moment they found out the taxi was being driven by my friend Dale Hansen.

Dale said, "Cheapskate didn't even leave a tip."

Still, with all the support we were gifted, and it was a lot, we had to prove ourselves. Truth is, we accepted the offer to move to Channel 8 knowing that it was only good for thirteen weeks. If the show caught on in that amount of time, we were golden. If not, we were out.

As those first weeks clicked off the clock, Jamie, Jason, Larry, and I were invited to join program director Bill Cox and others from the programming department for a Christmas lunch in late November at the Hard Rock Cafe on McKinney Avenue. It was great, and we were feeling like part of the team. Then Bill made the surprise announcement that Channel 8 had just acquired *Wheel of Fortune*, the number one syndicated show in America, from the NBC affiliate KXAS. The same show we had beaten in the last May ratings book. They would run it six nights a week at 6:30 P.M. It was going to be fabulous.

As the words came out of Bill's mouth, I think he suddenly realized this was not good news to the four of us who produced *8 Country Reporter*. Their new ratings blockbuster show was going to take the Saturday 6:30 P.M. time slot. Since we had been promised that time slot would be ours starting in January 1987, we thought we were out the door. It was the same time slot we had at Channel 4, and we expected it to produce better ratings.

We had no sooner returned to the station than Bill walked into our offices and shut the door.

"Guys, I'm so sorry to spring that news on you. It just had not occurred to me how this would affect you. Just know this: we don't have *Wheel* until September, so we still have time to figure this out."

When word got out that WFAA had won the bidding war for *Wheel of Fortune* in the Dallas–Fort Worth market, both Ed Bark and Bob Brock put together the fact that it was not a good way for *8 Country Reporter* to start the new year, knowing that we could only hold the Saturday 6:30 P.M. time slot for eight months. Was that going to be enough time to get the ratings back up to where they once were, and to find ongoing sponsorship for a local show?

In his *Dallas Morning News* column dated November 25, 1987, Ed Bark said of our predicament, "In a thriving economy, a class act such as *8 Country* would probably be kept on the air as a loss leader. But these are not those times."

He went on to say, "Whatever happens, the last best hope for this program is Channel 8. If I were [Bill] Cox or general manager Dave Lane, I'd hate to be the one to cancel what has been the best and most beloved local program in the history of Dallas television."

I went into the short Christmas break worrying about the future of our show. I was also feeling guilty because I had not only put my own future on the line by moving to Channel 8 with nothing more than a thirteen-week guarantee, I had upended the lives and careers of the three guys who made the move with me. Maybe I should have accepted Wendell Harris's offer.

I even started considering other options. A few days after our show was cancelled at Channel 4, I had received an interesting offer from a smaller-market TV station. In the early days of cable television, the programming from larger cities was carried on the cable outlets in smaller towns, and KDFW shows could be seen all the way from Shreveport to Lubbock and beyond. Essentially, the Dallas stations were seen in the northern half of Texas, while the Houston and San Antonio stations were seen in the southern half. So our show was known in those smaller markets, and as host of the show, so was I.

The interesting offer came from a very nice smaller market where one station was dominant. They wanted me to be their solo news anchor and they offered even more money than I was making at Channel 4. It included an apartment where I would live during the week (so I wouldn't have to completely move from Dallas) and use of the station's membership in the local country club "because we don't have any good places to eat here." The problem was that I still had no desire to be a news anchor.

Another possibility came from, of all places, St. Paul, Minnesota. After Channel 4 news director Wendell Harris and I got off to a rocky start, and shortly before he cancelled our show, I had applied for the job of executive producer for Garrison Keillor's *Prairie Home Companion* radio show. I told no one. For me, it was a worst-case scenario, but I needed to do something in case my dark feelings about what was ahead were right.

Garrison is a fiction and comedy writer who invented a town called Lake Wobegon for his radio show. In some ways, it was like a made-up version of *4 Country Reporter*. The search for the new *Prairie Home Companion* producer dragged on for quite a while; then, somehow, I made the short list for the job and was notified right after hearing that *Wheel of Fortune* was coming to Channel 8. But I never went to St. Paul to interview for the job because I realized I had no more interest in doing that than I did in being a news anchor. Besides, *me* in Minnesota? Doesn't it snow a lot there?

As 1987 began, I knew I needed a new plan—one that would not depend on the seasonal whims of any one television station or the possibility of our careers being held in the balance by the changing moods of any one person. I decided to make an all-or-nothing move that would either pay off in the end or push me over the cliff, possibly down a road that had nothing to do with what had become my life's work and my passion.

I asked for a meeting with Dave Lane. As soon as I entered his office, I unloaded all the fears and insecurities I had after being cancelled at

Channel 4 and then given only a thirteen-week trial at Channel 8. I told him I'd worked my whole adult life toward doing this one show. I told him that I had thought moving to WFAA was going to be the long-term solution to keeping the show on the air, but now I wasn't so sure. He sat and listened without comment while I vented my emotions. I laid myself bare right then and there.

"What do you want to do?" he asked.

"I don't want to work for you or for any television station," I told him. "I want to start my own production company and syndicate the show across Texas."

Dave stared at me for all of ten seconds, then said, "Great idea. And we will help you do it."

CHAPTER TWENTY-NINE

*I*HAD NO BUSINESS EXPERIENCE TO SPEAK OF, AND ON top of that, I had majored in the most non-business course of study I could find in college. Both my undergrad and graduate degrees have the word *art* in them. In those days that usually meant no foreign language and very little math and science were required. I had taken the path of least resistance because it was the only thing I thought I could do. Maybe the high school counselor was right when she told me to go to trade school, because I knew nothing about running my own business.

When it came time to "start my own production company," as I had told Dave I would, I literally did not know *where* to start. I kept thinking back to the movie *Shampoo*, in which Warren Beatty played a women's hair stylist who wanted to open his own shop. When he went to the bank to ask for a loan, the banker kept asking for his financials and his business plan. Beatty's character told him, "I don't need all that. I've got the heads. They'll follow me anywhere."

He did not get the loan, and neither would I. I had a feeling a banker would not care about my Q Score.

Then, shortly after talking to Dave about producing the show myself, there came a call from Obi-Wan Kenobi. His real name is Ward Huey, and his real-world title at that time was president of Belo Broadcasting and vice chairman of the Belo board of directors, but I figured he was actually a Force-sensitive Jedi Master and a member of the Jedi High Council because I thought he could do things no other human could do. His office, appropriately enough, was across the street from WFAA-TV, on the top floor of a mid-rise building we called the Death Star. That was the center of the Belo Universe, and that's the place from which the Belo Force emanated to all of its holdings. In short, Ward Huey was . . . well, like a god.

I was invited to join Mr. Huey on the top floor of the Death Star for a thirty-minute meeting. I had no idea what it was about, and I was . . . concerned. But when I walked into his office, the guy I met could have been any of the people I had met in my years on the back roads, except he had a large office and an expensive-looking suit. When he talked, he had an easy way about him and smiled a lot.

We started with some small talk, and he told me he had been a fan of our show for years. He warmly and sincerely welcomed me to the Belo family and asked a lot of questions about how we do what we do. They were the kind of questions we get from fans of the show that we meet in small towns all over Texas. I was starting to believe this guy was one of them. He even told me about an idea he had for a story, so I quickly wrote down the name of the guy he was suggesting.

Then, the great and powerful Ward Huey, Jedi Master and ruler of the Belo empire, quacked like a duck.

No, that's not quite right. He didn't quack. He talked like a duck. Donald Duck, to be precise. It was great, and it was the last thing I expected out of a person in a position like his. I don't even remember what he said, just that he did it.

"No wonder people love this guy so much," I thought. "He's just a great guy."

Before I left, Ward very casually mentioned that Dave Lane had told him about my plans for starting my own company and syndicating the show. He stared at me for about ten seconds before speaking again.

"We want to help you do that," he said, echoing what Dave said earlier.

And that was that.

I left Ward's office wondering what that visit had been all about. What I was working on was such a minor piece of the Belo empire that I couldn't imagine why someone in his position would waste part of his day on it. And I didn't think we had discussed anything of substance.

Later that day, I got a call from Sherri, Dave Lane's assistant, who asked if I had a minute to run up to his office.

As I walked in, Dave said, "I hear you met Ward."

There was no question, so I just said, "Yes, sir, what a great guy."

Dave handed me a piece of paper.

Printed on the paper were the names, titles, and phone numbers of people I had never heard of. There was a banker from Texas Commerce Bank, a lawyer from Jackson-Walker, a CPA from Ernst & Young, and the name of the man who did all the equipment purchasing for the Belo TV stations.

"These are the people who handle some of Belo's business. They already know you may call. Feel free to take advantage of their expertise if you want.

And when you're ready to buy your own production equipment, you should be able to piggyback on one of our orders and get the discounts we get."

What a start, especially for a guy who knew nothing about how to do all of that. The lawyers helped to form the corporation, the CPA set up our accounting, the banker opened a line of credit, and when it came time to buy equipment, Belo's buyer made sure we paid what they paid.

I did, indeed, feel like part of the family, and for the life of me, I still to this day don't know what I did to deserve that kind of treatment. Looking back on it, I now realize that Dave Lane and Ward Huey were just being nice guys, and they appreciated the work we were doing. They never asked for anything in return. Nothing—except honesty, loyalty, and hard work.

Then came the hard part, the chicken and egg game. You can't get sponsors for a TV show unless you have time slots on stations, and the only deal I had was with one station in Dallas, albeit the biggest and most powerful in the state. And you can't promise to produce a show and deliver it to TV stations unless you know you can afford to do that. That meant I had to find a sponsor to help pay the bills. Which should I do first?

The answer came in an envelope I found on my desk the next morning. In it were two reference letters introducing me and the show that we would be producing for statewide syndication. One letter was signed by Dave Lane, the other by Ward Huey. There was also a handwritten note from Dave that said, "Get your TV stations lined up first."

So that was the answer.

In his letter to the stations, Dave briefly told of the history and success of our show in the Dallas market and promised it would be a great addition to their lineup too. And he said, "I'm not sure if Bob has settled on a name yet, so I'm just calling it by the working title 'Texas Country Reporter.'"

Texas Country Reporter was born.

CHAPTER THIRTY

W HEN I WORKED AT CHANNEL 4, THERE WAS A MAN IN sales whom I respected named Dee Demirjian. He had recently gone to work for King World Productions, the one-time syndication arm of the CBS network and the company that partnered with Oprah Winfrey to form Harpo Productions, the company that produced and distributed Oprah's show. King World had a trifecta at that time because the top three syndicated shows on American television were *Oprah*, *Wheel of Fortune*, and *Jeopardy*, and distribution for all three was handled by King World. That meant the company could demand huge fees and dictate time slots and other requirements to the TV stations. If you wanted to play, you had to pay.

I called Dee and asked him how I should go about syndicating my show. It was only regional syndication, and I didn't have any money, but I wanted advice from the best of the best, and Dee was just that. He told me to do it myself, in person if I could. He suggested that I take a demo reel to every TV market in the state, a copy of an actual show, and the letters from Dave Lane and Ward Huey. I took his sage advice.

I started with the easy one first. KHOU-TV in Houston was owned by Belo, so I hoped my letter from their boss, Ward Huey, would not only get me in the door but get me a favorable time slot on their station. I met with Al Howard, the general manager, and clearing the show only took about five minutes. I'm pretty sure everything had been taken care of with a phone call from Ward before my arrival. Still, even if he did do that, he at least let me think I was doing it myself. Besides, it was good practice, because I had never done this before.

While I was in the area, I drove over to the Beaumont–Port Arthur–Orange market. KFDM-TV was in the 144th largest market in the country, but it was consistently ranked among the top three CBS affiliates in the nation. It had been owned by Belo until Belo bought KHOU; the FCC required them to sell the Beaumont station in order to purchase the Houston station. The long-time general manager of KFDM, Larry Beaulieu, greeted me warmly and cleared the show almost immediately.

Next up was the long drive down I-10 to San Antonio. Belo would later own KENS-TV there, but in the mid-1980s the station was owned by Harte-Hanks Communications. I met with the station manager, Jack Forehand, who was from North Carolina and a big fan of Charles Kuralt, who was also from there. When I described our show, he asked if I was familiar with Kuralt because my show sounded like his style of reporting. I told him that Charles and I were good friends, that I had gotten the idea for our show from watching his work, and that he had been my mentor.

Jack immediately cleared our show on KENS-TV, giving it the Sunday morning 9:30 A.M. time slot, immediately after the *CBS Sunday Morning* show, which was started by Charles Kuralt. Ultimately, we would draw our largest audience in syndication in the San Antonio market. I believe it was because of that time slot, and because the people in that particular market seem to love family programming.

The CBS network airs the political news show *Face the Nation* in that time slot, but our show was so successful on KENS-TV that they carried only the second half of it to make room for *Texas Country Reporter*. In 2019, that came to an end when CBS demanded that KENS carry *Face the Nation* in its entirety or lose their affiliation. We were pushed back to 10:30 A.M., a move that not only seriously affected our ratings but also angered the San Antonio fans of the show. But there was nothing KENS could do. Their hands were tied by Viacom/CBS.

The same day that Jack cleared the show for KENS-TV, I made the short drive from San Antonio up to Austin, where I stopped by the only VHF station in the market, KTBC-TV. It went on the air in 1952 as the first TV station in central Texas, and was then owned by the Texas Broadcasting Company (thus the call letters KTBC), which in turn was owned by future US president Lyndon Baines Johnson and his wife, Lady Bird, who had used her family's money to buy it and a couple of Austin radio stations. She operated those radio stations well into her eighties and became wealthy in her own right, independent of her husband.

The general manager at KTBC was a former KDFW-TV executive named Jack Harrison. He knew the show I was doing and also knew me, so that meeting was spent mostly exchanging old stories about Channel 4. He cleared the show in the first few minutes of our conversation.

Texas Country Reporter lasted only a few seasons on KTBC, which would eventually become a Fox network affiliate, then the NBC affiliate, then the new CBS affiliate, and, finally, the ABC affiliate, which was by that time a Belo station.

As I left Austin, I knew I had enough stations to cover more than 82 percent of Texas. Dee Demirjian had told me to clear the Big 4 markets of Dallas–Fort Worth, Houston, San Antonio, and Austin first. The remaining stations would be what he called "gravy." But little did he or I know how important those smaller-market stations would be as our show became popular across the state. I stopped by a station in Waco on my way back to Dallas and cleared the Waco–Temple–Bryan–College Station market.

My second and third trips to clear *Texas Country Reporter* for the 1987–1988 TV season took me to Tyler-Lufkin, Corpus Christi, Laredo, Harlingen/RGV, Wichita Falls, Abilene, San Angelo, Sherman/Denison, Amarillo, Midland/Odessa/Big Spring, Lubbock, El Paso, and Shreveport, Louisiana. Later, Victoria would become its own TV market (separate from San Antonio), and we cleared those stations too. *Texas Country Reporter* was now set to be seen in 100 percent of the households across the state.

When I returned home from my trips clearing stations, I felt good because I had signed up at least one network affiliate TV station in every market in Texas. I felt even better when I found out that that had never been done before. It's a good thing I didn't know that going in because that would have scared me to death. It is true that sometimes ignorance is bliss.

Photo by Kelli Phillips, © Phillips Productions, Inc.

Bryan Adams High School journalism teacher Ann Voss, the person who set me on the track to a career as a storyteller.

Photo by Martin Perry, © Phillips Productions, Inc.

Brian Hawkins, who has traveled the back roads with us for more than thirty years, shooting a segment of *Texas Country Reporter* with me.

With Kelli, shooting a story for *Texas Country Reporter* in an Austin candy store.

Recording a script for
the show as the editing
process begins.

Driving across the Regency Bridge, a Texas landmark that has been featured on *Texas Country Reporter* for almost thirty years.

In a familiar pose inside "the Flag," the Texas map- and flag-decorated vehicle seen on *Texas Country Reporter* every week.

The Phillips family—
Sue, Billy Ray, me,
and Leon—in happy
times, circa 1955.

The original crew for
8 Country Reporter and
Texas Country Reporter
(from left): Larry Ellis,
me, Jamie Aitken, and
Jason Anderson.

The current crew of
Texas Country Reporter
(front, from left):
Quintin Blackwell,
Jo Caudle, Kelli
Phillips, Mike Snyder,
and Brian Hawkins;
(back, from left):
Martin Perry, me,
Dan Stricklin and Ben
Hartmann.

A crowd gathers for "The Star-Spangled Banner" at the beginning of the annual Texas Country Reporter Festival in Waxahachie.

CHAPTER THIRTY-ONE

AT CHANNEL 4, AND DURING THOSE FIRST FEW MONTHS
at Channel 8, I only had to produce the show. The sales
departments at both stations handled the money end of things, bringing in
advertisers who would buy commercials to ultimately pay the bills.

Now that I would be putting the show together through my own production company, I was in the TV syndication and sales business as well.
I had just had a huge victory on the syndication side, but it would all be
for nothing if I could not do the same on the sales side. I expected that to
be even harder because this time I would be asking people to dig into their
company's pockets and pull out some cash.

The deal between my new company and the TV stations was done on
a barter split, meaning the TV stations paid nothing for the rights to air
the show, and I paid nothing for them to air it. Instead, the stations each
awarded Phillips Productions, Inc., half of the advertising time in each episode. Each station, of course, kept the other half to sell to local businesses.
When I added all of my advertising time together, I had statewide spots
I could sell.

But who would buy my statewide advertising time? I attacked that problem the only way I knew how: I sat down with one of those yellow legal pads
and made a list of Texas companies that covered all or at least most of the
state. It started like this:

1. Dairy Queen
2. Southwest Airlines
3. Dr Pepper

But I wrote the numbers all the way to twenty because I figured I would have to approach at least that many companies to get just one to love this idea as much as I did. Numbers four through twenty I would fill in later, after I made some test runs with the first three on the list. I was not unrealistic about how difficult this was going to be. Just getting in the door would be hard, much less getting them to commit to buying advertising. Even though I was selling commercials on a show that had a proven track record of fourteen years on one station and more than six months on a second station, I didn't fool myself into thinking these companies were just waiting for me to walk in the door.

A little research told me that the Dairy Queen account was handled by a company in Dallas called Berry Brown Advertising. I thought that would be the best place to start, not only because Dairy Queen was first on my list but because the agency was on McKinney Avenue, about a mile from WFAA.

After giving myself a pep talk, I made the call and managed to get the account executive on the phone. I told him who I was and that I'd like to drop by and discuss an idea with him, hoping I would not have to give away all the details until I could be in front of him. One of the sales people at Channel 8 had told me to always try to get a face-to-face meeting because it's harder for some people to turn you down in person than it is over the phone.

Lucky for me, the guy said he knew the show and invited me over to talk about my idea the next day. *Wow, that was easy.*

The next morning I was right on time for the meeting, and the Dairy Queen account executive sat down with me immediately. I gave him pretty much the same pitch I had given to the TV station executives when I was working to clear the show, except I made a bigger deal out of the ratings that the show had achieved over the years. He pointed out that there was no guarantee that the show would do as well in other markets, and I conceded that we did not yet have actual numbers since we were still a few months away from launching the syndicated version of *Texas Country Reporter*. I was mentally prepared for the "Get back to us after you have real numbers" line when the guy surprised me.

"I think this is exactly what Dairy Queen is looking for," he said. "I'll have to clear it with them, but I'm pretty sure they'll do it. Give me a month and I'll get back to you."

I walked out of that office feeling like I was in a dream. Did he just say yes? Or even a hard maybe? I think he did. I think I just got my first sale, and on my first sales call. We had even tossed around some dollar figures that he thought the DQ people would go for, and while it was less than

I had quoted, it was more than I expected. If this deal turned out, we were in business.

I was on cloud nine and couldn't wait to visit with Dave Lane back at Channel 8. He already knew of my success with clearing the show. Now I could report back that this thing was a go because we now had a sponsor.

I called the guy at Berry Brown Advertising one month later, just as he had instructed. I reached his voice mail and left a message. We had spent the past month working on the other details for *Texas Country Reporter*, and the time had flown by.

Three days went by with no call back from Berry Brown. Then four days. Then five.

At the one-week mark I was getting pretty worried. So I called back and left a heartfelt message saying I needed to know something about the status of things. And, surprise, a few minutes later the guy returned my call.

"You obviously don't read *Ad Age*," he said. "Berry Brown Advertising was fired from the Dairy Queen account. But don't worry. They'll be back. The agency that got the account can't handle it."

And that was it. My successful sales call was just a "we'll see," not a yes or even a hard maybe. This would be the first of many such experiences over the next thirty or so years. The difference later would be that I had learned to expect it and how to handle it. I eventually realized that there is no deal until there is a deal. This time I was devastated. I was worried. I felt like a loser. Stupid, stupid me.

Almost as soon as I got that bad news, another call came in, this one from Bob Isham. I had met Bob while I was still working at KDFW-TV. He owned the Fort Worth–based company Tra-Tech, a van conversion company, and we met when I was trying to get Channel 4 to make a deal to trade advertising for one of Tra-Tech's vans to use on *4 Country Reporter*. News director Wendell Harris was having none of that, so the deal went south. When we made the move to Channel 8, the second person I called was Bob to make a deal for a vehicle to use on our new show at WFAA. The first call went to my longtime friend Camille Keith at Southwest Airlines, because I knew we were going to need an airline deal as well.

Bob called me because he lived in Decatur, Texas, and one of the longtime Dairy Queen franchise owners lived there too. He owned dozens of DQs, and just by chance, Bob had mentioned our trade deal to him. He asked Bob to get in touch with me to ask if I would give him a call. I couldn't do it fast enough.

"Bob," he said to me, "I need you to call the president of the TDQOC."

I knew that was the Texas Dairy Queen Operators' Council, from the research I had done before approaching Berry Brown Advertising about sponsorship.

I made the call and talked to a man named Bill Hall. My impression over the phone was that this was one extremely sharp entrepreneur. But I had no idea at the time how much I actually underestimated him.

"Bob, we heard the details of your sponsorship opportunity," he said. "We fired our ad agency but we'd still like to talk to you."

I was about to hyperventilate, hearing those words. I also heard the words my mother said often to me.

"One door closes and another one opens."

I heard that a lot growing up. I was always surprised when the things my mom and dad said to me turned out to be true. Funny how the *older* I got, the *smarter* they got.

We set a date for me to come to Fort Worth to talk to the members of the TDQOC. Bill said he liked the idea, but that I would need to convince the DQ marketing board that this was a good opportunity.

I called Dave Lane and told him the latest update.

He said, "I'm going with you."

CHAPTER THIRTY-TWO

*I*N 1940 THE FIRST EVER DAIRY QUEEN OPENED IN Joliet, Illinois. It wasn't a restaurant per se but an ice cream place—even though they didn't serve ice cream but rather ice milk. The Food and Drug Administration says Dairy Queen's product doesn't have enough milk fat to qualify as ice cream. The company gets around that by calling its product DQ Soft Serve, based on a formula created in the 1930s. I grew up on the stuff and loved it then and still do.

Dairy Queen quickly moved its world headquarters to Minneapolis, and it remains there today. That's kind of funny because almost any Texan you ask will tell you DQ is a Texas company, but that's not so. What *is* true is that Dairy Queen has two marketing districts: Texas and the rest of the world. Funny, but lots of companies follow that same plan. Texas is, indeed, different.

Dairy Queen came to Texas in 1946 when a man named O. W. Klose from Missouri and his son Rolly Klose from San Antonio bought the franchise rights and opened a store on Guadalupe Street in Austin.

When Rolly and his daddy went to Dairy Queen's world headquarters in Minneapolis, they were seeking the franchise rights to Austin. The person who did the paperwork was accustomed to people from much smaller states, such as Iowa and Nebraska, getting rights to their entire state, so Rolly and his daddy were granted the franchise rights to the entire state of Texas. It was a mistake, but the deed was done.

Rolly then opened stores around Texas and hired people to run them who mostly had no experience running stores of any kind. Then, for some reason, those managers claimed Rolly quit servicing his DQ stores. They rebelled and even contacted International Dairy Queen's headquarters in Minnesota to complain.

IDQ ended up buying back all of the Texas franchises, then set out to sell them to other people. Rolly's former employees were given first rights, so, suddenly, many of the Texas DQs were owned by their former managers. And to make the deal even sweeter, IDQ offered them the same rates for buying the DQ Soft Serve mix that Rolly Klose had paid, which was pennies on the dollar compared to the then-current rates for the mix. The number of DQ stores in Texas grew as high as 862, which accounted for more than 20 percent of all the Dairy Queens in the world.

Rolly had also added food items to the menu, things like the Hungr-Buster burger, the DQ Dude (a chicken-fried steak sandwich), and chicken strips served with country gravy. Those items were not available in Dairy Queens outside of Texas. The Texas Dairy Queens used the name Texas Country Foods to advertise their non-dessert fare. That name would turn out to be a meaningful coincidence.

In the 1980s, Dairy Queen started attracting the attention of some well-heeled business people who had discovered in their research that there was a lot of money to be made in owning a Dairy Queen—even more if you owned several. One of those people was Bill Hall, a CPA who bought sixty-some stores from one of the old DQ franchisees and approached the Dairy Queen business as just that—a business.

A couple of the older franchisees who were around when I first got involved with Dairy Queen told me that in the early days, the DQ owners would go into a room with a big table and sit down together to discuss joint marketing plans. Eventually the table would be covered with bottles of booze, and one time the discussion ended up in a fistfight over their disagreements.

The new "MBA crowd" changed all that. At least, they eliminated the fistfights. Bill Hall rose to become president of the Texas Dairy Queen Operators' Council, and he pushed DQ's marketing efforts in a completely different direction. One of the results was the firing of longtime ad agency Berry Brown, the same one that had told me earlier that Dairy Queen would sponsor the statewide syndication of *Texas Country Reporter*. According to the account executive at Berry Brown, it was "a lock." I learned shortly after that there is no such thing.

CHAPTER THIRTY-THREE

*A*S DAVE LANE AND I DROVE WEST FROM WFAA-TV'S downtown Dallas facility, located across a shared driveway from the *Dallas Morning News*, we talked about a game plan for our upcoming presentation to the Texas Dairy Queen Operators' Council. As we progressed down the old Dallas-Fort Worth Turnpike, now known as Interstate 30, Dave suggested that I take the lead and give the TDQOC the same pitch I had given to the various Texas TV stations when I was syndicating the show. He explained that sponsors would be looking for pretty much the same thing the general managers of the television stations were looking for: a proven program that would attract viewers. Dave said he would be there for support and could answer any questions I couldn't. He explained that if these guys were very savvy about advertising, they might want to know more about the ratings and demographics of the show, and he could handle those things. I was happy to hear that.

When we arrived at the designated meeting place inside McStay-Regian Advertising, we were asked to wait in a hallway until we were called to the boardroom where the council members were already meeting. After a short wait, Bill Hall, the man I had spoken to on the phone, emerged from the boardroom and introduced himself. He was younger than I expected, a tall, nice-looking man who was extremely personable and very much a Texan. He was a no-nonsense kind of guy and told us that some of the people on the council could be a hard sell, but he knew there were others who would like our idea. He was among the latter.

"Just explain what you have in mind," he said, "and be ready to answer their questions."

We walked into the boardroom, and sitting at the long table were twelve or fourteen people—mostly men, but there were at least two women in the group. They went around the table introducing themselves, and we quickly discovered that they were all Dairy Queen owners except for Greg Regian, one of the owners of the ad agency. (I would later learn that Greg was a marketing genius, and he would play an important part in our show's success.)

A quick look at the faces and body language on display around that table told me these people had been around the block a time or two. They looked like they knew what they wanted, what they needed, and what they did not want or need. They also looked like people who would have no trouble telling us exactly what they thought about our presentation, especially if they did not like what we had to say. I was totally intimidated, and knew I probably had just this one chance to sell my show to the people at the table.

At that moment, Dave whispered in my ear, "Change of plans. Introduce yourself and the show *quickly*, then toss it to me. I'll handle it from there."

Thank God.

I did exactly as Dave told me and didn't bother asking why. I knew he had experience with situations that I had never even imagined. I was about to find out why this man ran the TV station and how he got to where he was.

Dave started by telling the group how long he had worked in television and about the reputation of the Belo Corporation. He let them know that his company didn't fool around with things that didn't work or with people who couldn't perform. He told them he had watched my work for years when I was employed at KDFW-TV, and he told them how the news director, Marty Haag, had been meeting with me for years trying to get me to move to their station. Then he told them how Channel 4 had cancelled *4 Country Reporter*, and how WFAA grabbed the show immediately with the blessing of the vice chairman of Belo's board of directors, Ward Huey, who was a big fan of the show. Then he told them about our ratings and demographics, and even got into something, psychographics, that I would later learn a lot about.

Then he said something that made me swell with pride. He said he had never been sorry that he brought me and my team to work at his TV station, that we were all hard workers, that we were all gentlemen, and that we were all nice guys. He finished by saying he knew Dairy Queen would look back at the day they decided to sponsor *Texas Country Reporter* as a major game changer for their organization. And he reminded them that they were essentially being offered the same thing Mutual of Omaha had been offered when they had a chance to sponsor *Wild Kingdom*. That partnership is one of the most famous sponsorships in TV history and lasted for decades. I thought that was brilliant and wished I had thought of it.

Along with Greg from the ad agency, the DQ owners, including Bill, asked several questions. Bill and some of the other owners were obviously intrigued by the possibilities, but I couldn't read the others. I figured it was going to take some time for them to sort out this deal and decide if they were going to sponsor our show. The problem was that I was running out of time. I had cleared our show on all the stations and promised there would be a program starting September 1, 1987, but to do that, I needed a sponsor to help pay the bills. I had a line of credit to help us get started, but at some point pretty soon, our status would need to change to pay-as-you-go. It didn't feel like that was going to happen that day. These things take time.

Then, just when we thought we were getting warmed up, Bill asked if we would mind waiting in the hallway while they discussed our proposal. We left the room and sat where we had sat before. We weren't there five minutes before Greg asked us to come back into the room.

"Bob," Bill said as he stuck out his hand, "you've got a deal."

CHAPTER THIRTY-FOUR

S TARTING ON JANUARY 2, 1970, AND LASTING ALL THE way until I walked out of KDFW-TV for the last time in October 1986, I was a part of the Channel 4 news department. The rules at the station were embedded in the cornerstone of the building and stated that the people in TV sales and the people in TV news were to have little or no contact. In fact, the news department at that time was located by itself in the building's basement, and the sales department was on the second floor. This was a system set up by the news director, Eddie Barker. The purpose was to keep the news people "pure" and away from the influence of the people and companies that purchased advertising on the station.

If you've never worked in journalism, this might seem like a strange rule. How often could there be a problem caused by news people and sales people hanging out together? More often than you might think.

In the early 1970s, several journalists walked out of one of the Oklahoma City TV stations because of an ethical situation brought about by mixing sales and news. The news department was doing a series of investigative reports on allegedly crooked car dealerships in OKC. The local car dealers' association did not like that, of course, and threatened that all of the dealers would discontinue their advertising on the station if the series was not halted. The station gave in to the car dealers, and the employees of the news department quit their jobs in protest.

It just so happened that, at that very time, Marty Haag was building his team after being hired to run the news department at WFAA-TV in Dallas. Marty was the strictest news director on the planet when it came to journalistic ethics. To him, the rules were black and white. There was no grey. Marty hired several of the journalists from that Oklahoma City TV station and brought them to work at WFAA. Several of them worked there most of, if not all of, the rest of their careers and made huge contributions to the station. Some left to work at one of the networks, supposedly the job every TV journalist wants, but some of those people came back to WFAA.

Shortly after the meeting that Dave Lane and I had with the Texas Dairy Queen Operators' Council, Greg Regian, the owner of McStay-Regian Advertising, invited me to lunch to talk about an idea he had.

"I want you to become DQ's spokesperson," he said. "I want you to appear on their commercials."

This was something that had never occurred to me. After all, for fourteen years I had produced the show as a member of the KDFW news department, and no one in news could endorse any product or person. Some journalists have been known to take that ethical commitment so far as to not vote in elections while working as reporters so that they can't be accused of being biased. My journalism advisor at SMU encouraged all of his students to avoid being what he called "joiners."

"If you're a member of a fraternal organization or even a charitable organization," he told us, "you will develop opinions about that organization. What if you are called on to report news involving that organization to which you belong? Can you be fair and unbiased?"

That suggested course of action made a lot of sense to me, so I have to this day never been a joiner. When Greg asked me to become the spokesperson for Texas Dairy Queens, I immediately filtered that question through my seventeen years of news experience. I told him that I needed time to think and wanted to talk to a couple of people about it. He was understanding and said he would wait for an answer.

As I drove back to my office at WFAA-TV in Dallas, I thought about the conversation I had with Marty when I first moved to the station. He had called me into his office and asked if I wanted to be part of news or programming. I had assumed it would be the same setup we'd had at Channel 4. He told me that while he would like to have me in the news department, he was wondering if our show, and I, should be made a part of WFAA programming. As it turned out, that's where we ended up, and we reported to Bill Cox, the director of programming.

Still, I had not crossed any lines of journalistic ethics, and I remained part of Marty's news department. When big stories came up, my guys and I were called in to help, and we were honored to do so. Fact is, the adrenaline that news reporters experience is a hard thing to explain. It never stops pumping. I still get that rush even today.

Now I was faced with a decision that could be irreversible.

The first person I turned to for advice was Marty Haag.

"Bob," he said, "this will change everything. Once you cross this line and endorse a product, you can never go back. Not here in my news department anyway. I'm not saying you shouldn't do this, just to think long and hard about it."

I next went to Dave Lane.

Dave's attitude was different.

"Why wouldn't you do this, Bob? This is an opportunity of a lifetime."

"But I won't be able to work in news anymore," I complained.

"So what? You turned down the chance to anchor the news at Channel 4 to come here and continue producing your show. It seems to me you made this choice several months ago."

He then gave me the practical side of things.

"Texas Dairy Queen buys about $10 million in advertising every year. Your name and face will be on every station in the state. This will introduce you to the audience in places where they've never heard of you or seen your show."

Then I called Greg and told him I was honored that he had asked me to be the DQ Dude, and that I was ready to get started. I had no idea at the time how important this move would be to the future of *Texas Country Reporter* and to me personally. I would soon find out.

Dave was right when he gave me the advice to step across the news line and become an advocate for the sponsors of *Texas Country Reporter*. And Greg had indeed given me the chance of a lifetime with his offer to be DQ's spokesperson. By itself, it wasn't that lucrative monetarily, but that opportunity would mean the difference between life and death for a newly syndicated TV show. And it would set me on a course that continues to this day. Without it, I doubt *Texas Country Reporter* would have survived.

And it all started when DQ's Bill Hall said, "You've got a deal."

CHAPTER THIRTY-FIVE

O N SEPTEMBER 12, 1987, *TEXAS COUNTRY REPORTER*, the syndicated version of our show, debuted in every Texas market except Dallas–Fort Worth. WFAA-TV made the decision to stick with the name *8 Country Reporter* to capitalize on the equity the show had built up over the past sixteen years in DFW.

The first year of *TCR*, the shows were made up of stories that had appeared on the first season of *8 Country Reporter*. The statewide shows would later catch up to the programs that aired in the DFW market, so every viewer in every market now sees the same show each weekend. Eventually, in 1999, WFAA-TV chose to drop the *8 Country Reporter* name and started airing the same show that aired in the other Texas markets. By then the syndicated version had become very well known, even in the DFW market, so Channel 8 saw a certain wisdom in having just one name on the show statewide. It made our lives much easier because, until that change, we had to shoot two versions of everything so we could customize the show for the DFW market.

Shortly after the statewide debut of *TCR*, the first Dairy Queen commercial with me as their spokesperson started airing across the state, even on the TV stations that did not carry our show. That first commercial featured a chicken-fried steak sandwich called the DQ Dude, which can only be found in Texas Dairy Queens. It had a humorous theme, as did all the spots we did, and it was memorable, but it wasn't my best work as I was pretty green at that kind of thing. The endorsement scenario still felt strange to me. It would get better.

That TV spot, however, along with others (for the Peanut Buster Parfait, shot in a peanut field in Comanche County; the Banana Split, shot as longshoremen unloaded a ship full of bananas in the Houston ship channel; the

Hungr-Buster, DQ's giant burger; and most of their other products), made me a household name almost overnight. And because I was identified on those spots and lots of others as Bob Phillips of *Texas Country Reporter*, it made the show a household name almost overnight too.

But it was one particular DQ spot that somehow started a slow rumble that erupted into a full-blown earthquake that triggered a volcano, a hurricane, and a tsunami all at one time. At least, that's the way it felt to me, to ad man extraordinaire Greg Regian, who created the spots, and to lots of DQ owners. Here's how it went:

Video	Audio
Snow shoes in the sand	Harmonica intro
WS Bob (in snow suit) in sand	You know what they say about West Texas weather . . .
CU Bob lowering snow goggles	It can change in the blink of an eye . . .
WS DQ sign/Bob walks across parking lot to front door	EXCEPT at Dairy Queen, where there's only ONE forecast:
Bob opens DQ door/hit with snow in the face	BLIZZZZARDDDD!!!
Product shots	The orginal Blizzard flavor treat, swirling with your favorite candy, fruit, or nuts!
Turning Blizzard upside down	It's upside downright thick and delicious!
MS Bob o/c	Whatever the weather, at Dairy Queen you'll always find . . . a Blizzard!
Hero shot of product/DQ logo	Music stinger

The Blizzard spot aired on our show and on every TV station in Texas. The Dairy Queen stores filled up. The calls and letters poured in. It was an instant hit, and I got to be the messenger. It was a magical moment in my life, in the lives of everyone associated with DQ, and in the life of a new show called *Texas Country Reporter*.

"Have you seen that commercial where the guy is wearing a full snow suit with goggles and snowshoes as he walks across the West Texas sand hills?"

And, for whatever reason, the line that made the spot so popular almost didn't happen.

The cinematographer and director for many of the DQ commercials was the very talented M. L. Nelson, a great guy out of Dallas who had a lot of experience shooting food spots. He still does that today, and is considered to be one of the best food shooters and directors anywhere.

M. L. was, and is, a perfectionist. Just good enough isn't good enough for him. He shoots until he is absolutely positive he has that "thing," whatever it is, in the can.

For the DQ Blizzard spot, we did about fifty takes on the Blizzard line, the part where I open the door and get hit in the face with wind and snow, then yell "BLIZZZZARDDDD!!!"

Except in those first fifty takes, I simply opened the door and *said* "a Blizzard"—the way it was written in the script.

At that point, M. L. huddled with me and Greg and said he felt like we had it, but *something was missing.*

"Something's just not right."

We all thought and thought and thought. M. L. asked me how it felt when I opened the door and said the line. I told him that the only thing that had occurred to me was that if there was a lot of wind and snow, maybe I wouldn't just say "a Blizzard." Maybe I would yell it because the wind is howling, and the snow is flying, and it's all kind of noisy.

M. L. said, "Give that a try."

On take fifty-one of the now famous DQ Blizzard TV spot, I opened the door and yelled "BLIZZZZARDDDD!!!" at the top of my lungs.

And that's the one that was chosen when the commercial was edited. Just like that. Fifty previous takes left on the editing room floor. Take fifty-one was the magic.

And there was another response besides long lines filled with customers wanting Blizzards in Dairy Queens across Texas—a response that none of us expected. Everywhere I went, and I mean everywhere, people kept asking me to say "BLIZZZZARDDDD!!!" Except they didn't always say it that way. More often, they just giggled and told me, "Say it! Say it!" And even though Dairy Queen has not been a sponsor of *Texas Country Reporter* since 2000, it still happens today. Almost daily, someone brings up Dairy Queen or calls me the DQ Dude, or asks me to yell the now famous line. And that spot was shot in the late 1980s.

Back then, though, I was quick to clue in to what people wanted me to do, so I just did it. It always brought a fun response. Besides, it was catapulting *Texas Country Reporter* into a completely different stratosphere, and the weather was different up there.

Eventually, all of this attention did more than just help *Texas Country Reporter*. Viewers constantly asked if they could tag along with us when we went out to shoot our stories, so we created a tour company to let them have a similar experience. Texas Country Tours, Inc., was born in 1988, and we took thousands of people to all corners of Texas, often showing them things they wouldn't have been able to see on their own. Texas Country Tours also operated a boutique hotel and spa near Kerrville called Escondida, the Texas Country Reporter Hacienda, with fans of the show from all over the world booking stays with us. It was a lot of work and a lot of fun.

In the mid-1990s we started a gathering that we first called the Texas Country Reporter Reunion. The idea was to bring together people who had been featured on the show so they could meet each other as well as fans. That first gathering attracted about 4,000 people, but after we moved it to Waxahachie, Texas, four years later and changed the name to the TCR Festival, it exploded into the largest single-day festival in Texas, attracting 60,000 to 70,000 fans year after year.

The success of our show also led to Phillips Productions producing other shows, the first being *Gardening Texas*, which starred super plant guy Neil Sperry. Like *TCR*, we syndicated the show in every market in Texas. We also produced a series called *TEXANS* that spotlighted famous people from the Lone Star State, much like one of those Barbara Walters specials except our guests were all Texans. We syndicated that show statewide too, and our featured guests included Governor George W. Bush, Willie Nelson, Charlie Pride, Don Henley, Walter Cronkite, Jimmy Johnson, Phylicia Rashad, Tanya Tucker, and many others.

Some programs we did in partnership with Belo. Michael Grant, who years later came to work for Phillips Productions, was the vice president in charge of Belo Productions back then. I remember hearing him tell Ward Huey, "Phillips can syndicate the entire state with a phone call." It was an exaggeration . . . and a challenge . . . and I felt proud that we had come that far.

We also branched out into corporate production. That started when a feisty woman appeared at my desk at WFAA-TV (I still don't know how she got past the guard) and said she worked for Neiman-Marcus and wanted to hire us to help tell their stories. I had no idea what she wanted us to do, but she was so insistent that I finally said, "Okay, we'll give it a shot."

For almost twenty years we traveled all over the world for Neiman-Marcus and Carolyn Cobb, the woman who hired me to help her Dallas-based company, and she became one of my dearest friends. The places we went and the things we did could easily make a separate book, except you probably wouldn't believe the stories. It was a magical time.

Our corporate clients included American Airlines, Southwest Airlines, the Centex Corporation, Balfour-Beatty Construction, lots of colleges and universities, many not-for-profit agencies, and so many others I won't bore you by naming them all. For years we had a separate division of our company just to handle the corporate work.

And one more very important thing came out of all of this, though many years later. In November 2000, I got a call from a guy named Patrick Gottsch. He said he was about to launch a cable and satellite network and was looking for programming.

By this time I was used to getting calls from people who were "about to do something or other," and I usually listened to them with a degree of skepticism.

"Where did you get my cell number?" I asked Patrick.

"From Willie Nelson," he told me. "I just visited with him about getting license to air some of the old cowboy westerns he owns."

Okay, I thought to myself, I could easily check this out. Patrick went on to explain that when Congress passed a bill that allowed for the use of digital satellite systems in consumer homes, there was language that said the service providers would dedicate some programming to rural America.

"Nobody is doing that," he told me. "So I'm going to do it. This network, the RFD-TV Network, will serve farmers and ranchers and people who live in small towns and even suburbs."

Now he was talking my language.

"When do you go on the air?" I asked.

"December 15," he answered.

"So we have a year and a month to get this put together and get RFD-TV up on satellite?" I asked.

"No," he said. "We have a month. *This* December 15."

The next day Patrick visited our studios in Dallas and moved in that afternoon. He was from Omaha, Nebraska, where he grew up the son of a successful farmer. Pat Gottsch had two or three farms and a feedlot, and was well respected by other farmers and ranchers. But he'd been through some hard times too, the kind that farmers and ranchers are all too familiar with, and now his son Patrick had dedicated his life to providing services that would help America's farmers and ranchers.

"Communications is the first thing to tackle," he said.

This was a cause we could get behind, so I told Patrick we would gladly help in any way we could. We launched RFD-TV on Dish Network on December 15, 2000, right on schedule, with six hours of daily programming that repeated four times. Eventually, that schedule would expand to 24/7, and RFD-TV would be known to anyone who lived in rural America or small towns, worked in the ag industry, or had a farm or ranch. The programming in the early days was all shows that had been produced for other TV stations, like *Big Joe's Polka Show* and *Miss Lucy's Kitchen*. There was lots of agricultural news and even cattle auctions. The network even found a sizeable audience among people living in big cities, giving credence to my long-held belief that skyscrapers are filled with people who long for a life in rural America.

We helped Patrick with RFD-TV until the network added DirecTV and lots of other cable systems across the country. It grew so much that it needed more than we could offer, so we packed up all their stuff in a U-Haul and moved the network to Nashville, where it would take over the former studios of *Great American Country* on Music Row. Now, when you turn on to Music Row, the first thing you will see is a big building with a sign that says RFD-TV. The network's tagline is one of the truest I have ever seen: "Rural America's Most Important Network."

We still work with Patrick and help when he asks or when we know there is a need, and we still support the cause that he took up decades ago. His passion for helping rural America is unparalleled, and we applaud it. *Texas Country Reporter* is an original show on RFD-TV, and we are proud that we are still on their network, where all of America can see our show. We get lots of email from all over the country, and even from other countries where the network is seen online. Our RFD-TV audience is very special to us.

Of course, back in 1987, we had no idea that all of these "other things" would come to us; we were just hoping to make it through a season of syndication without being cancelled. We knew we were in a business that loves you today and hates you tomorrow. And we were always aware that even one misstep in the world of television, and you and your show are history.

But we did start thinking *Texas Country Reporter* just might beat the odds in syndication and have staying power. At least, maybe it wouldn't be cancelled in its first season of syndication like so many other shows. We were cautiously optimistic.

We had no idea.

Part Five

SETTLING IN FOR THE LONG HAUL

CHAPTER THIRTY-SIX

I WISH I COULD TELL YOU THAT *4 COUNTRY REPORTER* started out as the show we wanted it to be, but that would have been very difficult. That's because, looking back, we didn't have a clue what we wanted it to be. All I knew was that it would be stories about people— nothing too serious, I hoped—and stuff that would make the audience laugh or feel good, or just think, "That's cool."

In today's TV world, you don't get the luxury of making your mistakes as you go. But what we were doing was groundbreaking television in its day. The 1960s was an incredible decade of growth for television as it introduced such things as color, the space race, and *Star Trek*. But it was also a period of grave concern for the same audiences, who witnessed assassinations, riots, and wars being fought halfway around the world right there in their living rooms. People truly had a love/hate relationship with this new member of the family.

When I started working in television at the beginning of 1970, the medium was, in many ways, still defining itself. Advertisers already knew its power, and audiences knew how it had changed their lives, but there was also still room to try new things without too much scrutiny. I have often said that if we were to try to create our show today in the same manner we did then, it would be a colossal failure. Today people expect a new show (or a movie or a song) to be an instant success when it goes on the air. If it's not, they'll move on. Back then we could put on a stinker every now and then, and the viewers would just say, "Maybe the next segment will be better . . . or next week's show."

I hate to admit this, but we were probably nine or ten years into the program before even *we* could define it.

Think of it this way: if *Texas Country Reporter* was a book, in what section of the library would you find it? History? Culture? Fiction? Nonfiction? Who can say?

I was asked that question once by Ed Bark of the *Dallas Morning News*, and I couldn't answer him . . . because I had no idea. Luckily, he didn't use my non-answer in print. In fact, Ed was always very kind to our show, and now I think maybe he understood what we were doing . . . or trying to do . . . before we did.

Then, in the early 1980s, we finally got it together enough to start asking ourselves what this thing we were doing was all about. We began to define what *Texas Country Reporter* was . . . and what it was not.

In the earliest days of the show we followed the advice of the TV consultant who made our idea possible. Frank Magid, owner of the market research company Frank N. Magid Associates, told our bosses to put small-town Texas on TV and to stop pretending that Dallas and Fort Worth were the only places that mattered. In support of that theory, we often started our stories with pictures of our *4 Country* vehicle traveling down back roads, beauty shots of Texas cotton or wheat fields or cattle grazing, and people going about their lives in small towns in our viewing area.

We even employed a trick to make life look somehow simpler and less hectic in those small towns: we shot the show on 16mm transparency news film, pretty much the same stuff as the Kodachrome that people used back in the day to take pictures for slides. This film gave us rich, color-saturated images that, as Paul Simon sang, "make you think all the world's a sunny day." Today you might compare it to an Instagram filter.

Add that to the fact that we usually filmed people walking or driving around those small towns at 36 or even 48 frames per second. Film is normally shot at 24 or even 30 fps, but when shot at 36 or 48 fps, then projected at the normal speed, it makes everything . . . and everybody . . . slow down. People look like they are gliding through life. They look like they are going about their lives while taking it easy and having a pretty good time. It was a technique that produced images of people who almost appeared to be in a dream state.

Add the appropriate instrumental soundtrack to those pictures and you've created a kind of nirvana, which allows viewers to dream about having a life like that.

"If only my hurry-up, workaday life was like that."

I always believed that downtown Dallas and Fort Worth (and now all the downtowns around the country where our show is seen) are full of people in high-rise office buildings who watch *Texas Country Reporter* and live vicariously through the people featured on the show, whose lives look somehow simpler and happier.

In the early days that's probably because we made the people on the show look that way. In later years it's because we eventually realized that showing *simpler lives* is one of the key attractions for the kind of people we hope to draw for the show. As we started trying to categorize what *TCR* is all about, the desire to live life to the fullest was right at the top of that list. We wanted to appeal to people who had lived one particular lifestyle, such as working a high-paying job in corporate America, only to find that they longed for something more. We still try to attract people like that today, probably even more so.

I remember the first story I produced for the show that made me start thinking about people seeking a better quality of life. It was one of the few stories we ever did in the middle of a big city, and this one was smack-dab in the middle of downtown Dallas. It was about a guy who had a popcorn stand in the Dallas Underground.

For those who don't know, there are extensive tunnels that run all over downtown Dallas. Some parts resemble a mall, with shops, kiosks, and restaurants. And in one of those areas, close to one of the entrances to the Dallas Underground, sat that popcorn stand. It was owned and operated by a happy young guy who wore a straw hat and a red-striped blazer that made him look kind of like Meredith Wilson in *The Music Man*, or like my dear friend Jerry Haynes, who played Mr. Peppermint, host of the long-running children's show *Mr. Peppermint* (later *Peppermint Place*).

All through the lunch hour and often after work, the young man would be there at his popcorn stand, smiling and filling up bags of the treat for people who wanted not only a snack but something that made them feel like . . . well, like they weren't at work.

Now, on the surface this wasn't an earth-shattering story. It was simple: a man selling popcorn, not in a movie theater but in a major metropolitan area. It was the kind of thing you might see at the end of the newscast, one of those ten- to fifteen-second stingers or kickers (as they call them) with the news anchor saying, "Hey, would you look at that? What a guy! Can you believe he makes his living selling popcorn? What a wonderful world! That's it for tonight. We'll see you tomorrow on 6 News at Ten!"

But that's not at all what the story was about. And to know that, all you have to do is look deeper, ask the right questions, and then do something that few people do. *Listen.*

I spent the whole morning shooting film of the Popcorn Man and watching him work, listening to him talk to his customers, and chatting with him about his life. And the longer I listened and watched, the more intrigued I was.

The Popcorn Man, it turned out, had given up a six-figure salary at a big Dallas tech company. He had gone to college to study to be a technology genius so he could make a lot of money and live a happy life. And it seemed like a happy life—until it didn't.

One day he woke up and realized that, yes, he made great money, and, yes, he could pretty much buy whatever he wanted. But he also realized he was not happy. He started thinking about what would make him happy. The answer, he finally decided, was that he liked to interact with people and make them happy, make them smile. He also realized that his high-tech job gave him little opportunity to do that.

Then, while munching popcorn at a movie theater, the idea hit him. Why did people only buy popcorn when they went to see a movie? What if they could have a bag of popcorn right in the middle of their workday? Wouldn't that be kind of a morale boost? And what if he could make a living giving people what they want, giving people that morale boost? What could be better than that?

And so the Popcorn Man was born—or, more appropriately, the man behind the Popcorn Man reinvented himself. He gave up the six-figure salary for this ludicrous idea called . . . *happiness.*

HAPPINESS IS AN ELUSIVE THING. IT COMES IN ALL KINDS of shapes and colors and experiences, and those things are different for each and every one of us. For some, it's as simple as selling popcorn to people in a big city. For others, it's getting as far away from the city as they can get. Over the many years of producing the show, I can't tell you how many times I've heard the line "I was born a hundred years too late." I guess now they would say, "I was born a hundred and fifty years too late," but I always want to ask, "Do you actually mean that?"

Every time someone recites that line to me, I cannot help but wonder if they have thought it through, if they have picked over the list of all the things people didn't have 100 or 150 years ago. Would they gladly give up those modern-day conveniences in order to live like people did in those times? Would they forsake the value of modern medicines that allow us to live longer lives? Would they want to wash their clothes in a creek and take a bath just a few times a year? I can easily tell you I would not. But I know a few people who would.

Dick and Bonnie Cain didn't just wish they had been born in the pioneer days. They made it happen . . . sort of. First, there's the location where they live. Parts of Big Bend are considered to be among the most remote places in the lower forty-eight states because they are farther from a commercial airport than most any other spot. The place that Dick and Bonnie Cain have chosen to live is one of those places. After driving about an hour south of Alpine, Texas, to a turnoff from the state highway that leads part of the way to their house, you still have quite a ways to go down a dirt road—if you want to call it that. I think of it as more of a trail, and that suits Dick and Bonnie just fine. Not many visitors would want to go to all the trouble that's required in order to see them. They don't care.

You see, Dick and Bonnie think the world took a wrong turn way back . . . well, way back. Maybe it was 100 or 150 years ago, or maybe it was before that. Thing is, they have decided to reject the world that most of us think of as modern. They don't care how you live your life. They are going to live their life together just the way they want.

That way of life consists of living in a house that most people simply wouldn't want to live in, with no central heat and air or swimming pool or three-car garage. Not only do they not have access to the internet, they don't even have a phone, and they don't want one either.

To them, this place is a mansion. Their mansion, a hideaway from the rest of the world that went so wrong—and that they want no part of.

Dick told me, "I was born in this kind of country and whatever you're used to, that's what you like. I'd love to have been born a hundred years ago but this is my lot, so I make the most of it."

Bonnie added, "It's so quiet, so peaceful. Sometimes it's so quiet, it hurts your ears. I don't know how to explain it but it's very addictive. I have never had a boring day. I can always find something to do, something that I enjoy doing. There's nothing I do that I hate doing."

We watched as Bonnie cut some bread from the loaf she made fresh in the wood-burning oven just that morning. Then, in that century-old adobe homestead, she cracked an egg and listened to the sound of another day in the desert. First there was only the sound of the wind blowing under the door, then bacon crackling in a cast-iron skillet, and finally the metal clink of her hungry husband's spurs. He'd already been up for hours tending to chores. Bonnie, too, but now it was time for their ritualistic morning coffee together, something she had been looking forward to since he rode off at daybreak to check on the cattle out in the desert.

"I miss him so much," she told us, "that even when he goes out riding or something, I'm like a little kid. I can't wait for him to get back home."

As they sat and sipped coffee and chewed the fresh bread hot out of the oven, they talked about the morning. Bonnie had already washed the desert sand out of some of Dick's clothes and hung them out on the line to dry, and Dick found a cow he'd been worried about, acting like she'd never been gone.

You won't find a four-burner electric oven or automatic dishwasher in Bonnie's kitchen. Those modern marvels require electricity and running water.

"I never did like electricity," Bonnie told us. "Seem like that's when all the trouble started." Bonnie said the words as if, surely, we have thought them too.

"Seems like people didn't sleep anymore because they could stay up around the clock, and to me, it just took so much away from our society."

Dick continued, "You can cut out a lot of frivolous stuff if you want to. There's a lot of stuff that people think of as necessities that aren't necessities when you get right down to it. And I'll tell you what, right to this day, if I had to choose between a good horse and a pickup, I'm afraid the pickup would lose."

As Dick saddled up and headed out into the desert again, Bonnie got on with her chores.

"When I wash, I wash by hand, and I can either make soap using lye or I can use cactus, and I'm kind of partial to the cactus soap. I do some hand sewing and I do some with my treadle sewing machine. I've had it for thirty-five years. It's like an old friend."

Seventy miles from civilization's nearest outpost, this simple life is no reality television show. On this day, Dick's son had come all the way from town to help round up some cattle, a family endeavor that goes back many years. Old-fashioned doesn't begin to describe Dick and Bonnie.

"I like this lifestyle, and we keep it as cheap and simple as we can because we ain't got any money," Dick explained from the back of his best horse.

Money is another thing Dick and Bonnie don't think of as a necessity. They don't have much in the way of material things, but they are rich in spirit, happy just being together far away from the city lights. Dick and Bonnie are quietly sending a message to mainstream America, a reminder of where we came from and what's important.

As the evening sun set, Bonnie picked a guitar and blew into a harmonica strapped around her neck while Dick tapped the toes of his dusty boots and smiled at his bride like they were just married yesterday.

"Everybody has to find what makes them happy," Bonnie explained.

> And the simpler it is, the more time you have to sit out on the porch and watch the sunset or look up at the stars, just the simple things people don't have the time to do in our rush, rush society.
> And so many people get to the end of their journey and they find out that life wasn't about all those things they were seeking, and they see the vanity in it all, and I've heard about people who spent their

lives trying to get those things they thought would make them happy only to find there is no happiness in things.

Dick and Bonnie Cain have found happiness. They have found it in their bare-bones life, or, as Bonnie says, the living, loving, and laughing found only in simplicity.

Maybe true love does conquer all, even greed, envy, and the almighty dollar. For Dick Cain, a West Texas sunset is money in the bank, and for Bonnie, a happy home is all the insurance she will ever need. Out here, life is what you make it. It's just that simple.

"I'm on a journey," Dick told us before we headed back to the comfort of our air-conditioned motel rooms in Alpine. "And, you know, it's not about money. It's about peace and tranquility and the joy Bonnie and I have found. And, if the Good Lord's willing, I'd like to finish up right here. I love it. I love it."

The Popcorn Man and Dick and Bonnie Cain seem about as far away from each other as you can imagine, physically and in many other ways. Truth is, they are alike, at least the way I see it. They are seeking their own kind of happiness in life, and they are willing to go to what many of us would consider extreme measures to find it. There would be many more people like these that we would meet in our travels.

In fact, after we had been on the air for a number of years, we started noticing something we came to call "the *TCR* effect." We were now, frequently, coming across people who were doing something in life that made them happy in addition to or instead of doing things that made money. People were chasing dreams and, in some cases, giving up much easier lives to do something they considered to be more meaningful. And over and over again we heard them tell us they got the idea to make such a radical move by watching other people on *Texas Country Reporter* who had done just that.

CHAPTER THIRTY-SEVEN

WE HAVE A SAYING AT *TEXAS COUNTRY REPORTER*: "It's not about what it's about."

In journalism school, they teach you to never bury the lead. In the first paragraph, preferably the first sentence, you're supposed to sum up the crux of the story. We almost never do that.

Instead, we like to romance it a bit first. We like to set the scene, then take you down a road and make an abrupt turn. Suddenly, you find yourself where you least expected.

Or maybe we give you some information up front, but then make you wait for things to resolve. We love to bring the story full circle so you find yourself just sitting back with a smile. We like to make you work for it. That way, it means so much more to you. *We love to take you on a journey.*

The story about the Popcorn Man is a perfect example of "it's not about what it's about."

First, it ain't about popcorn. That has almost nothing to do with the real story.

But wait, he's making popcorn and selling it, right?

True. But he could have been selling almost anything. He could have been selling lemonade or those little chameleons on a string they used to have at the State Fair of Texas, or . . . widgets.

It doesn't matter *what* he's selling, because the story is about the fact that this man is on a journey to find happiness in life while making others happy as well. Same with Dick and Bonnie Cain . . . and lots of folks we feature on the show.

When we are discussing a possible story internally, trying to decide if it's a good one for us or not, we often use the widget example. Around the *TCR* office, you'll hear one of us say on a regular basis, "She's selling widgets!

I don't know! Does it make any difference *what* she's selling (or making or collecting or . . .)?"

It's not about what it's about. It's about the story behind the story. That's what *Texas Country Reporter* is all about.

I recently received an email from a viewer who was partially lamenting days gone by and partially complaining about a story that had just aired on *TCR*. Her email mentioned the story on Mr. B, who worked at the legendary Highland Park Cafeteria in Dallas for decades. He'd been there so long that he was working there when I did my first story about the eatery, which aired on November 28, 1981. And he was still there when we went back a few months ago, although "there" is now across town, since the real estate at the original location became much too valuable to support a cafeteria. It is also no longer owned by the family that made the place famous back in the day.

Before the second story aired for the first time in early 2020, Mr. B had decided to retire from his job at Highland Park Cafeteria. No harm. He had been there almost his entire adult life. It was a good story about a good man, and the first airing brought a ton of mail from people wishing him well. And the cafeteria picked up a lot of new customers, which often happens when we feature places to eat. All was well.

Then the COVID-19 pandemic hit, and Highland Park Cafeteria, like so many other businesses, had to close down. Just prior to the rerun of the story, the owner of the cafeteria announced they just couldn't make it and the famous cafeteria would not reopen, but the repeat episode ran as scheduled.

The email I received from the viewer said how sad it was that we could no longer go to the cafeteria, but regardless of that, this was now a story without relevance.

I read the email and shook my head. After all these years, I'm used to hearing from people who just don't "get it." I wrote back and told her I hardly thought a story about Mr. B's life was irrelevant and that I thought she had missed the point: that the story was about a man who gave his life to a job he loved and did well, and it had made lots of people happy, including Mr. B. I said I thought that story would be relevant for years to come because it is timeless.

The email I received back said she didn't know that you had to have an advanced degree to watch and understand our show. So sorry she sees it that way. Case closed. No further reply from me.

I know I'm probably dwelling on this too much for some people, but this is what I'm talking about: the story isn't about what it's about. Translated: stop, listen, and watch, and you'll probably learn that there is a hidden gem somewhere in that story. It's often not about an eatery that's been around for a long time, but about someone who is passionate about the place.

Why? Because (and this will shock many of you) we don't do stories about places. We don't do stories about festivals or towns. We do stories about *people*. It's something we decided way back in the early 1980s, when we finally got around to trying to figure out who we are and what kind of stories we do on *TCR*—and what kind of stories we don't do. We do not do news stories because the world is already saturated with too many of those, along with, these days, an unhealthy dose of too much of someone else's opinion to go with them. We don't do politics of any kind. We stay as far away from controversy as we possibly can.

Many times each month I'll hear from a viewer who says something like, "I would have thought you would have run out of stories by now! How do you keep finding them?"

And my answer is, "As long as they keep making new people, we will never run out of stories."

My dad would have called that a "horse's ass answer." He probably would have been right. But I don't mean for it to come across as sarcastic.

Another thing we hear and read frequently is, "I like it when you do those stories about small towns." This is a comment that goes all the way back to what I was talking about earlier. In the early days of the show, we frequently started off with footage of the town where the story was taking place, making that town look, feel, and sound like the perfect place to be. We still do that today, though maybe not as much as we used to.

In response to that one, I just smile and thank them, even though I usually think, "How closely do you watch the show? We don't do stories about small towns." I think the reason I don't have a horse's ass answer for that one is because it at least tells me they watch the show, and have probably been watching for a long time.

Maybe I am a horse's ass.

But when you've been doing something for as long as I have, it comes to mean so much to you, and you want other people to feel what you feel. I want the viewers to get the full experience that we get when we visit the people featured on the show because, at least most of the time, it's a wonderful thing. And because so many people do get it, it makes it all worthwhile. We do it for them. We do it for us. We do it because we love it, and we know others do too.

Often, as we are about to leave, I will say to the person we have just spent an entire day with, "I promise you're going to like the story we tell about you." And I mean that, because we don't do negative. The story we tell about each person that we feature is as important to me as it is to that person. My job is to tell their story in the best way I can. And remember, everybody has one. It's important to me that the people we feature feel like they are important when they see the story we produce about them—because each one of them *is* important. They are the cogs in the wheels that keep the world turning. They aren't famous, and most don't want to be. But they *are* important.

My best buddy, Brian Hawkins, whom I mentioned earlier in this book—the guy who, as of this writing, has traveled the back roads of Texas with me for more than thirty-one years—says it this way:

> There is no routine, no "average week," no set amount of tasks to craft a finished segment for *TCR*. Those of us who work on this show (and I have had the immeasurable blessing to have been a part of this family for thirty-one years) know the incredible feeling we get after completing a day's filming and driving miles and miles to another location, re-living the hours just shared with yet one more unique individual. For me, it's the windows rolled down, the images once more passing through my fresh memory, watching the sun go down across a shifting horizon . . . and another day passing in this journey that, thankfully, seems to have no destination. This is what I love. This is why I do what I do.

Ditto, BH. Ditto.

CHAPTER THIRTY-EIGHT

WE WEREN'T WITHOUT DIRECTION OR GUIDANCE AS we started the show in the early 1970s. I had lots of thoughts about what I wanted the show to be, or what I thought it should be, and so did other people that worked on it. If anything, we probably had too many ideas. What's the old saying? Too many cooks in the kitchen? When that happens, it's hard to get focused and point something in the right direction. Creative differences and egos get in the way, and you end up with a hodgepodge of "stuff." As we struggled to define what the show was and what it was not, we tried lots of different things. Still, the ratings were good, so it's not like we were chasing anyone away.

Then I met Charles Kuralt.

Charles Bishop Kuralt, the man who inspired my idea for *4 Country Reporter*, was born in 1934, during the Great Depression, in Wilmington, North Carolina. His family moved to Charlotte in 1945, and it was there that Charles's interest in journalism took root. He was something of a child star in the field and by his early teens was one of the youngest radio announcers in the country. He attended the University of North Carolina at Chapel Hill, was editor of the *Daily Tar Heel*, and then became a reporter for the *Charlotte News* after graduating. He went on to join the CBS Network at the age of twenty-three and covered stories all over the world, including the Vietnam War.

I first met Charles Kuralt in person when he came to the Dallas area sometime in the mid- to late seventies. We had spoken on the phone a few times prior to that meeting, the first time when I was at home in bed with a bad case of influenza.

On that day Kuralt was in town to speak at the Radio-Television News Directors' Association annual meeting. I had wrangled tickets to the luncheon where he was speaking just so I could hear the man in person, with hopes that I would be able to meet him.

On the evening before Kuralt's speech, I was running a high fever and felt like I'd been run over by a train. The next morning I was even worse because the train kept running over me. I was absolutely heartbroken that I could not go to the event to hear, and possibly meet, Charles Kuralt. He was my idol, my inspiration, the very guy from whom I had "borrowed" the idea for our show. I felt like we would hit it off—if he didn't hit me in the mouth first. I had no idea how he might feel about the show we were producing. It wasn't a rip-off, but more of a tribute to the kind of journalism he pioneered. We never, ever copied a story Kuralt did, and still have not to this day. To me, that would be like plagiarism, even if we put our own spin on the story. I know something about that subject, because *Texas Country Reporter* has been copied a lot over the years, with some imitators almost identically reproducing stories we'd already aired, right down to the same shots and almost identical scripts.

Sometime that afternoon my home phone rang, and I managed to answer it as I fought my way out of a fitful sleep. The voice of the man on the other end was friendly but also businesslike.

He said, "May I speak to Bob Phillips?"

"Speaking," I said, thinking it was a telemarketing call or something annoying like that.

"Bob, this is Charles Kuralt."

I knew immediately that this was a prank call from some of the guys in the Channel 4 newsroom. They knew how much I was looking forward to Kuralt's speech, and they knew I was at home, sick in bed. I rarely called in sick, and everyone knew I wouldn't miss seeing and hearing Kuralt if I could help it. This was a bad joke.

They expected me to believe that Charles Kuralt was on the phone?

"Like hell it is! Come on, guys, this isn't funny!" I shouted.

I slammed down the phone.

Have you ever said something, and even as the words are coming out of your mouth, you want to reel them back in because you know you're making a fool of yourself?

I looked at that telephone, amazed it was still in one piece after how hard I'd slammed it down, angry at the guys in the newsroom who were having some fun jerking my chain. But at the same time, my brain said, "That voice sure sounded familiar."

I was fully awake by the time the phone rang again.

I sheepishly answered, and a more gentle, caring, but very straightforward voice said, "Bob, this *is* Charles Kuralt."

I have no idea what I said next, but it probably involved stuttering and stammering some kind of excuse for my previous behavior. All I remember was that he understood and didn't care about that.

We talked for several minutes. I found out later that the news director at KDFW-TV had attended the luncheon and heard Kuralt's speech, and managed to talk to him after the event. He told him about the show we were doing and that he, Charles Kuralt, was my greatest inspiration. And he told him I was home sick. Then he asked him if he would give me a call, and the great man agreed.

I barely remember the conversation that afternoon, but I do know that Kuralt offered his phone number, his assistant's name at CBS in New York, and his mailing address. He invited me to keep in touch and let him know how our show was going, and he said maybe I could join him sometime when he was shooting an *On the Road* piece in our area.

He also said people sent ideas to him every day and that he couldn't possibly do them all. If I was interested, he said, he would send some of the Texas ideas to me, and he asked if I would do the same if we ran across something that didn't work for our show but might work for his.

Suddenly I was feeling a lot better.

Our first in-person meeting occurred some months later when Kuralt was in the Dallas area with his crew—Isadore "Izzy" Bleckman, the photographer, and Larry Gianneschi Jr., the sound man—to shoot a story for *On the Road.*

Besides my respect for Kuralt, I also admired Izzy Bleckman, who is famous for much more than the million-plus miles he traveled and the hundreds of stories he filmed with Charles Kuralt. He was present that day in Dallas when Lee Harvey Oswald was brought through the basement of the Dallas Police headquarters and Jack Ruby stepped up and killed him on live television. It was Izzy shooting the film for CBS News that day. And the news rush that still ran in my blood made me want to meet this person who had been present for a big story like that.

At the time I wasn't sure why Kuralt was in Dallas and at my TV station, but the day he and I met in person, he'd stopped by KDFW to meet with someone in the station's promotions department.

Word travels fast in TV stations, and someone said, "Hey, Phillips, your hero is upstairs." I didn't have to ask who they were talking about, but I wasn't sure if I should barge in on the meeting or if maybe I could just happen to be walking down the hall as he was on his way out. I opted for the latter and had to walk up and down that hallway several times. Finally, Kuralt and the promotions guy were walking to the elevator just as I happened to turn the corner—and there we were, face to face.

By this time it had been several months, maybe more, since our initial telephone conversation, but we had talked on the phone a couple more times. I remember one of those times was when Kuralt's assistant called to ask if I knew anything about Hopkins County Stew. It just so happened that we had produced a story at the Hopkins County Stew Cook-off, so I was familiar with the stuff and told her what I knew.

Hopkins County Stew originated in the late 1800s, when it became a tradition in the northeast Texas county for families to gather at the county seat, Sulphur Springs, to make a big pot of stew at the end of every school year. Some people would bring vegetables and some would bring meat, if they had it, and they'd just throw everything in the pot. No one ever knew exactly what might be in there, and that, of course, became kind of a joke around Hopkins County. Eventually, someone with some marketing savvy turned the legend of Hopkins County Stew into an annual event in Sulphur Springs.

I don't remember if he was considering doing a story about Hopkins County Stew, but after talking to his assistant, Charles himself got on the phone to thank me for my help. If he ever did that story, I did not see it, and I cannot find any mention of it in the archives. Maybe I scared him away.

Sometime after that I was invited to be a judge at the Hopkins County Stew contest. Everything was great until one of the cooks—jokingly, I hope—mentioned that it was the best roadkill stew he had ever made. I'm not sure what was in that pot of stew, but it started me thinking, and I pretty much swore off of judging any kind of cooking contest after that. Except for pie. What can you do to pie?

That day I met Charles at KDFW-TV, he mentioned he was going to grab a bite to eat before meeting up with Izzy and Larry and asked for a recommendation, someplace that served good Texas cooking. The problem was that he was in kind of a hurry, so I suggested he go directly across the street from the station to Joe's Barbecue, on the corner of Pacific and Griffin. It wasn't very big, and you'd smell like smoke for the rest of the day after going in, but the food was decent. And it was simple and quick: you would go through a line, order your barbecue sandwich or plate, say yes or no to chips and a drink, and you were set. The place closed after lunch, and it was almost that time, so Charles said he was going to grab a sandwich and be on his way.

Then he invited me to go with him. I jumped at the chance, even though I knew it would be quick. I was eager to hear more about his adventures, but I knew this would not be the day. Still, I was honored that I had been asked to have lunch with my idol.

We ended up sitting in Joe's until Joe finally told us he had to lock up and leave, probably almost an hour after we walked in the door. I remember

Charles asking me a lot of questions about my background, about where I grew up and why I got into journalism. I remember that because I was kind of amazed that he would ask those questions. Why should he care? He was the one who had achieved great things. I wanted to hear his story, not tell him mine. But as I got older and more experienced, I realized that was one reason Charles Kuralt was so successful at what he did. He was a listener, not a talker. He was just interviewing me the same way he'd interviewed hundreds of other people.

During that conversation I told him about growing up in Old East Dallas and about the silly book I wrote about my dogs when I was eight or nine years old, thinking I was going to be some great writer when I grew up. He immediately told me about winning a prize for a story he wrote for a local newspaper when he was thirteen or fourteen. It was about a dog that got loose on the field during a baseball game. We laughed about the similarities in our backgrounds. I pointed out that my book had won no prizes.

He wanted to know how I came up with the idea for the show I was doing, and I told him that his reporting style was the inspiration. And I told him how I had begged my bosses for a long time to let me try my idea, to let me do just one show, and how I was repeatedly turned down, until one day they suddenly decided to give it a try—with someone else as the reporter.

He laughed at that story and said it was very similar to his own at CBS. Seems he, too, had begged to do stories about ordinary people doing extraordinary things only to be constantly turned down by his boss, until one day management told him he had three months to prove it would work. He never looked back, and now that was his primary job at the network.

I asked why he wanted to be a traveling features reporter, and his answer was that he simply longed to do stories like the ones he had done when he was a reporter with the *Charlotte News* and wrote a column called "Charles Kuralt's People."

"Let me give you a piece of advice before I go," he said as we headed out the door. "Keep your head down, stay out of the fray in the newsroom, do your job, and fly below the radar. In fact, the best-case scenario is if your bosses never think about you. And if you need some free advice about all of this, I don't mind giving you mine, for what it's worth."

"You don't mind if I call you with questions?"

"Not at all," he said with a laugh. "The trick will be finding me in the office."

It's funny now when I think back on Charles's advice because, while his plan worked for me for a long time, it's the very thing that angered Wendell Harris, the Channel 4 news director, and caused him to give me the "I don't know *who* you are or even *where* you are" speech shortly before canceling 4 *Country Reporter* that fateful day in 1986.

Keep in mind that all of this was long before the internet and email. Besides, Charles Kuralt was a letter writer, and I'm not sure he would have fully embraced email even if we'd had it back then. Shortly after our conversation at Joe's Barbecue, I received a handwritten note from Charles, saying he enjoyed our lunch and that he found it amazing how much he and I had in common, citing the early writing attempts about dogs and the similar experiences we had in getting our bosses to accept a reporter who concentrated on so-called fluff instead of hard news.

And he told me we should get together again when he was in the area, maybe Izzy and Larry would join us, and that I should be thinking about where we could get great fried chicken and country cooking.

I had just the places in mind. More importantly, I felt that Charles Kuralt and I had become friends.

CHAPTER THIRTY-NINE

O VER THE YEARS, CHARLES KURALT AND I STAYED IN
touch. He sent quite a few story ideas to me because he only
did a fraction of the number of stories that we did . . . and still do. Charles
probably got around to no more than twenty-five or thirty stories a year,
while our show required three stories every week. If he knew he wasn't going
to get around to a particular story, he would jot it down on a piece of paper
from a reporter's notebook, a napkin, or the back of his business card and
send it in the mail. Sometimes he would just forward a letter that someone had sent to him with a quick note scribbled on it, like "Take a look at
this" or "Maybe this is something you can use." He occasionally called, but
Charles wasn't much for talking on the phone. Most of the time those calls
were to ask a question about something in Texas or about a particular story.

A few times I got to visit Charles and the crew as they filmed part of a
story in Texas or Oklahoma, but that was kind of a sensitive thing. Charles
would mention that they were going to be in the area and I was welcome to
come by, but he always cautioned me to keep some distance while they were
working. I never knew if this was a CBS policy or if maybe he didn't want
to make his coworkers angry by having some kid hanging around, but I can
easily buy either or both of those reasons. The latter reason definitely applies
to me and my crew: when you're working on a story, you can't afford the
distraction of people hanging around in the background.

But the great thing is that Charles, who had accepted the job as my
mentor ("I'm glad to share what knowledge I have with you, Bob"), would
always follow up with some explanation for why or how they did certain
things I might have witnessed on one of those stories. Keep in mind that
I was still very young at that point. Truth is, they didn't do things that differently from the way we did (except that we could never afford a separate

sound man), but the way Charles explained things always kind of put them in perspective as I was honing my craft. He was a very giving instructor. He didn't have to give me the time of day, but he did.

Besides his job doing *On the Road*, Charles was also one of the founders of *CBS Sunday Morning*, a ninety-minute weekly news show that began on January 28, 1979, with Charles as its host. The show has Kuralt stamped all over it, with in-depth profiles of people, both famous and not so famous, and deep reporting of current trends and situations in society, art, music, and more. The show has always ended with what is called a "moment of nature," where pictures from the great outdoors are quietly and reverently presented before sign-off. The production is never flashy and reminds me of reading the *New Yorker*. Perhaps that was its inspiration.

After doing his *On the Road* series for more than twenty-five years and hosting *CBS Sunday Morning* for fifteen of those, Charles shocked the world by announcing his retirement at the age of sixty. Though he had been at CBS longer than any other on-air personality at the network, he was still five years away from the age when most folks think about retiring.

When asked, Charles often said that after telling other people's stories for most of his adult life, he simply wanted to see America through the eyes of a patriot instead of those of a journalist. He has been quoted as saying to himself, "You have at least one good long trip in you yet." He spent several weeks alone in his cabin in North Carolina atop Grandfather Mountain, where he wrote *Charles Kuralt's America*. He called his time there "part of the most memorable year of my life."

Shortly after the publication of his last book, at the age of sixty-two, Charles was admitted to New York-Presbyterian Hospital, suffering complications from lupus. He wrote notes to some of his friends that said things like, "Something is dreadfully wrong and I fear I may not make it out of here." He did not. Charles Kuralt died on July 4, 1997, and was buried on the grounds of the University of North Carolina at Old Chapel Hill Cemetery.

A few months after his death, I made a trip to North Carolina—a kind of pilgrimage, I suppose—to pay my respects and to think about the life of Charles Kuralt. I visited the site where he was buried and thought about where my own life might be had it not been for the guidance I had been given by this great man. And I thought about the gift he had given our country by telling its untold stories.

That trip also included a visit with my dear friend and colleague Brian Hawkins. He is also originally from North Carolina, and it was partly our mutual admiration for the work of Charles Kuralt that bonded us as we worked together to tell the stories of the people of Texas. He was in North

Carolina visiting family and suggested that I stop at Grandfather Mountain. Little did I know what he had in store for me to do there.

At that time the mountain was privately owned by Hugh Morton, who built the famous Mile High Swinging Bridge, the highest suspension footbridge in America, to join two of the mountain's peaks. Hugh was a close friend of Charles and kept a special cabin there for him called Anvil Rock. Charles once told me it was there that he felt most at peace, high above the valley, in the midst of the incredible natural beauty of his home state of North Carolina.

When I arrived at Grandfather Mountain, Hugh Morton greeted me, said he knew I was a friend of Charles Kuralt's, and asked if I would like to stay the night in his cabin, something he said no one else had been allowed to do. To this day, I believe that this invitation was one of the highest honors I could have been given. It was there, and not at the cemetery, that I said good-bye to my friend. There were lots of tears shed that night, but they were happy ones because I had no doubt that Charles was beginning another journey on another of life's unknown back roads.

Two years after he died, Charles Kuralt's decades-long relationship with a woman in Montana named Patricia Shannon became public after she made claim to some land that was adjacent to a house that she and Charles had shared for many years. That assertion was later upheld by the Montana Supreme Court based on a letter Charles wrote just before he died, telling Patricia he wanted her to have the land.

Charles had been married twice. His early, short-lived marriage of six years to Sory Guthery produced two daughters who now lived on the East Coast. His much longer marriage to Suzanne "Petie" Baird lasted thirty-five years. She lived in New York while he lived much of his life on the road. He told me he had missed far too many birthday parties and special family events because of what he chose to do for a living. He cautioned me not to do the same.

After the story of Charles Kuralt's secret life became public, I heard stories about people who refused to buy his books because he was a cheater, a sinner, a man of low moral character, and on and on. What was so confusing to me is that prior to the discovery of his long-term affair with a woman other than his wife, Charles was practically a national hero. I think that may be part of the reason why people responded to the news so harshly. The contrast between "the two Charles Kuralts" was more than some people could wrap their minds around, so they took the easy way out and said, "I'll have nothing more to do with him."

I don't support Charles's so-called cheating, if it was indeed that. But I find it hard to believe that his wife had no knowledge of it. They were married for thirty-five years, and for twenty-nine of those he had been in this other relationship. Is it possible to keep something secret for that long? Secret from a person you love? And consider this: Charles and Petie had no children together. She seemed content with the fact that he was always gone, even on holidays. Is it possible that the two had worked out some kind of . . . arrangement? I always remember what I was taught as a teenager: there are lots of ways to live a life. And just months before she died, not long after Charles's death, Petie said, "He was the greatest man I ever knew." This came *after* she supposedly found out about his years with Pat.

Why else do I think people knew about this even though they claimed not to? Because I knew about it, and I was not his closest friend, not by a long shot. We were casual friends and colleagues, not best buds. There is no way that Izzy and Larry didn't know about it: Pat Shannon's son had an internship at CBS and sometimes traveled on the road with them. And I have firsthand knowledge of the fact that nothing could have been kept a secret in that little Winnebago. Nothing.

How did I know about his other relationship? Because Charles and I shot a TV promo together while he was in the Dallas area back in the early 1980s, the second time we appeared on camera together promoting our two series. I picked him up at DFW Airport and was conflicted about what I was going to do if he decided to smoke in my brand new car. Charles was from North Carolina, the land of tobacco farms. In those days most people from that part of the country still smoked. I did not, but I hated the idea of telling my hero that I didn't want him to smoke in my car. It turned out not to be a problem because he never attempted to light up that day.

We went to the hotel at the Fort Worth Stockyards and shot the following spot, which, by the way, was pretty much ad-libbed by the two of us as we walked through the lobby in a single scene. We had a script, but Charles suggested we try winging it, so we did, and the director from KDFW's promotions department liked it. It went like this:

> Charles: "The old Stockyards Hotel. I like this!"
> Bob: "A lot of Texas history here . . ."
> Charles: "Maybe you have noticed, Bob and I do pretty much the same thing . . ."
> Bob: "Traveling around, meeting the people who make up the fabric of America. Charles, I think we ought to divvy up the territory."
> Charles: "Uh, you would want Texas, I suppose . . ."
> Bob: "And you could take the rest of America."
> Charles: "I don't know, I've always liked Texas."
> Bob: "Okay, we'll share." (Bob + Charles shake hands)
> Announcer: "Phillips and Kuralt, only on Channel 4!"

The spot was shot in the late afternoon, so Charles and I went into the dining room at the Stockyards Hotel and had an early supper. He was pretty tired from being on the road for several days and wanted to go to bed early, plus I had a story to shoot early the next morning and wanted to get back to Dallas to try and get a decent night of sleep.

One thing I had learned was that Charles had at least three vices: drinking, smoking, and eating. And when he did things, he often did them to excess, so he drank too much, he smoked too much, and, the one vice we shared, he often ate too much. After I started traveling with the show, it only took a year for me to put on twenty pounds over what I had weighed all through high school and college. Too many great cafes.

That night we gorged on steaks and baked potatoes and hot bread, and Charles poured down a few alcoholic beverages while I drank iced tea. By the end of supper and conversation, I was drunk on the joy of being in the presence of my friend, mentor, and hero, and he was slightly drunk on his booze of choice that evening, perhaps chased by a feeling of guilt. Charles started talking.

He asked a lot of personal questions about my life that were uncharacteristic of the Charles Kuralt I had come to know in previous conversations. I didn't mind sharing with him and thought nothing about it. I told him about my parents' divorce, something I rarely talked about, and how it had affected me. I also told him that I believed it takes two to make a relationship work, and two to make a relationship end, something that helped me get over the "Who's to blame?" game I used to play in my head when thinking about my mom and dad. He said he agreed, but then he dropped a bombshell.

"I'm in love with two women."

And that was it. He didn't tell me who the two women were, though I assumed one of them was his wife. I didn't ask. I just listened. He moved on from that to talking philosophically about life and about the expectations of society. I remember that he said it was harder for a person who lives their life in the public eye because people have expectations for how other people should act, and Charles said he wasn't always a good example of the kind of virtuous people he featured on TV.

I remember telling him that, to me, he represented Everyman, a term I use to describe the most common among us, the salt-of-the-earth people who make the world go around. I told him he was entitled to make the same mistakes that we mortals make every day. That was about as far as my attempt at advice went because I didn't have any for him. He was my hero and that was that. I wasn't going to judge him, and I wasn't going to pry. Maybe I didn't want to know more.

I didn't learn anything else about what Charles meant by "I'm in love with two women" until the rest of the world learned about it. He never brought it up again, and never acknowledged bringing it up that evening. It was something in the past and a moot point between us. That was that.

I didn't judge Charles that evening, and I still don't judge him. My opinion of him was never challenged by this information. For one thing, it simply was and is not any of my business. Who among us gets to judge? But it's also because I don't expect my heroes or my friends to be perfect, and I know that I wouldn't have any friends if they expected me to be perfect. I am far, far from it.

A writer named Ralph Grizzle, who knew Charles very well, put things in perspective with an article he wrote called "Forgiving Charles Kuralt." It's worth a read if you care about this topic, but the part I want to point out is how he decided to deal with what some think of as Charles's "betrayal."

> Kuralt enlightened by seeing the good in us—not because that was all there was to see but because he chose to. We praised him for his good-news approach, even bestowing him with 13 Emmy and three Peabody awards. It is unfortunate that when we discovered that all the news about his own life was not good, we chose to lash out at his memory. What does that say—not about Charles Kuralt, but about us?
>
> Kuralt could have as easily chosen to be a muckraking journalist, but his style was not to be brutal or harsh. "You know, most reporters can't go back to the towns they wrote stories about," he told me in 1994, and then added thoughtfully: "I never wrote that kind of story."

I have decided that, like Ralph Grizzle said, Charles Kuralt was simply a good man with some excesses in his life. He drank too much. He smoked too much. And, I suppose, he loved too much.

I hope that when my time on this planet is done and I'm laid to rest in the Texas State Cemetery in Austin, people will judge me not for the many missteps I've made in my life but for the body of work and the feelings I will leave behind. It's not perfect, because it is the product of an imperfect man. That's how I decided to feel about Charles Kuralt.

He is still my hero.

CHAPTER FORTY

SEVERAL TIMES AFTER CHARLES KURALT AND I FIRST MET
face-to-face and had lunch at Joe's Barbecue, he came back to
Dallas, always looking for some good food. Over the years I introduced him
to the original Henderson's Fried Chicken at Thomas and Hall, where two
pieces of white bread were placed in the bottom of every chicken basket to
absorb the grease from the chicken and fries; Adair's, then located on Cedar
Springs Road, where the waitresses called everyone "hon" and referred to the
owner as "Mother Adair"; and the crown jewel of country cooking, Ginnie's
Bishop Grill, where they must have put some kind of magical drug in the
chicken-fried steak batter because you couldn't stop eating it.

Ginnie's was Charles's favorite, and we ate there on more than one occa-
sion. I produced stories on all of these eateries over the years. Stories on cafes
and greasy spoons have always been a staple of *Texas Country Reporter*, going
all the way back to the beginning.

Ginnie, the owner of the grill, was my friend. For some reason she
decided I was a struggling, starving journalist, and on Fridays she would call
me before shutting down the diner for the weekend and tell me to "come
pick up your box." If I was in town and could get away, I would, and the box
would be loaded with much more food than I could have ever eaten over
the weekend, so I usually ended up sharing it with people in the newsroom.
I tried several times to refuse the box, but it seemed to make Ginnie happy
to give it away, so I finally just gave in, and I certainly never minded eating
her cooking.

There were only a few small tables inside Ginnie's Bishop Grill, and hungry diners routinely queued up at the place, with the line snaking down
the block from the front door at 321 North Bishop in the Oak Cliff section
of Dallas. She always snuck me in the back door so I didn't have to wait in

the line, and Charles said circumventing the line was a "guilty pleasure" that he enjoyed.

On one particular trip to Ginnie's with Charles, we were sitting at one of the tiny tables, both of us enjoying the chicken-fried steak with gravy, mashed potatoes, and whatever veggies Ginnie gave us, along with an unlimited supply of her incredible yeast rolls with butter, when I felt a kind of emotional chill run through my veins. By this time, Charles and I were comfortable enough around one another that we didn't always feel the need to talk, so when the food arrived, we had taken a break from the chit-chat to eat.

This was another similarity between Charles and me. My dad, having grown up on a farm where the noon meal was called dinner and was usually served at straight-up twelve o'clock, always ate like he had to hurry back to the fields to get the day's work finished before dark. One bite of everything on his plate went into his mouth before he chewed and swallowed. That was always followed by a drink of iced tea, then repeat. Little talk, if any, happened unless it was the evening meal, when he would push back from the table and talk about the day before going to bed. Charles said it had been pretty much the same way at his house.

That day at Ginnie's I looked across the table and saw my friend, my mentor, my hero—Charles Kuralt—sitting there being Everyman, chewing his chicken-fried steak, and suddenly I felt the need to tell him what I was thinking. I wanted him to know that I was grateful for the interest he had taken in helping me with my career over the years.

I blurted out, "Charles, I don't know if I ever told you this, but you're my hero."

Charles hardly reacted, but put down his fork, cleared his throat, and said, "And just who might your other heroes be?"

I was not expecting that response. I thought he'd say something like, "Aw, thanks, Bob, that's nice," or even come back with a joke like, "You need to get your priorities straight, kid."

But, no, he asked me a serious question, one out of left field, and I wasn't ready with an answer. Still, I knew I had to come up with something to say, something that wouldn't make me feel as stupid as I was feeling at that moment. Wishing I hadn't blurted out the hero thing, I did just what he did and put down my fork, cleared my throat, and proceeded to tell him all about the garbage man. THE GARBAGE MAN.

He listened, because Charles was always polite. Come to think of it, I never heard him say a bad thing about anybody. He truly was a gentleman, and someone who believed in his heart that all people are created equal.

I think he understood what I was saying about the garbage man, or at least he pretended to.

Then he said, "But tell me who your other heroes are now, at this moment in time."

Whoa! My lame answer about my first hero when I was six years old was not going to suffice, and he apparently wasn't going to cut me any slack here. He wanted an answer. In retrospect, I think the question he asked was a good one, because if someone tells you that you are their hero, it's probably a good idea to find out what company you're in—just who this person's other heroes might be. You could find out you don't want to be their hero. Now I felt the pressure to say something semi-intelligent, something thought-provoking.

"Charles," I said with a philosophical tone in my voice, as if the words coming out of my mouth were well thought out, "I don't think there are any heroes left in this world."

ZING! Charles shot me a look over the top of his little half glasses that said, "You poor, pathetic excuse for a man. You ignorant creature, you. Did you just say what I think you said?"

Maybe he didn't mean for that look to say all of that because, like I said, I never heard him utter a rude thing the whole time I knew him. But that's what I was feeling about myself at that moment, so I probably interpreted it to be the way he felt too.

Then came the lesson. Charles—like Coach Landry, Eddie Barker, and my mom—was a great teacher who believed in showing you the way to the answer instead of giving you the answer. You know, the old "give a man a fish" versus "teach a man to fish" thing. He never gave you any fish. He pointed you in the direction of the nearest pond (or tank, as we call them in Texas).

Charles's verbal response to my "no heroes left" moment of ignorance was simple.

"I know that you know better than that. Don't speak to try to impress other people. Speak from your brain, and if you can't do that, just speak from your heart."

Those words were forever burned into my brain cells. I learned a great lesson that day, one that would serve me well from that moment on. Then Charles issued the challenge, something with which I was familiar because he had given me "homework" a few times before that day at Ginnie's Bishop Grill.

Think about what you're doing for a living and why you are doing it. Think about the people you feature on your show, the people I feature on my series, the people we both admire enough to tell their stories. Think about why we bother to do it, and why it's important that we do what we do. Then break it all down. Put those people into categories if you must, but think about their lives, their accomplishments, what's important to them and about them. Then get back to me on this hero thing. Take this seriously, Bob, or go back to reporting fires and wrecks and politics. These people deserve your devotion.

When Charles stepped away to the restroom, I grabbed a napkin and wrote down what he said as well as I could remember it. I was near tears but couldn't let him see that, though I doubt he would have judged me for being deeply affected by his words, a condition with which I'm sure he was familiar.

After lunch, I dropped Charles off at a hotel near DFW Airport. He was taking a flight out later that day—and leaving me with a lot to think about. That was nothing new, because I think that was at least part of the essence of his work. He gave us all a lot to think about.

CHAPTER FORTY-ONE

*I*T WAS AFTER THAT DAY AT GINNIE'S BISHOP GRILL,
after Charles Kuralt left me with a challenge to give deep
thought to what I was doing with my life and why I was doing it, and to what
was important about the people we both featured in our work, that I started
spending a lot of time, for the very first time, contemplating the answers.

As I look back on it, I now feel that up until that lunchtime conversation in 1982, I was just doing a TV show. I was enjoying the ego boost that
everyone who appears on television feels from time to time. "Hey, look at
me, ain't this cool what I get to do?"

But now, maybe for the first time, I knew there was a lot that I hadn't
even considered about my chosen life's work. What's more, it was then, and
only then, that I finally realized that this WAS my life's work. Up until that
point, I wasn't sure if it was what I wanted to do forever, so I'd always kept
my options open, telling myself that if a better deal came along, I might
take it.

And the way the TV station where we started the show did things back
then helped me with that attitude. It felt like everything was always tenuous,
like they could just suddenly pull the plug at any moment. Fact is, when
4 Country Reporter went into summer reruns at the end of May every year,
I did a "Good-bye, it's been great" show because I just knew they wouldn't
let us keep doing it again next year. When the show did come back each
fall, I had to do a "Well, they're allowing us to do one more season." This
went on for at least seven or eight years before my boss told me to stop
doing it.

Coming up with the answers to the questions that Charles had asked
and the challenge he'd issued wasn't an overnight thing. He wasn't expecting

an answer, but I had to know for myself. It took me a while to compile my "list," and even then, and even now, that list is always up for revision as we constantly plow new ground. And it's not like this list is even written down. It's just something in our heads. We are very aware of the types of stories that easily fit into our show, the stories that the audience has told us over time they like best. But we also occasionally produce stories that we know some of our audience may not like, stories that challenge the way people think. And we love to do that.

It was during that time of self-examination, with the self in this case being not just me but also the show, that I began feeling that what we were doing was so much more than just a good time and a way to have a fun career. After hearing what Charles had to say, I gradually came to realize that for some people, this show was important. For some people, having a TV show that honored Texas and Texans was a serious thing and something that was sorely needed. Since the early days of television, it had mostly been about famous people and people who had important jobs, often people with lots of money and the prestige that goes along with that.

4 Country Reporter and, later, *Texas Country Reporter* were always about people that most viewers had never heard of: they weren't famous or rich, and they didn't seek the limelight. It was, and is to this day, about the everyday men and women who wake up every morning, get dressed, and go out and get the job done. They aren't athletes, or movie stars, or politicians, or, for the most part, people who have made some incredible contribution to society that will change it forever.

But most of the people we feature on the show are *important*. They probably don't consider themselves to be important; in fact, it's usually quite the opposite. Many of them, when we first contact them, ask us, "Why would you want to do a story about *me?*" That attitude is often further confirmation for us that this is probably someone we want to feature on the show.

What's important about these people and, consequently, about them being featured on our show is that they are important to *someone*. Sometimes it's a lot of someones. Just because you never won a Nobel Prize or came up with a new vaccine or started a company that changed the world doesn't mean you're not important.

Think of it this way: we all know the names of the important and giant corporations, the Apples and Microsofts and Googles of the world. Still, it's small businesses that drive the economy, and it's small businesses that make the big businesses possible, not the other way around.

The people we feature on *Texas Country Reporter* are, in a way, the small businesses of the American character. Their influences may be slight, their circles may be small, and most of them will never become household names, but they are important to our world. And they are important to those of us who produce this show. They are the bread and butter of *TCR*. Their lives, their feelings, and their contributions humble us every day. To us, they are the real heroes.

CHAPTER FORTY-TWO

*T*HE FIRST RULE OF *4 COUNTRY REPORTER* (AND, LATER, of *8 Country Reporter* and *Texas Country Reporter*) has always been this: the people who are featured in the stories we tell are the "stars" of the show.

Since I first sat down in the driver's seat of the *4 Country Reporter* van, I have been the host of the show. Not the star. The host. I'm the storyteller whose job it is to convey the stories of these often great Texans to those who watch our show. It's as simple as that. And for that reason I'm the one the audience gets to know, the one whose face they see week after week.

And for decades it had just been me driving that vehicle and asking you to "hop in and travel with me."

But a few years ago, that changed.

In May 2005, I walked into the KFDM-TV newsroom in Beaumont, Texas, where my dear friend Larry Beaulieu was the general manager and 6 o'clock news anchor for well over forty years—the only GM in American TV who also anchored the news. Ever since it first signed on, that station's ratings had been so high that it was almost as if no other stations existed, especially when it came to news.

I was visiting Larry and his station as part of a special one-time series we did on *TCR* called "Texas Country Star." It was a singing competition that we came up with as a means of promoting some of the talent we often saw on the back roads and giving them a chance to shine. My crew and I traveled all over the state producing concerts at local venues and hosting a kind of battle of the bands with one act emerging as the winner at each venue. Later that year the winners then met up at the Texas Country Reporter Festival in Waxahachie, where my good friend Tim DuBois, who at that time was running Universal South Records, would pick a winner and give them a recording contract.

Tim is a Nashville songwriter and music executive whose resumé is far too long and detailed to go into, but you should look him up. Among other things, he's the guy who created the musical group Restless Heart (probably the best act ever at the TCR Festival, a few years back), and he's the guy who put Brooks and Dunn together. He also discovered and signed the artists Alan Jackson, Brad Paisley, Blackhawk, Pam Tillis, and Diamond Rio, all within an eighteen-month period. He wrote five number one country hits, the biggest being Alabama's "Love in the First Degree." He also co-wrote Vince Gill's first hit, "I Call Your Name." Getting a record contract from this guy was the real deal. If you can't tell, I have always been impressed by all those things my friend Tim has done.

By the way, the winner of the Texas Country Star competition was a band from San Antonio called 10 City Run. They had a unique sound and an attitude similar to that of Cross Canadian Ragweed, another Tim DuBois discovery. We made a music video for their first release, which was called "City of Angels." It was also their last release, since the band broke up just months after getting their recording contract. You should look up the music video on YouTube anyway, because it's very different and entertaining. And the runner-up? A seventeen-year-old girl from the Tyler area named Kacey Musgraves.

Anyway, back to that visit with Larry Beaulieu. As we chatted, I followed him into the newsroom, where he said, "Kelli, I want you to meet my good friend Bob Phillips. He's here to be on your noon news program."

Kelli wheeled around in her chair and stood up, and my jaw must have hit the floor and partially knocked me out because I don't remember much after that. I know we did a live interview on her news set about the show and the music competition tour, but beyond that, I'm clueless. I would later find out from Kelli that she was in the same shape I was in and doesn't remember that interview very well.

Do you believe in love at first sight? I do now. It took until autumn of that year, but Kelli and I eventually got together, and almost three years after first meeting, we got married. I had been married before and it didn't work, so, after a divorce way back in 1991, I made a vow to myself that I would never do that again. Now, here I was breaking that promise, and I can't tell you how happy I am that I did. All these years later, we are still on our honeymoon, and I think we always will be. Funny how you can go your whole life thinking one way and then, just like that, change your mind. Never say never.

Kelli kept doing her news job, and I kept working on *Texas Country Reporter*, and our relationship required a more than four-hour commute, but we made it work *because it's what we both wanted*. My mother always said to me, "We always have time for the things we put first."

IN 2013, I WAS IN MY TRUCK, FOLLOWING BEHIND THE *TCR* vehicle as we traveled from Bastrop to Lockhart for some barbecue. We were in a construction zone, and BAM!!! I didn't know what had hit me on the passenger side, but I distinctly remember thinking, "I'm not sure what's happening, but I doubt I can survive this."

A few seconds later I heard Dan Stricklin yelling my name. All I could see was white, so I wondered if I was dead, but it was the airbags, and 6-foot, 8-inch Dan was pulling them out of the way and pulling me from my truck. Miraculously, I walked away from the accident, and so did the other guy. Turned out the construction crew was supposed to have put up a traffic control device but didn't, so we both thought we had the right-of-way, and neither of us could see the other.

A few days later I experienced numbness in my hand and arm, and I eventually had to have surgery to repair broken discs in my neck. When they opened me up, the doctors discovered my entire cervical spine was in bad shape, so my expected two-hour surgery became a seven-hour surgery. Now I have titanium rods and cadaver discs from C1 all the way to T2. Every doctor who saw the x-rays told me I should be dead and didn't know why I wasn't. I spent months rehabilitating, but we never shared this story on the show. At the time it was just deeply personal, and I didn't know how things would turn out.

I came out of this experience a new man. While I recuperated at home, mostly in a drug-induced daze to keep me still while I healed, I thought a great deal about life. I thought about what makes me happiest, and the top thing on that list was Kelli. I then spent the next three years trying to talk her into quitting her news job and joining me as co-host of *Texas Country Reporter*. Most of the reason behind that was I simply wanted to spend as much time with her as possible. When she finally agreed, in 2016, we went from seeing each other over long weekends to being together 24/7. It's been bliss, even when it wasn't. The other reason for wanting Kelli to join me was that after the wreck, I realized that had I died that day, *TCR* probably would have died with me, and I think the show is too important to let that happen. Kelli was not only the logical person to make sure the show goes on, she was the only person I trusted with that job.

I told Kelli to expect some pushback from a few of the *TCR* fans. One thing I have come to know over the years is that lots of people hate change. They want everything to go on forever as it always has. I told her to expect some negative emails from viewers who did not like the new addition but not to worry about it, because another thing I had learned about the people who watch our show is that most of them are good people. Still, I never expected some of the emails that came in, filled with horrible, hateful comments, even threats.

I was right about most of the viewers being good people, though, because for every hate letter we received, we got five hundred positive comments. I have never given much thought to hate mail because, first, we have never received much of that stuff, and second, because I just don't care. If someone has that much hate inside, I would just as soon they don't watch the show. We don't do it for those people. But I hated the way it made Kelli feel. I constantly reminded her to give it time.

Today the ratings for the show are higher than they were before Kelli arrived, and the only mail we get on the subject now is from people who tell us how much better they like the show. Lots of viewers have told us they love the relationship they see, and that they feel our joy. Kelli is the most genuine person I have ever known, and she brings a breath of fresh air to *TCR*. I have always been aware of the need to slightly reinvent ourselves from time to time, but I have done that with caution. Adding Kelli was the biggest single change I had made in the show since its inception, and it has been the most positive, both for me and for the experience we want to give our viewers.

Kelli has brought about incredible changes to the way we do what we do. She has streamlined some things about our workflow that make it possible for us to keep on keeping on, even though some of us are no longer young and spry. But the biggest thing she has brought to *Texas Country Reporter* is a new sense of wonder and reverence for the people we feature on the show. It is contagious. Her respect and love for our subjects constantly amaze me.

I am often hesitant about making changes—to the show, to my personal life, everywhere. But now I sometimes find myself looking back over the years and asking, "What if this or that had not happened?"

There is a long list of "what ifs," and I suppose it could go on forever, but here are just a few.

One of the worst days of my life was when my parents' marriage fell apart and I was in the middle of it, but what if that had not happened? What if I had not gone to live with my girlfriend's family, the ones who gave me the confidence to pursue my dreams?

What if my high school counselor had not told me, "You're not college material," a statement that challenged me to bite off more than I could chew, then chew like hell?

What if my high school journalism teacher had not told me, very specifically, what she wanted me to do with my life? What if she had not given me a plan for doing it, or I had not followed it?

What if I had not met Eddie Barker and asked for a job? What if he hadn't given me the chance to prove myself?

What if I had not been offered the job traveling with the Dallas Cowboys and had not become friends with Coach Tom Landry, the man who constantly reminded me that "the goal is to make the transition from being a good boy to becoming a good man"?

What if I had not pursued my dream of creating a TV show that featured ordinary people doing extraordinary things?

What if Dairy Queen had not agreed to sponsor the syndicated version of our show, and what if Greg Regian had not come up with the idea for me to become their spokesperson, catapulting my show to a new level of recognition across the state?

What if these and lots of other things had just never happened?

A very dear friend tells me time and time again, "Sometimes the planets line up and things happen, but you usually don't know it at the moment. You can only connect the dots looking back."

Looking back, I can only say it's all been a dream come true.

Part Six

STORIES FROM THE BACK ROADS

*I*LOVE THE ENGLISH LANGUAGE. THAT'S PARTLY BECAUSE, I am embarrassed to say, English is the only language I know. I can tell just by listening to them that I would also love the Spanish language, and the French language, and lots of other languages if I could speak them. I envy people who are bilingual or multilingual. I guess that means that what I love is words, in whatever language, and I love what we can do with them.

With words, we can paint pictures, and create moods, and describe scenes to the point that the reader or listener can imagine they are right there in that place and time. And that's what we try to do on *Texas Country Reporter*. We want you to be able to close your eyes and picture what we are talking about and who we are talking to without seeing the video, and still feel you are right there with us. One of the greatest compliments we frequently receive is from people who cannot see, who tell us they enjoy listening to our show. That means we are accomplishing what we are trying to accomplish. A lot of time is spent on the words we use on the show, and they're something we are proud of because they're not something that is totally necessary.

Television is a visual medium, and we could get by with just some standard news-style writing to go along with the pictures you see on the screen.

Let me give you some examples of how we write to paint a picture and how we seek out ordinary people who are going about their lives to feature on the show. Keep in mind that our end goal here is to point out that these people's lives are not ordinary, that there's nothing ordinary about them because, in some little way, there is something extraordinary about the way they live their lives. We want you to realize by the words we use that they are important.

I'll grab one from the early 1980s, some forty years ago. Just read the words, minus the pictures and minus the things the subject of this story had to say, and see if we painted the picture we intended to paint.

MAILMAN RALPH

Daybreak in the little East Texas town of Winnsboro. Looks like it might rain. Then again, maybe not. Ralph White's lived here most of his seventy-one years and he still doesn't presume to guess what kind of weather Mother Nature will serve up this time of year. He just makes sure he's prepared for anything. What's the old saying? Neither rain nor cold nor dark of night? Well, nothing's ever kept Ralph from making his appointed rounds. Ever. And that's something to raise your eyebrows at because Ralph's been covering 98 miles of rural mail routes six days a week for thirty-two years now. Never missed a day. Never missed a box. And that's a lot of boxes.

[Ralph goes on to talk about his rural mail route and the things he sees and does every day, the things he has come to know.]

Back in 1949, Ralph beat out forty-five other people for a job as the rural mail carrier for route number four out of Winnsboro. He drove Route 4's country roads through Wood and Hopkins Counties for ten years before switching to Route 3 for a change of scenery. He's been on this new route now . . . for twenty-one years.

[Ralph talks about the people on his mail route.]

Since he started delivering the mail, Ralph has spent most of his waking hours in his car. A few years back, he was awarded a commendation from the US Postal Service, a million miles without an accident. Not bad, considering Ralph has driven every one of those miles sitting in the passenger seat.

[Ralph talks about why he sits on the right side—so he can put mail in the roadside mailboxes without stretching across the seat or getting out of the car.]

The old Dodge here is Ralph's own car. All the rural carriers drive their personal cars. They put in their own steering gizmos and pedal gadgets, and Ralph won this neat light setup at a rural letter carrier's convention in Richmond, Virginia. Working the same job for so long has sort of made Ralph's whole life one big mail route. It's just habit.

[Ralph talks about driving on the right side even when he's not delivering the mail.]

When he's on the road, Ralph White IS the post office. Folks out on the rural route might not get to town for weeks at a time, and as far as they're concerned, Ralph is the Postmaster General himself.

[Ralph talks about getting to know the people on his route.]

Yep, there's something about a rural route that sets it apart from the city deliveries. The fresh air, the trees, the things people send through the mail.

[Ralph talks about delivering live chickens and other farm animals.]

But mail and assorted livestock isn't all Ralph delivers. Like every other mailman, Ralph carries a little charge of excitement in his bag, and he deposits it in the mailbox along with every letter or paper or package. In the tiniest sort of way, it's like Christmas every day and Ralph is Santa Claus. When folks on the rural route gather for the daily delivery, it's a time to catch up on the news, laugh about the latest, and wonder if Ralph's got anything in his bag for me.

[Ralph talks about the anticipation on people's faces when they see him coming and about the disappointment he sees on their faces on days when he has nothing for them.]

Ralph's been at this long enough to know that he's an important part of a lot of people's lives out here. More than just the mailman, he's what sociologists call a "constant." Ralph's here, the mail is here, all is right with the world. Ralph isn't much for sociology, but he knows these people depend on him.

[Ralph talks about how seriously he takes his job and knows he represents more than just a delivery to many on his route.]

The community of Little Hope is an intersection of two East Texas farm roads. About noon, Ralph swings into the gas station and country store for a quick break. He's got a couple hundred boxes left to fill with circulars, newspapers, letters . . . a little hope.

As we followed Ralph around all morning, folks asked us what's so important about old Ralph. You guys must be hard up for stories. But as the morning wore on, and as we slowed Ralph down by tagging along, there was a noticeable relief on the faces of people when the old grey Dodge swung into view. Even when there wasn't any mail.

What's so important about old Ralph? Gee, I don't know. He's just a mailman . . . on the rural route.

COULD YOU SEE IT? COULD YOU SEE OLD RALPH, THE GREY Dodge, the country roads, the people who were waiting by their mailboxes?

Could you feel the anticipation building, the concern mounting, when old Ralph was a little late?

Now, add pretty motion pictures to go along with these words, and add in what Ralph had to say about his life, his work, and what these people and this job mean to him, and put in some music that's just right to match the mood of the story about old Ralph—and edit it all together in a pleasing way that *takes you on a journey.*

Then, think about it. This is a story about a common man who got lucky and landed a job back in the 1940s delivering the mail on the rural route.

It was just a job. Until one day it wasn't. One day, or maybe it was a little bit this day and a little bit that day and the day after, Ralph realized some things. He realized that as ordinary as he thought his life was, as mundane as he thought his job was, he was important to the people he served. He realized his job was more than just a job to those people, that sometimes he was carrying magic in his bag. And he realized that sometimes he was carrying sorrow, and other times he was carrying concern. But, more than anything, he was carrying the constant message that life goes on no matter what, that people are just people, that we are all in this together.

Ralph took his job seriously. The people around him took Ralph seriously.

When I was trying to talk my bosses at the TV station into letting me do this show, they asked many times what the stories would be about. It was a question I had a hard time answering, and even after all these years, it's still hard. It happens all the time.

"Hey, Bob! What's gonna be on the show this week?"

"A story about a mailman in Winnsboro!"

And every time it happens, I can hear the sound of channels changing on that person's television. I can see the disappointed look on their faces when they don't hear the words they wanted to hear. Because they're looking for me to say something titillating, something juicy and rich, something outrageous, or even something extremely heartfelt.

"A story about a guy who went down every road in Texas on one of those little clown bicycles like the Shriners ride in parades!"

"A story about a woman who saw a man standing on the corner with a sign that said 'I need a kidney,' and even though she didn't know him, and even though she was in poor health herself, she gave him one of hers!"

"A story about (insert name of very famous person here) and how he is sending a million dollars to every man, woman, and child in Texas."

Let's face it, we have become conditioned in our pop news society to being spoon-fed manufactured emotions about pop stars, and athletes, and people who are famous for being famous.

What people don't want to hear is, "It's a story about a mailman in Winnsboro."

But then they watch that story the next weekend, and at least some of them sit back when it's over and maybe sigh and smile, and feel like those people on the rural mail route felt every time they saw old Ralph.

All is right with the world.

This is what we do: we use words and pictures and music and pacing to tell stories about people. And the stories we tell sometimes elevate that person just a little in the eyes of many of the people who know them and, just maybe, in their own eyes too. Because most of us live our lives with a little bit of doubt about whether we measure up, whether we're as good as others, whether we're . . . important.

Then, *Texas Country Reporter* comes to town and says, "Wait a minute! Take a look at what this person does for our world. Listen to how this person feels about this planet we all share together, about how this person feels about her neighbors, about how much this person cherishes his family. About how important this person is."

We don't make these people into something they are not. We hold a light and a magnifying glass up to them so everyone else can see them for who they are.

You could say it this way: *We connect the dots.* We show people how important all of us are and how our stories intersect and interweave to make this beautiful tapestry called life.

And when you remove the controversy, the negativism, the politics, and even the hatred that is often the highlight of news stories—and life in general—we all look a little better, a little different to the people around us.

I picked this story about Ralph the mailman, which was produced for the show ages ago, because it's the perfect example of what we so often did and still do, and because it's the perfect example of what I told my bosses when they constantly asked me what the show would be about.

After being asked and asked and never having a great answer, I finally blurted out, in what I'm sure was the very defensive tone of a kid, "It will be about ordinary people just living their lives and how their lives affect the lives of the rest of us—because I can pick any stranger off the street and tell a good story about that person!"

Okay, I've been proven wrong a few times on the last part of that statement because we have encountered a few . . . very few . . . people about whom even we could not craft a positive, feel-good story. But it's only happened a handful of times in almost fifty years, so I'll take that as an almost true statement and a victory.

I stick by my words, the ones that were originally the words of my daddy. *Everybody has a story.*

CHAPTER FORTY-FOUR

SOMETIMES THE STORIES WE TELL AREN'T DEEP AND meaningful, at least not on the surface, at least not at first. And there are times that we accept things at face value and tell the tale of a person who does something with their life that is simply different, maybe even a bit humorous. Some stories are just for a good chuckle.

Keep in mind that even though I said we "never say never," one thing we never do is make fun. Never. The only person on our show who is allowed to be the brunt of a joke is me. I can take it, but I won't dish it out.

Some of the stories we tell are primarily to make the rest of us sit up and say, "Well, I'll be darned. Would you look at that!"

Christine Londenberg was one of those stories. Christine worked for Puremco, which at the time was the last manufacturer of dominoes in America. They were there on the side of the road in Waco, and Christine had what may have been the most important job in the entire company.

Christine was a dot painter. THE dot painter. In all of Puremco, there was only one, and that was Christine.

Christine was a model employee. She punched in every morning at precisely 7:30 A.M. You could set your watch to her arrival. Like clockwork, she would head directly to her station, no chit-chat, and get to work. She was meticulous about that job.

The dominoes, of course, were mostly made by machines, and so were the dots. But Christine was the first to tell you that machines are only human. They make mistakes.

That's where she came in. Her job was to inspect every set of dominoes to make sure the dots were . . . well, all there. And if they weren't, or there were too many, or they were in the wrong place, into the trash bin they would go.

If there was a Domino Dot Painters' Union, Christine would have been the president, secretary, and only member. She was serious about dominoes.

Then there were the snooty domino players. Those people who didn't want some machine painting the dots on their dominoes. No sir, they were serious about their domino dots, and for those people, only dots painted by Christine would do. So she dripped drops of paint into domino divots . . . more than four thousand times every day. And all that work produced only nine or ten complete sets of dominoes.

It's a good thing there was no boss in the back filling out a productivity report. Not because it would have revealed the tiny number being turned out, but because everyone knew that you better not give Christine any grief about the job she was doing or she'd just go home. Christine didn't need that job. For her, it was a calling.

The pre-painted dominoes that Christine inspected are produced in China. She not only looked for bad dots, but also duplications. You can't have two double sixes in a set. Christine said she figured the Chinese probably don't play dominoes and might spend time wondering what we Americans were doing with those little dot-covered rectangles.

"Let 'em wonder," she said. "We know."

In these days of mass-produced, machine-made overseas imports, we never expected to find a woman hand-painting dominoes. I had to try my hand at it. It wasn't easy.

"That's not enough paint, Bob," Christine told me after I presented my first domino.

"That's too much paint, Bob," Christine told me after I presented my second domino.

"You see, one drip isn't enough, and two drips is too much," she explained. "You have to finesse it."

Turns out, domino-painting is best left to the experts, or should I say THE expert, Christine Londenberg. It may not be a very glamorous job, it may not be something anyone else ever wanted to do, but domino dot-painting was good to Christine for more than fifty years.

We think that's pretty special.

DOWN IN SERBIN, TEXAS, WE FOUND ANOTHER WOMAN WITH a job that might make you scratch your head. Her name was Hattie Schautschick, and before you go trying to pronounce it and turn it into something a little obscene-sounding, it's pronounced "CHOW-chick."

When we first met Hattie, she was in a large room surrounded by . . . noodles.

You see, Serbin is a Wendish community. The Wends were a group of German citizens, but they were German only because they lived inside the borders of Germany. They were Slavic people with a language more like Polish or Czech, and they were treated in Germany like second-class citizens and were not allowed to advance educationally or economically.

So in 1854 a group of Wendish people got on a boat and made their way to Galveston Island, eventually settling in an area that they named Serbin after paying fifty cents an acre for 4,000 acres. They set aside some of the land for a school and a church, and Wendish people flocked to the community. It was the center of the Wendish world in America.

Over time, the town of Serbin dwindled down to just a dot on a map— *some* maps—but the church is still there, and once a year the descendants of those original Wends come back for a kind of celebration. And for noodles.

Hattie explained that the noodle recipe has to be exactly the same every time. You can't vary it even a little bit. If you do, the texture won't be right, and the noodles will be too soggy or too dry. She preaches this constantly to the other ladies in the room who come to help her make the noodles.

Make no mistake about it, Hattie is the Noodle Master.

When I asked Hattie how many pounds of noodles she had made in the past twenty years or so, she said she'd have to check her book. She has a book? A book about noodles? Yes, she does.

I noticed Hattie's daughter and a niece doing something strange to the noodles after they came out of the water, so I had to ask exactly what it was they were doing.

"I'm fluffing the noodles," the daughter explained.

"Fluffing the noodles? I never knew noodles had to be fluffed."

"Oh, yeah," she said. "Otherwise the noodles might stick and dry all clumped together."

"And you don't want that?"

"Oh, no-no-no-no-noooooo," the daughter said.

"So you are fluffing the noodles," I repeated. "And that would make you . . ."

"I'm a noodle fluffer," she said with a giggle.

By now Hattie had consulted "the book."

"We usually make twenty-one batches for the Wendish Fest," she explained. "It depends on how the eggs are, but it's 250 to 260 pounds a week. So if we make them for four weeks, that's a thousand pounds of noodles."

All I could think was, that's a lot of noodles.

Hattie told us she would be eighty-eight in November, so she was training her daughter and niece in *exactly* how to make the noodles because it has to be done *exactly* the same way every time. We'd heard that before.

When I asked Hattie what the noodles taste like, she gave me a sample. I said they didn't have any taste.

"That's because they're just plain, but when you put a lot of butter and chicken broth on them, they taste good."

I said, "I think a hammer might taste good with enough butter on it."

"Yeah, some people only use butter."

So much for joking about the noodles.

Before we left Serbin, Hattie the noodle cooker took us to the cemetery where her husband and most of her family members were buried. She also took us to the 150-year-old Lutheran church that still fills up some Sunday mornings. Hattie said the famous Texan crooner Lyle Lovett has Wendish ancestors.

"He told *Texas Monthly* our church is his favorite place in all of Texas," she said proudly.

According to Hattie, there are quite a few people of Wendish descent in Texas, but you wouldn't know one of them just by looking.

"They look and sound just like everybody else."

But she went on to say that if you talk to them and ask about their heritage, their faces will light up and they will tell you. She went on to say that Wendish people are very proud of where they came from and how they got here.

As we pulled out of Serbin, it occurred to us that without all the different cultures here, Texas would be like . . . well, noodles with no butter. Tasteless, without texture or flavor.

Thank God for all the different kinds of people that make up Texas. And thank God for Hattie and her noodles.

CHAPTER FORTY-FIVE

W HEN YOU THINK ABOUT IT, LOTS OF TEXANS ARE
pretty adamant about keeping the past alive. I don't think
it's because we as a people don't want to advance, or that we want to seg-
regate ourselves. In fact, I think most Texans truly want to make sure our
cultures mix together like a good stew with lots of veggies, resulting in the
whole being much better than the individual parts. (In Hispanic and Latin
cultures, people call such stews *olla podrida*.)

But we also want to honor our past, to stay in touch with what those who
came before us went through, what they sacrificed for the rest of us.

Sometimes a determination to never forget the past comes from not
wanting to repeat parts of it, and to do whatever you can to make sure
others don't go through some of the things you went through. Shirley Perry-
Church is one of those people determined to not forget the past.

Shirley is a retired teacher. These days she is an artist and writer, and she
visits schools near her Pearland home to talk to children and young adults
about how to become an author and an artist, and about what happens
when those two worlds collide, as they did for her.

Shirley's goal is to make sure young people understand that if you can
become familiar with art and literacy, there is nothing you can't do with the
rest of your life.

She said, "It's crucial to cultivate creativity in young people."

This is a lesson she learned later in life, but she wants to make sure today's
students learn it now. She lives in a world surrounded by her own original
art, *most of it made from cardboard.*

"I like cardboard because it has character," she said. "I tried canvas, but it
absorbs the paint in such a way that it doesn't feel good in my hand. Cardboard bends and flexes and does what I want it to do."

As you look at Shirley's art, you quickly notice that every piece has a message. There is a staircase that she calls "Life's Climb," and when you look closely, you notice that some of the steps are broken and cracked, and some are missing. Every piece of cardboard art in her house has a similar message, but the one piece that sums it up best is probably the one she calls "The Lighthouse within a Lighthouse."

"There's something about a lighthouse that is symbolic of our journey here, about our need for a guiding force that is somehow representative of that path that you need to be on."

As her story unfolded the day we visited, we found out that Shirley's childhood is a time she remembers well but it's something she has had to come to terms with, so now her goal is to help young people get through their own tough times. Shirley's early life was difficult for her, but by keeping her past alive instead of burying it, she believes she can help guide today's kids, and herself, to a better future.

"Don't destroy the past," she said. "Learn from it."

Here lies an important point about what we do on our show—and what we don't do. Although Shirley told us she had a difficult childhood, she did not elaborate beyond that. In our interview I gave her plenty of room to tell us more . . . *if she wanted to.* I realize that by not pressing Shirley to give us "the dirt," I was breaking one of the seemingly sacred rules of modern-day journalism, but we didn't think it was important for us, or for you, to know exactly why her childhood was difficult unless she wanted us to know. But some news outlets, and many social media outlets, would make a big deal out of Shirley's misfortune with salacious headlines and on-air promos.

"Local teacher and artist spills the goods on terrible childhood! More on the 10 P.M. news!"

Suffice it to say that we don't believe that is necessary.

Shirley Perry-Church's art is for all people, but especially for one little girl who could have really used it: Shirley herself. She knows that had she had it then, she would have felt more hope and more inspiration during those tough times she went through.

And even though she can't change the past, she is doing the next best thing by changing the future, one child at a time.

We wish there were more people like Shirley.

UP IN NORTH TEXAS, IN A LITTLE SPOT OFF HIGHWAY 380 between Decatur and Denton, Bill Marquis is saving the past in his own way. Bill has always liked hearing old stories, and he would much rather talk to people who experienced history firsthand than read about it in a book.

The old-timers he knew as a kid are all gone now, but thanks to Bill, much of their hard work still stands.

Bill makes his living by restoring old structures all over Texas—*only in Texas*—and works to put them back together exactly as they were originally. For him it's truly a labor of love. He goes to great lengths to find old boards and nails exactly like the ones that were used way back when. He has made an entire career out of rebuilding historic structures for other people, but now he's working on something that hits a little closer to home.

As we stood in the middle of the intersection of two country roads, Bill pointed out that we were standing smack-dab in the middle of the world as he once knew it: the town of Stony, Texas, where he grew up. He was raised in the house on the corner, and he could walk to the general store right across the street, a store you can still find today . . . in Bill's front yard, just a half mile down the road.

Today that store is faithfully stocked with the same fixtures and merchandise it had when he was a kid. For Bill, it's like walking into his past. The original store was open until 1963, when it was abandoned. So many trees and shrubs grew up around it, you could no longer see it . . . until Bill Marquis took it apart board by board and saved it. Every board, every nail, every memory he could call up.

"I can't understand why you wouldn't save it," Bill told us. "We gotta know our past to understand our future, is the way I look at it. You gotta know the way things were in the past and how people lived to understand those people."

Bill has restored some of Stony's other buildings, including the First Baptist Church, which he now uses as a workshop. And he's just started restoring the old school he attended as a child.

Bill says it would be impossible to save all of the old places, but too many people don't want to save any of them. His constantly growing scrap pile is proof of that. It's full of nothing but boards, glass, and nails.

But Bill says every structure those things came from also had a soul. No one knows where he keeps those, and he's never seen one on a blueprint. Yet somehow every time Bill Marquis finishes a project, he puts the soul of that building right back where it was.

"I believe we were all put here for a reason," Bill told us, "and I was put here to do what I can to save the past. I hope this is what I'm doing when my time comes."

Somehow, I think Bill's wish will come true.

SOME PEOPLE HOLD ON TO THE PAST SIMPLY BY HONORING it. That's what's going on at the Buffalo Soldiers National Museum in

Houston, where Captain Paul J. Matthews says they're not big on *content*. They care more about *context*.

"You take every item in this museum," he told me, "and you build some type of story that makes it real. Most museums have a little thing on a big wall. Here we have a lot of things on a little wall."

As Captain Matthews showed us around, it occurred to us that if the relics on the walls of the Buffalo Soldiers Museum could talk, they would have a lot of stories to tell: whispers of wars once fought and other tales of old times. Captain Matthews says the stories told in the museum are about one of the most important groups of people in American history.

"At the end of the Civil War," he told me, "the US Army created six all-Black units: the 9th and 10th Cavalry, and the 38th, 39th, 40th, and 41st Infantry. Those units went on to become what we now call the Buffalo Soldiers."

Seems these Black soldiers reminded the Cheyenne of the spirit of the buffalo, so the name stuck. They went on to build camps, forts, and railroads and became an important part of America's western expansion. It represented a shift in the opportunities that were given to African Americans in the United States.

"A lot of what you have to show and teach here at this museum deals with the most shameful time in American history," I said to Captain Matthews. "It seems like that could be a negative message to people who visit this place, but I don't feel that. How do you do that?"

"Because we tell history as it was," he said. "We don't try to rewrite it. And you don't put a 2015 face on an 1866 activity. It's like a building with a thousand windows in it. You can't just look out one window and say this is American history. You have to look out the other 999 windows. Then you have American history."

It's easy to see when you visit the Buffalo Soldier Museum and hear the stories told by Captain Matthews that his desire is to make the past relevant to today so we can all learn from it. It's a worthwhile lesson.

He said, "When I go speak to schools today, I always end my presentation with a poem titled 'God's Minute.' The poem goes like this:

> I have only just a minute. Only sixty seconds in it.
> Forced upon me. Didn't seek it. Didn't choose it.
> But it's up to me to use it. I must suffer if I lose it.
> Give account if I abuse it.
> Just a tiny little minute, but eternity is in it.

"It's simple but profound," he said. "And my charge to students and anyone else is, 'What do you plan to do with your minute?' Amen."

Amen, Captain Matthews.

SOMETIMES, HISTORY IS PERSONAL. SOMETIMES, THOSE WHO don't want to turn loose of the past are holding on tight because it is *their* past. They don't want to forget it, and they don't want you to forget it either.

On August 18, 1973, outlaw country singer Jerry Jeff Walker gathered his Lost Gonzo Band and some other folks in the Luckenbach Dance Hall to record an album called *Viva Terlingua*. It was a live album filled with several songs that are still played on the radio today, and the words to some of those songs are pure poetry. If you listen to "Desperados Waiting for a Train," for instance, you will likely have a better understanding of the relationship I had with my dad in his later years.

4 Country Reporter had been on the air less than a year when *Viva Terlingua* was recorded, and I had not yet ventured to the Texas Hill Country or the unincorporated "town" of Luckenbach, thirteen miles from Fredericksburg. But as soon as I heard Jerry Jeff's album, I knew I had to go.

I had heard about this "kind of crazy" guy who called himself the mayor of Luckenbach, but the town wasn't a town at all, and therefore it had no mayor. It's been said that Hondo Crouch bought the place so he'd have somewhere near his ranch to drink beer, listen to music, and play dominoes. If that's what he was trying to create by buying Luckenbach, he did a great job, because that's what it still is today, decades after Hondo's passing.

Hondo had been a championship swimmer at the University of Texas and was friends with John Connally, a fellow student who later became secretary of the navy under President John F. Kennedy and secretary of the treasury under President Richard Nixon. Most people in the Lone Star State at the time of this story knew Connally as the thirty-ninth governor of Texas.

When I was eleven years old, before I knew the slightest thing about politics, I volunteered to deliver yard signs in my neighborhood for John Connally's gubernatorial campaign. My dad, a yellow-dog Democrat his whole life (even when my brother worked for President Ronald Reagan and President George Herbert Walker Bush), was proud that his son was following in his footsteps. I didn't know anything about that. I just wanted something fun to do, and putting signs in people's yards was the fun du jour.

Connally was riding in the presidential limousine when John F. Kennedy was assassinated in Dallas, and he was seriously wounded. Somehow, shortly after, I was invited to meet Governor Connally during a reception for workers at his campaign headquarters in Dallas. It was at the top of the Southland Life Building, at that time the tallest in Dallas, and my mother took me to meet the man whose yard signs I had been delivering. All I remember about that day is going through a line and shaking hands with Connally, who had one arm in a sling from the attack in November.

When I think about the fact that just over seven years from that day I would be a reporter and photographer for the TV station where the man who first announced President Kennedy's death to the world served as news director, I get chills. How did I go from being that goofy little kid to appearing on television for one of the top CBS affiliates in the country? Me?

Back to 1973. When Hondo Crouch—who had been getting a lot of press, especially after the Jerry Jeff Walker album, and who would again later, after Waylon and Willie sang about Luckenbach—attended a UT football game in Austin, he ran into his old buddy John Connally, who by that time was a household name.

As the story goes, Connally said, "Hondo, I see you've made a name for yourself as the mayor of Luckenbach!"

And—again, as the story goes—Hondo replied to his now famous friend, "That's right. What you been up to, John?"

The story was confirmed for me by Hondo's daughter about forty years after the fact. Becky Crouch Patterson told me, "I know at least some form of that story is true."

I don't remember the year I first met Hondo, but I know it had to be sometime in the mid-seventies, at least a couple of years after the Jerry Jeff Walker album came out. We still didn't have permission to travel outside of Channel 4's immediate broadcast area to shoot stories for the show, but I had already been stretching that limit by including places from Shreveport to Tyler, Waco, Abilene, Lubbock, and even Hobbs, New Mexico, where *4 Country Reporter* appeared on early versions of cable TV. I knew the number of viewers in those places might add up to only fourteen or fifteen, but I still figured it was a good argument for going outside our 150-mile radius. Luckily, it was never a problem.

At the time I was also doing *Young 4 Country* (remember that?), and I had a possible story about a high school kid from a small town near Dallas who was a page in the Texas Senate. I actually sought and received permission to travel to Austin for that story, so I thought, "Why not take a side trip to the town of Luckenbach?"

We shot the story in Austin, then hightailed it west on Highway 290 toward Fredericksburg before turning back to the southeast on FM 1376. Luckenbach was just a few minutes down that road. I remember that we almost passed it because it's tucked away on a little dirt road that circles through the so-called town and back to the farm road, and there was no road sign. That's because after Luckenbach became famous, the road signs disappeared as fast as TxDOT could put them up. In fact, I'm not sure they even bother with the signs anymore.

That day I walked up to the old Luckenbach post office and store and saw a man with a white beard who was wearing a funky hat, standing on the porch, and leaning on a post. I had called ahead and told Hondo that I wanted to come down and meet him, but I'm betting by that time he'd grown pretty tired of reporters coming to his town just to jump on the Luckenbach bandwagon and didn't pay much attention to calls like mine.

I said, "Would you be Hondo Crouch?" To which he replied, "I be!"

I quickly introduced myself, and Hondo stared at me for a few seconds before asking, "Are you as disappointed as I am?"

Talk about breaking the ice! This guy had it going on. He took me for a quick tour of "his town" and pointed out the most important parts, which were the areas where people played music (pretty much anywhere they wanted) and the ones where you could buy beer or play dominoes (pretty much anywhere you wanted).

We did not spend much time together because Hondo had important things waiting on his attention, including a game of Texas Moon he intended to sit in for.

I visited Luckenbach many more times over the next forty or so years, and we shot several stories there about this and that. But my absolute favorite was in the spring of 2018, when I went back for a guided tour of the life of Hondo Crouch and his beloved Luckenbach, given by his daughter. She was busy writing her latest book, *Luckenbach, Texas: The Center of the Universe*, when we arrived.

One of the first things Becky showed us as we entered her house on the old Adolf Stieler Ranch, where she grew up, was "the laptop" she used to write her books: a legal pad that she held in her lap.

"I don't know how to use a computer," she told us, "but on this laptop I have written three books, all on legal pads with a pen because I like the feel of ink on paper."

Adolf Stieler was Becky's grandfather, and back in the day they just called it the Home Ranch. Here you will still find wide open fields, folks working cattle, and lots of horses, just like a hundred plus years ago. Inside the little house, Becky is almost always busy making art on the land that has been in her family since the 1890s.

"I've been an artist all my life," she said. "I was mainly a painter, but then I started making banners for my church, and I thought, wow, rags are cheaper than paint, so I ended up doing machine-appliquéd tapestries."

From piles of fabric to designs and paintings, everything Becky touches turns into art. Her reputation has earned her some big assignments along the way, like the project she did to help San Antonio celebrate its 300th birthday: designing a Ramone signature scarf to commemorate the Ramone Expedition of 1716.

As you look around Becky's home, the lines between history and art disappear. She showed us a map mural on the wall, a piece that she would be using in the book to tell the stories of things that happened on the ranch. The entire house is full of old deeds, maps, and memories, from the old ranch ledger to Becky's childhood bedroom. This is the story of Becky's life.

And then there's her daddy, Hondo: the man, the myth, the legend. Becky says pretty much all of the stories you hear are true.

"We never called him Daddy," she said. "We just called him Hondo."

Who better to give us a personal tour of Luckenbach than the daughter of the man who owned it, the daughter who grew up here? We had seen Luckenbach many times, but on this day we saw it with different eyes.

"It's kind of like a shrine to Texas music is what it is," she told us. "When Jerry Jeff met Hondo, BAM! . . . They met and then he drug his whole crew out here. Some of the greatest songs were written and sung on that album. Gary P. Nunn, Ray Wiley Hubbard, Guy Clark, oh my gosh! Texas's best songwriters are on that record, and some of those songs were written while they were sitting out here under these oak trees."

No, you can't talk about Luckenbach without talking about Hondo Crouch. It's a whimsical place of humor and imagination that could have only been dreamed up by someone who was more legend than man. Becky says growing up with Hondo was just magical.

"He always wanted to be that folk hero, a teller of tall tales," she said. "And there was something about watching him sing that was just inspiring."

Becky thinks it's beautiful that people still remember Hondo, that he is someone who is remembered and loved on and on—a true folk hero.

And here on the wooden walls of Becky's old ranch house in Luckenbach, and in the strumming of an old guitar, you will find traces of the man who dreamed up this little town, this magical place. Though Hondo has been gone for years, Becky knows that part of his legend lives on here in Luckenbach . . . and in her heart.

This is her history and the history of her people, and she doesn't want any of us to forget it.

CHAPTER FORTY-SIX

O NE OF THE MOST GRATIFYING AND REASSURING
things for those of us who travel Texas in search of the stories we tell on *Texas Country Reporter* is seeing how many people do things
strictly out of the goodness of their hearts. We meet them every day—
and please don't think that is an exaggeration. For people who watch the
news, it would be easy to slip into the belief that this world has just gone
to hell and ain't coming back, but the people we meet make us stop and
reconsider.

That's good not just because it's uplifting for us but because we believe
our show has that effect on many of its viewers. We constantly receive emails
from people telling us just that: how much they enjoyed seeing this story
or that one, or, in many cases, most of the stories we tell because it makes
them feel better about the world we live in. It seems the worse the news of
the day gets, the more people gravitate toward *TCR*.

And that's just what we hoped for when we started the show.

We call the people we feature—who do things just because it's the right
thing to do, or because it helps others—our angels. They come in all shapes,
sizes, colors, and creeds. Like heroes, angels do not wear identification
badges. You judge them not by their words but by their actions. We know a
lot of them.

Our first angel had already been given that name before we met him. In July
1981 I received a book in the mail with no note and no indication why it was
sent to me. It was called *Border Angel*, and the author was a newspaper man
named Bill Starr. I had received books and magazines and newspaper articles in
the mail before, but the previous items were always accompanied by a letter or
note of explanation. And they were always sent with the intention of convincing me to put someone on our show. This had none of that.

I suppose the fact that there was a mystery attached to this particular book caused me to leaf through it. I won't say I read it at that point, but I flipped through the pages until I had an idea about why this book was written and just who the Border Angel was.

Then, shedding light on the mystery, just a few days later I received an envelope with this short note:

> Bob,
> My name is Bill Waugh. I am the founder of the Taco Bueno restaurants and I've been told you frequent one of our stores on Lemmon Avenue in Dallas.
> I am a fan of your show and love the work you do.
> You may not know it, but you have a ministry.
> Please read the book I sent about Frank Ferree. It's a story you need to tell. Your story will do a world of good for the recipients of this struggling charity in the RGV built by one man, The Border Angel.
> I truly believe God wants you to do this story.
> Sincerely,
> Bill

The note included a phone number, so I called Mr. Waugh, and he asked if I would meet him for lunch at one of his Taco Bueno restaurants. I went to them a lot because it was Tex-Mex food that didn't cost a lot of money or take a lot of time, yet it was, to me, as good as most other Tex-Mex. I still eat there occasionally.

I don't often go to lunch with people who are pitching a story idea because (1) you then feel like you owe them something, even if the story is not one you would do, and (2) if you accepted every lunch invitation in my business, you would never have time to get your work done.

But there was that line that said God wanted me to do this story.

I met Bill Waugh at my favorite Taco Bueno, and he was truly a great guy. He was very conservative in appearance and, I would later learn, in just about every other way. He was a graduate of Abilene Christian College (ACU today) and had founded his taco chain in Abilene while he and his wife were living there with his mother-in-law. He had first tried to make a living with a dry cleaning shop but quickly found out that the people in Abilene in the 1970s had little use for a dry cleaner. Tex-Mex, however, was something they could wrap their mouths around.

Bill was a very religious man and told me about the work of Frank Ferree, who had moved to Harlingen, Texas, when he was much younger. Frank was now eighty-seven years old, and over the years he had witnessed the plight of hungry families on the Mexico side of the border in Matamoros and Reynosa and had been moved to do something about it.

So even though Frank lived in poverty himself, he founded a group that provided food to the hungry. His best sources for supplies were bakeries that could only sell their goods when they were fresh, so they allowed Frank to pick up their day-old bread and other pastries for free. He also approached restaurant owners and begged for the food they would throw away at the end of the day.

I asked Bill why he was asking me to do this story, and he said, "That's simple. I had a dream that God told me to get you to do the story. So I'm doing what I was told."

Two weeks later I traveled to the Rio Grande Valley with Bill, breaking another rule I had set, to never let people tag along when we were producing a story. Why did I break my own rule? To this day I cannot tell you. I think perhaps I was just intrigued by this man who was so honest and open about his message from God.

Frank turned out to be more than Bill promised. He was a strange-looking man, very tall with a huge, bulbous nose—and an even bigger heart. I learned that he had been a soldier in World War I and had served in France, that he had been employed by the US Postal Service and delivered mail on horseback for almost ten years, that he was very interested in faith healing, and that he had made a deal with God when he was in his forties. It seems he was very sick and believed he was dying. He prayed for God to heal him and promised he would dedicate his life to serving the poor. He told me he was healed almost immediately and was now doing what he had promised God he would do. There seemed to be a lot of that going around.

The story about Frank Ferree, "The Border Angel," aired on *4 Country Reporter* on September 19, 1981. I cannot remember a show receiving as much mail as that one. We routinely receive letters from folks who comment on stories we air, but the letters about the Border Angel were almost overwhelming. We sent out information to lots of people who wanted to donate to the cause, and forwarded a lot of checks that were sent directly to us. Some people just wanted to meet him.

Frank Ferree died a year and a half later, at the age of eighty-nine. His Border Relief agency has continued to grow and do wonderful work over the years, though they are still just as strapped for cash as they were in the early days.

Bill Waugh became one of my dearest friends. In addition to his Taco Bueno restaurants, he founded Casa Bonita Mexican Restaurants and

Crystal's Pizza and Spaghetti. He sold those businesses to the British company Unigate for $32.5 million shortly after we met, and he later opened the Burger Street chain. Bill then spent much of his time giving his money away to worthy causes. He died in 2015 at the age of seventy-nine.

I will always remember Bill and Frank, not just because they were both incredible human beings who genuinely cared about others, but because they were responsible for pointing out to me that there were lots of stories we could tell that could go a long way toward helping those in need. It was a lesson we still live by today.

JUST AFTER THANKSGIVING IN 1944, DR. ARCH MCNEILL made a house call to the home of an older woman on Irving Boulevard in Dallas. Mrs. Birchfield was known in the neighborhood as a sweet lady who always kept a pot of beans simmering on her stove so she could feed anyone who was hungry, whether it be friend, family member, or passerby.

Mrs. Birchfield was also known for putting up a Christmas tree every year so anyone who wanted to could come celebrate with her. She knew most of the families in that area could not afford Christmas presents, so she did her best to keep a few small toys under the tree. Doc noticed that there were no gifts under the tree that year and volunteered to make some toys in his workshop so that Mrs. Birchfield could hand them out to children who might otherwise have nothing come Christmas morning.

At that time the neighborhood was known as the Trinity Bottoms, and it was one of the poorest sections of Dallas. Time was short, so Doc called up some friends and asked them to help him in his workshop. The response was overwhelming, and that Christmas they passed out a hundred wooden toys to children. The following Christmas, two hundred children received a toy.

This went on and got bigger every year. Eventually, Doc's toy-making became a year-round regular thing, with the toy-makers meeting every Thursday night at Doc's workshop.

Just after Thanksgiving in 1981, more than thirty-six years after Doc started his group to make toys for underprivileged kids, I got a call from him. He said he'd been watching the show since it started about nine years earlier and was puzzled as to why we had yet to visit him and the elves in his workshop. I told him we had never heard of his group but would like to know more.

Since the show had been on for a while and had become well known, we would often get calls or letters like this—and we still do. Lots of times it's from someone who wants to be on television to make money or to achieve fame of some kind, so we are always careful when people blow their own horn. But there was just something about Dr. Arch McNeill that made me want to find out more.

"Come out on Thursday evening after supper," he told me.

Dr. McNeill's workshop was a huge building, nothing like the tiny home workshop I envisioned. A cameraman and I pulled up as close as we could get, which wasn't very close because of the number of cars parked around the building and on the street. We wandered inside.

You should know by now that you can't trust everything you see on television. Christmas specials would have you believe that Santa's helpers have green shoes, pointy ears, and high-pitched voices. But in a workshop in Garland, Texas, we found out what Santa's elves really look like. There were dozens of men of all ages scurrying around between different machines, each one of them making wooden toys. It sounds like a cliché, but with all the men going about their jobs like they were elves on Christmas Eve and the sleigh still had to be loaded, it really did look like Santa's workshop.

And right in the middle of them was Santa himself—or rather, the angel Dr. Arch McNeill—barking orders, shouting words of encouragement, and making sure everything stayed on track. He was a little, balding man and had a short, unlit cigar sticking out of his mouth. I don't know if I ever saw him without that cigar. He did not fit my image of an angel, but like I said, elves and angels rarely look like we think they should.

And the elves? They were known as the Hobby Crafters, and they were doctors, lawyers, managers, and mechanics who were giving up a few days each month to make toys for the needy.

The solid wooden toys they made were simple and rugged by today's standards: powered by hand, animated by imagination, and tough to break. They were reminiscent of the kind of toys that . . . well, the kind that Doc might have had when he was a kid.

We featured Doc and his Hobby Crafters on the *4 Country Reporter* Christmas show that aired on December 19, 1981, telling the story of the angel Arch McNeill and his elves. One thing I'd asked Doc in the interview for the show was how he'd convinced so many men to give up every Thursday night of the year to make toys in his shop, and he said it was easy because every one of his elves had a big heart. He said he'd even started soliciting his patients during their office visits to help with the cause, telling them, "What you need is to breathe a little sawdust" before handing them directions to his workshop.

The story about Dr. Arch McNeill and his Hobby Crafters was well received by our audience, and the project grew even bigger. More volunteers, more gifts, more Christmas spirit.

We moved on, as we do after every story. Then, sometime in the late 1990s, I heard that Dr. Arch McNeill had died after a couple of strokes and heart attacks, and after spending a long time in a nursing home. I thought the Hobby Crafters were probably a thing of the past and wondered about all those kids who would have no toys without them. I wondered, but I quickly put those thoughts aside and worried about something else. Like most of us tend to do, I decided that "surely someone had stepped up to the plate."

Now here's the part of the story that could only happen when you've been around a long time, like *Texas Country Reporter* has. In the fall of 2017 I got an email from someone who wanted to remain anonymous: "Bob, thirty-six years ago you aired a story on your show about Dr. Arch McNeill and his Hobby Crafters group that made toys for children who might not have any Christmas. Even though Doc died almost twenty years ago, our group stayed together and we could sure use your help."

The fact was not lost on me that Hobby Crafters had been around for more than thirty-six years before we ever heard about and did a story on them, and that it had been more than thirty-six years since we did that first story. We seemed to have fallen into a pattern. Rod Serling's theme song was playing in my head.

We looked up the Hobby Crafters and found them in Garland, Texas, still making toys. The shop was newer and nicer than the one at Doc's house, but there were still a lot of old machines being held together with shoestrings and baling wire. And there were still lots of elves running around like it was Christmas Eve and they were on a deadline.

We found out that all kinds of things had happened shortly after our original story and in the years since. The most important was that Doc's homegrown charity had outlived its founder; he made sure of that before he died. His last official act was to hand the baton to his trusted lieutenant Jerry Reichert.

When Doc McNeill got sick in the mid-1990s, he called his top ten guys together and told them he had to go to a nursing home so he wouldn't be a burden on his wife. He said he needed one of them to step up and take charge to keep the group going. Every one of the men present promised to help keep it going, but no one volunteered to be in charge. Then Jerry took the job.

By now Jerry had kept the lights on and the saws spinning for more than twenty years, and every time Hobby Crafters had been in peril, it seemed a Christmas miracle was just around the corner.

There was a story about their roof leaking, and the estimate to repair it was $14,000. Their entire annual budget was only $5,000. Everything else that kept the place running was the result of donations and volunteer hours. Then, out of nowhere, a $14,000 check made out to the roofing company showed up in the mail. They still don't know who sent that check.

There was the story of losing their workshop after Doc died. Then, almost out of nowhere, a former Hobby Crafters volunteer donated a place for the group to make their toys. He had left it to them in his will, along with some money.

Another story involved an expensive cable that fed electrical power to the workshop, a cable that could only be purchased by a licensed electrician and at great cost, much more than the group could pay. But a foreman for an energy company heard of their plight and suggested they leave their parking lot gate unlocked. They found the repairs mysteriously made when they returned the next day.

Stories like these go on and on and on. Almost every time there had been a need, the problem had been mysteriously solved.

We also learned that Jerry Reichert had learned a valuable lesson from Dr. Arch McNeill: the Hobby Crafters must go on. When Jerry felt the time was nearing for him to step down, he took a page from the Book of Doc and decided to train a new leader for the group. That was underway during our last visit.

The sign out front says "Volunteers Always Needed." Jerry has faith that will always be true. The Hobby Crafters have made and given away hundreds of thousands of toys, and they've built a kindness that's bigger than any one person, bigger even than any one angel.

Somehow, just like the magic that happens in Santa's workshop every year that allows him to take toys to children all around the world, the Hobby Crafters keep going. And it's all thanks to Dr. Arch McNeill and a group of dedicated volunteers and wonderful supporters who recognize that what this group has done, and is doing, is important on so many levels. Somehow, it just keeps on going, seventy-six years and counting as I write these words.

The second show about Dr. Arch McNeill's Hobby Crafters aired on *Texas Country Reporter* the weekend of December 16, 2017, a mere thirty-six years after we first told our audience about this extraordinary group of people.

We have marked our production calendar to check back with them again in 2053, thirty-six years after our most recent story, seventy-two years after our first. We expect the Hobby Crafters will still be going strong.

SOME ANGELS PREFER TO WORK ALONE. SOMETIMES PEOPLE see a need and just decide to do something about it.

We had been in Big Bend shooting some stories and decided to avoid the interstate (we often do) and take Highway 90 back over into the Hill Country and South Texas. We had gone through Langtry and Comstock and across Lake Amistad, and were driving down Veterans Boulevard in Del Rio. Just after we crossed 15th Street, something caught our eye.

Veterans Boulevard is a long, wide street with a large median running down the middle. And there in that median was a little man mowing the grass: *with a push mower.*

Normally, that wouldn't be a thing that would get your attention, but we noticed he had other mowers, carts, and wagons sitting off to the side, and they were all tied together with ropes in a train configuration. And every time he finished mowing one section and moved on to the next patch of grass, the train of equipment moved too, with that little guy acting as the engine. He would pull and tug and force all that equipment to follow him as he went about what appeared to be his job.

But wait a minute, we said. Wasn't this the job of the City of Del Rio? Or maybe TxDOT? Or . . . whose job was this? Surely it wasn't the responsibility of that one little man? We had to find out.

Turns out, just about everybody in Del Rio, Texas, knew about the guy with the mower—the hardest-working man alive, one person told us. But not many said they actually *knew* him, until we found the man who just may be his best friend.

Russell Stidham was born and raised in Del Rio, and he knows the border city like the back of his hand. He runs his family's security company, and we found him in the parking lot of a fast-food restaurant along Veteran's Boulevard, supervising the installation of some new security cameras. When we asked Russell if he knew anything about the man who was mowing the median, he lit up like a Christmas tree.

He told us he had watched "the mowing man" for a long time before approaching him to find out more.

"I probably did what a lot of people do," Russell told us. "I dismissed him as a homeless person or a vagrant. Still, I had a feeling there was something more, something special."

And Russell was right. He found out the man could not talk and had been disabled his entire life. He told us the man's name was Chito, and that for more than a decade he and his long train of mowers, carts, and tattered tools had been a fixture along the highways and side streets of Del Rio. He said Chito mowed those medians because he wanted the city to look better and knew whatever official city or county or state agency was supposed to mow them didn't have the budget to do it very often. So Chito did it . . . for free.

We found out that Chito was an uncomplicated man whose twisted limbs made even the simplest of motions painful. But despite his disabilities, Chito had become a one-man landscape crew at all hours of the day and night all over Del Rio.

"He does this for hours on end, on the hottest of days, in the middle of the afternoon," Russell told us. "It seems crazy to us, but it makes perfect sense to Chito."

Other people saw us hanging out on the median with Chito, and some of them stopped to talk to us.

"He works all hours of the day and night," one man said. "I've seen him mowing at three in the morning."

"He never takes a break," a woman at the convenience store said. "He just keeps going."

As we watched Chito pick up a large piece of cardboard, another Del Rio citizen stopped, got out of his car, and said, "A lot of people would take that piece of cardboard and make a sign from it, then use it to beg for money, but not Chito. He's going to take that cardboard, put it on one of his carts, then put it where it belongs—in the trash."

"Everybody nowadays knows him as Chito," Russell said, "but his actual name is Jose Anjil Martiarena, and he's a good man, and I'm proud to have him as a friend."

The town of Del Rio, it seems, has decided Chito should be an example for all of its citizens. They created a new campaign called "Del Rio Doin' Right" and intend to recognize one citizen every year for . . . well, for being like Chito. The first recipient of the annual award was, of course, Chito.

While we and our cameras were watching Chito work at mowing the median on that warm day, suddenly he fell to the ground. Russell tore away from us and ran across the boulevard, stopping traffic as he made his way to Chito. Within seconds, two police officers, one on a motorcycle and another in a cruiser, sirens blaring, were on the scene. Cars pulled to the side of the road, and it seemed that everything in Del Rio came to a stop as word spread: Chito was hurt.

But because he couldn't speak, no one trying to help him could figure out what was wrong until his old friend Russell finally broke through the grunts and groans that Chito was emitting as he was lying on the grass. Turned out, Chito had changed to new shoes that morning, and they were killing his feet. His bent and misshapen hands hadn't been much help in fixing the problem, and he had fallen in a desperate attempt to get those shoes off his feet. It made us realize that Chito did, indeed, live in a different world, one much harder than our own.

After a change of shoes and a quick drink of water, Chito went back to work, sorry that he had caused such a fuss. Truth be known, we suspect that people in Del Rio welcomed the chance to come to his aid because no one knows how to help him. He has repeatedly refused any kind of government assistance.

We talked Chito into taking a break to sit on the tailgate with us for a few minutes so we could attempt an interview, but after just one question, he started crying.

"Chito, why do you do this? Why do you mow the grass for free?"

As he sobbed, so did we. Then Russell, also wiping tears away, once again came to the rescue.

"I think what he's trying to tell you is that he does this to take care of his mother and his family," Russell said. "His dad passed away and now Chito is the breadwinner."

We then learned that Chito's free median-mowing had caught the attention of some people in town, who had hired him to take care of their lawns. He didn't make much, but he was able to provide for his family, and that made him proud.

Then Chito got back to his mowing, to the place where he feels needed and wanted and . . . normal.

Russell Stidham tried to explain Chito's mindset, telling us, "Chito was called to cut grass, and Martin Luther King said it best." He paraphrased: "If a man is called to be a street sweeper, he should sweep streets just as Michelangelo painted or Beethoven played music or Shakespeare wrote poetry. He should sweep streets so well that all the hosts of Heaven and Earth would say 'Here lived a great street sweeper who did his job well.'"

So if you find yourself in Del Rio, Texas, look for the flags, the orange cones, and the wagons strung out along the pavement, and you are bound to see a man called Chito. Watch him for a while, and we believe you will understand why, even though his bent and twisted body is barely five feet tall, Chito is a man who many people in this part of the state look up to.

We think the world needs more people like Chito . . . a true angel among us.

CHAPTER FORTY-SEVEN

While most of the TV world spends its time talking about what's new, what's cool, what's popular—and the people who are new, cool, and popular, whether they be celebrities, athletes, or people just famous for being famous—we tend to spend a lot of time talking about ordinary folks and about what used to be, or even what is but will soon be no more.

There are some things in this world that probably need to no longer be— things for which we truly have no further need, such as rotary dial telephones and eight-track tapes.

But it's just as true that as far as we're concerned, some things in this world deserve to go on forever, whether we *need* them or not. We love discovering those things, even if we are there to pay tribute in their final days. That's where we found ourselves on this next story.

In the 1880s, Texas ranches were moving from open range to fenced pasture. This was after a long battle between ranchers on opposite sides of the issue. Up until this time, ranchers had allowed their cattle to roam on open land so they could find the best grass. The open range practice is what gave rise to the use of cattle brands, allowing ranchers to easily identify their cattle in mixed herds grazing the same pastures.

One of the most important advances that allowed ranchers to switch to fenced pasture was barbed wire. It was introduced in Texas by John F. "Spade" Evans and Judson P. Warner, who formed a corporation and bought twenty-three sections of land in the Panhandle. Warner, who was in the business of selling barbed wire, supervised the fencing of the land's pastures, then he and Evans sold out to Isaac Ellwood, co-owner of the barbed-wire patent with Joseph Glidden. The fencing of Texas pastures was by then becoming an accepted practice, and the Spade Ranch was completely surrounded and cross-fenced with barbed wire.

Eventually some of the Spade Ranch was sold off to farmers, and in 1924 the town of Spade sprang up near the old ranch headquarters. Most of the land surrounding the town was under cultivation by then, with 84 percent of it purchased by Texans who borrowed the money from the Federal Land Bank.

That's interesting to me, because the longest-running sponsor of *Texas Country Reporter* is Capital Farm Credit, the largest of the borrower-owned cooperative credit systems that emerged from the Federal Land Bank. Again, small world. They, along with our other sponsors, have kept us on the road doing *TCR* for the past twenty years, picking up where the Dairy Queen sponsorship left off. I love this thread running from 1880 to 2021 because connecting all the dots is a passion of mine, and even if all the background doesn't make its way into the story we tell on the show, it's important to me to know how everything lines up and fits together.

The town of Spade had a store and cotton gin, which were the center of the community, as well as a post office, two churches, several businesses, and enough young people to open their own school.

That school was a single building for students in every grade, from pre-kindergarten through twelfth, and it served the kids from the town and the surrounding farms and ranches for years. Spade School was cherished by the locals for a number of reasons, one of the most important being their 5:1 student-teacher ratio.

In 1948 a student named Sherman Jones quit Spade School to join the army and found himself a world away from the South Plains of Texas in a place called Korea. His regiment was nearly wiped out in battle, and he ran out of ammunition. After being taken prisoner by the North Koreans, he suffered one of the worst atrocities of that war: a horrific thing called the Korean Death March, a forced march of prisoners all the way to North Korea that left 50,000 to 90,000 soldiers dead. Sherman was shot twice, once in the foot and the other time behind one ear. The second bullet went through his skull—but exited from his cheek. He was one of only three from his unit who survived.

While Sherman's classmates at Spade School were receiving their diplomas, he was lying in a ditch in Korea, shot in the head.

In 2006, teacher Ashley Martin was in charge of organizing the graduation ceremonies at Spade School. We were invited to attend. That night a grand total of six students would march across the stage in the school auditorium, and Cassidy Chapman would be valedictorian of the only school he had ever known.

"This place is more of a family than it is a school," he told us.

One of the students who would walk across the stage at Spade School was an unlikely candidate: Sherman Jones, the same Sherman Jones who quit school to fight a war on the other side of the world. He would finally receive his diploma, right behind the other students. He had been invited to participate in the commencement exercises by Cassidy Chapman and his fellow graduating seniors, including salutatorian Dustin Garrett.

"It's not fair that he didn't get to graduate, and we feel that he deserves to walk with us for all the service he gave to his country," Cassidy told us.

The opportunity for Sherman to finally graduate from Spade School came just in the nick of time.

Fifty-eight years after Sherman quit Spade School, the school board decided that the tiny school just couldn't make it alone. It would become a part of the nearby Olton Independent School District. Tonight the school would hand out diplomas to the final graduating class, then they would shut it down.

Seventy-five-year-old Sherman Jones would be the last graduate of Spade School.

"I was a dumb farm boy from Texas," Sherman said. "I always wanted a high school diploma, and now I'm getting one."

Ashley Martin gave her graduating seniors a final word before starting the ceremony.

"Understand this: when you walk down that aisle and across that stage tonight, you carry one thing that nobody else carries. You are the last graduating class from Spade. Honor that. Be proud of that. And walk with pride."

"This will be the end of all things for our school," Dustin Garrett said. "After tonight it's just going to all be over."

We stood in the auditorium in the midst of what must have been the entire population of Spade and maybe even Lamb County that night, joining the crowd that was there for one last glimpse of history, and one last glimpse of an American hero from their hometown, a man who still carried the scars and nightmares from a terrible war so long ago.

Then the moment the senior class was waiting for arrived, and their names were called one by one by Ashley Martin.

"Martin, Jessica, Dustin, Cassidy, Joanna."

And, finally, more than five decades after he last attended classes at Spade School, "Mr. Sherman Jones."

The Class of 2006 then marched out, taking with them more than seventy years of history. Marching with them, although moving slowly, the last graduate of Spade School made his way through the crowd. Everyone waited patiently as the war hero took the walk he had always dreamed about.

On that night the people of Spade, young and old, decided the last page in their school's history should be reserved for Sherman Jones, the man who never gave up.

Once again, we were honored to be there when it happened.

THEN THERE ARE THOSE STORIES THAT DON'T HAVE A FIRM end date; you don't *know* that you better do it now, but you do know the clock is ticking.

We find stories in the funniest of places, and this one ranks up near the top. It was the mid-eighties and I was getting a haircut at a little one-chair joint near Red Oak, Texas, called Jack Weir's Barbershop when I spied a handwritten note on the back of a box top that was tacked on a bulletin board by the barber's sink.

The note read, "I grind corn, call J.D." and had a phone number.

Funny place to advertise your corn-grinding business, I thought, but what the hey, I'll give 'em a call.

The directions on the phone took us to a field somewhere south of Dallas, and out in the middle of that field was an old wood and tin shed. Scattered all around, in piles and in the weeds, we saw ancient farm implements looking like something the earth had coughed up, but definitely not like something anyone would be using anytime soon . . . or ever again.

But inside that shed we saw a sixty-seven-year-old Fairbanks-Morris engine that sounded like *it* ought to be out in the middle of that field. The guy running the machine noticed us looking at it like it was from another planet, and I guess he felt obligated to defend his hard-working machine.

"Give it a little choke, a little gas, a little time," he said, "and this old Fairbanks will fool ya. It chugs on today like it was made yesterday."

Welcome to the farm of J. D. Russell, famous for box-top business cards of the "I Grind Corn" variety stuck on the wall of Jack Weir's Barbershop. And, yes, the man minding the motor in the middle of the room was J. D. himself.

And what do you think he was doing? J. D. was grinding corn.

He told us his six-horse Fairbanks-Morris and a bushel of kernels would get you a pretty fine mess of cornmeal. J. D. will guarantee that, which is especially notable when you take a look at what he's got to work with. Like everything else around the place, the mill is ancient. The Fairbanks has been coughing and chugging for sixty-seven years now. The grindstones are closing in on a hundred. That's a lot of corn gone through the mill. And it's a lot of time and a lot of memories.

"If you want old-fashioned corn meal," J. D. told us, "this is the place to get it. Can't find it much anymore."

Once you look around the place, you can see that the corn mill is the last vestige of a dying business. Used to be J. D. had a dairy farm and 1,500 acres of corn and wheat. What he's got left is twenty acres and an amazing crop of bygone-era farm gear . . . all the stuff he never bothered to sell or trade away.

"But just about all of that stuff is still good," he told us. "Most of it will still shake, rattle, and roll."

Fact is, most anything you see around J. D.'s place will still shake, rattle, and roll. Forget that it's not the prettiest thing you've ever seen. When the tourists come around, J. D.'s buddies like to come over and make bets that this tractor will start or that motor will kick over. And they win more than they lose.

During our visit, J. D. ground up seventy-five pounds of corn meal, and it didn't seem like it took any time at all. But then, time has a way of coming and going at J. D. Russell's place. The years sort of drift in, drift out. Some years never make it back here at all, while others never leave. And if Father Time never comes to collect, J. D. just stores those good ole days back here in the shed with everything else.

There are some who would say that speed is inevitable, a modern-day fact of life. They'd say cornmeal comes from a grocery store, and J. D. Russell's relics are beyond recovery. If I were a bettin' man, I think I'd have to bet against that.

Still, that clock keeps on ticking.

IN THE ALMOST FIFTY YEARS THAT WE'VE BEEN TELLING stories on *Texas Country Reporter*, we have probably produced about ten or fifteen about boot makers. Cowboy boots are one thing that makes a handful of states in the United States different from all the others, Texas being one of those few. It's part of who we are and what we are all about. Even if you don't personally wear cowboy boots, you can't deny that they're a major symbol of Texas culture.

I remember that the first boot-maker story I did was in Meridian, Texas, in the mid-seventies. The man's name was Magdaleno Trujillo, and not only was he a boot maker, his father and his father's father were boot makers too. One of them (I can't remember which one; maybe it was all of them) used to have a job in the old days of Hollywood when they would turn out a western movie a week on the back lots at the big studios. It was Trujillo's job to make boots for the people acting in those movies.

The most famous boot maker in the world had to be Charlie Dunn in Austin. He became famous not just because he was a good boot maker but because Jerry Jeff Walker wrote a song about him. The first time I heard the song "Charlie Dunn," it must have been the early seventies, but it was January 1983 before I would get around to meeting the man in person and featuring him on the show.

Charlie was a funny little guy who always wore an apron and a beret. I guess he liked to look the part, especially after Jerry Jeff made him a folk hero. (Funny how Jerry Jeff is responsible for making so many people and places famous through his music.)

We produced a piece on Charlie for the show, but as with lots of other stories we've done over the years, it was the follow-up piece that I liked best. When we first visited Charlie's shop, he had a new apprentice. I thought it was kind of funny that this world-famous Texas boot maker had a guy working for him, making boots right alongside him, who was from Vermont.

Some twenty-five or thirty years later we went back to the little boot shop on College Street in Austin to see how that boy from Vermont was getting along. Charlie had retired (for the second time), and Lee Miller, his apprentice, had taken over the shop a couple of decades earlier.

Well, there he was, still making boots in that same shop using lots of tools and machines left there by Charlie. He told us that his boots now start at $2,900, and that if you want a pair, you'd better not be in a hurry, because his wait list was three or four years long.

And, yes, Lee Miller's boots are just as good (and maybe better) than Charlie Dunn's boots. They are worth every penny. We were happy to see that Charlie's legacy lives on because of Lee. Whatever happened to the apprentice system? Well, in some places it's alive and well. Lee had an apprentice the last time we visited him. She was from Vermont, just like him.

But of all the boot stories we produced over all the years, the one that most sticks in my head goes under the category "End of an Era." It's the story of Dave Wheeler, the proprietor of Wheeler Boots in Houston.

They say few things in life are guaranteed, and maybe that's true out in the wider world. But behind a nondescript storefront in southwest Houston, you can bet the farm on a pair of Wheeler boots. You are guaranteed to be measured personally by owner Dave Wheeler himself, you are guaranteed to have to wait for your boots, and the boots are guaranteed to look not just good, but *real* good. That's the legacy of Wheeler Boots.

Since Dwight David Eisenhower was president, a Wheeler has been stamping the family name into custom-made, one-of-a-kind boots. After nearly six decades of making boots, their reputation has grown into a legend. Customers are used to waiting years to get a pair from this shop that began with Paul Wheeler, the original boot maker, and Dave's dad, who made sure to pass down the craft of boot making.

"My dad always told people, and I adopted it later, that we're not for folks who *need* a pair of boots," Dave told us. "We're for people who *want* a pair of boots. If you want some special, one-off boots made just for you, we're the ones. But you've gotta be patient."

We had heard that Dave was pretty . . . uh, picky about the boots he will make. We had also heard that no matter what you may want in a pair of boots, Dave will make them his way. He told us that's not true. Well, "Sort of true . . . I guess."

"I may make some suggestions," Dave admitted.

"Strongly suggest?" I asked.

"Very strongly suggest," he responded. "Like, *those two colors do not go together!*"

"And they listen to you?"

"They listen," he said. "They're thankful. They say, 'Well, you're not gonna let me make any ugly boots, are you?' And I say, no, because I don't want my name on an ugly boot. It may not be something I would make for myself, but I want to be proud of it when it goes out."

Dave grew up in this boot shop, and when he was twelve years old, he was told he would be working there, that he was to report to the shop after school and on Saturdays.

"Be honest with me," I said. "When you were twelve years old, did you love it or hate it here?"

"Hated it. I came here kicking and screaming because I wanted to be on the baseball field, but that's the way things were back then. Parents were on you from the morning you woke up until you laid your head down at night. They expected more from their kids."

Dave said he now realizes his dad was strict, but he says he learned a lifetime of trade skills as a teenager and joined the shop crew full-time in his twenties. Father and son rode the ups and downs of the business together, through oil booms and busts, the *Urban Cowboy* craze, and eventually his dad's retirement.

"I was thirty-four at the time. He said, 'My hands hurt and my shoulders hurt, so just go on without me.' I said okay, but I was scared. He was always right there next to me, and suddenly I'm the guy."

And Dave has been "the guy" ever since, earning the ultimate recognition among boot makers—inclusion in Tyler Beard's book of the best. Suddenly Dave was boot-making royalty.

Now it was time for Dave to follow in his father's footsteps once again. And a pair of Wheeler boots was about to become even more rare. Dave said he was about to hang up the apron for good.

But boot making isn't the kind of business where you just one day hang a sign on the door that says "Closed" and walk away.

Dave had to give serious consideration to exactly how he was going to retire. It wasn't going to be as easy as it was for his dad, because Dave didn't have someone to take over his shop.

"We stopped taking orders four years ago," Dave told us.

Yep, for the last four years, Dave had been working on the last of the Wheeler boots. When we were there, he almost had it all sewn up. One day soon the antique machines in this storied shop would fall silent. It's no small thing to take over your father's life's work. After sixty years, Dave Wheeler could walk away knowing that he had filled some mighty big boots.

"Nah, all I had to do was not screw it up," Dave said. "This was all set up for me. He figured it all out."

"But you didn't screw it up."

"No," he said. "I feel like I even took it to another level, and one day he told me that. He said, 'You know, I could never do all these things that you've done with the boot shop.' It's hard to get compliments from people from that era, but I'll remember that forever."

As we pulled away from Wheeler Boots, those words "people from that era" ran around in my head. We would just as soon places like this stay around forever—again, whether we *need* them or not—doing what they do and changing nothing. But we are always honored when we are invited to be there to witness the end of an era when the end comes calling.

This, indeed, was truly the end of an era.

CHAPTER FORTY-EIGHT

*J*UST THE OTHER DAY I OPENED AN EMAIL FROM A viewer who wrote, "Just wondering if there is a particular reason you do so many stories on art and artists. I'm not complaining, just wondering because I love art."

Well, yeah, there is a particular reason for that. We discovered early on, probably sometime in the first year of the show, that artists are . . . different. They often look at the world through different eyes than the rest of us. Where we see a mess, for instance, many artists see . . . well, art. And most of the time we find that artists have thoughts that are more interesting then the things we mortals think about. We love artists on this show.

It was December of 1986 when we met Iness Arey. Now don't ask Iness about expressionism or abstracts or color temperature or composition. Those are artsy words, and Iness doesn't use them. You want to talk to Iness, you keep it plain and simple. You talk about things she knows. You talk about her life.

"These are just pictures of my life the way I remember it," Iness told us. "I never picked up a paintbrush until I was old."

It's true. Iness never picked up a paintbrush until she was in her golden years. After she retired from Woolworth's at sixty-five, Iness figured she'd have to find something to do to keep her out of trouble. So she did what she did as a girl. She worked on the farm, chopping wood, hanging clothes, hauling hay. And she remembered.

"I guess I just started painting my memories from the farm."

When she took up painting, eight years before our visit, the naïve and primitive farm scenes were nothing more than one lady's way of passing time. Alone, there in her living room, Iness had no idea that she was living and painting a mirror image of the life and work of America's greatest folk artist, Anna Mary Robertson Moses, better known as Grandma Moses.

Grandma Moses didn't pick up a brush until she was eighty years old, but she still became famous for her work. Her pictures were also naïve and primitive, a self-taught artist's look at growing up on a farm, with scenes of chopping wood, hanging clothes, hauling hay.

"Did it surprise you, seeing how much your art resembled that of Grandma Moses?" I asked Iness.

"Of course," she said. "I had never seen her work, but she obviously had similar experiences to mine, there on the farm."

That farm was the stage where almost half of Iness's life unfolded. So it's not surprising that the house she grew up in is the center of so many of her paintings. The scenery may change, and the characters may come and go, but the house remains the same. Her friends have carried paintings of that farm all over the country.

And in each painting is a piece of Iness Arey's life, a life she thought we needed to know about . . . and not forget.

Iness kept her brushes busy over the years, keeping herself out of trouble. And while she never achieved the fame of Grandma Moses, it wasn't because her art wasn't as good. It's because that's the way life works. Some people achieve fortune and fame, some do not. But on the day we visited, and on the day she first appeared on our show, Iness Arey was a star.

That's the way *our* world works.

LOTS OF ARTISTS, IT SEEMS, PAINT, SCULPT, OR DRAW WHAT they know. Lots of artists, it seems, paint, sculpt, or draw their homes . . . if they remember them. Some create works of art that are similar to what they wanted their homes to be or what they thought they might have been like . . . if only they could remember.

Our homes are an extension of who we are. They reflect our personalities and soothe us with what makes us comfortable. It's like Dick and Bonnie Cain, the pioneer couple in Big Bend, said.

"What you know is what you like."

The house where Enedina Vasquez lived was pretty much the same as every other home in her modest San Antonio neighborhood, but when you stepped inside you found yourself in Enedina's world, one of color and art, reflecting her thoughtful philosophy of life and love. Those were the things that brought peace to an artist who struggled to create everything that was conjured in her mind.

"I can't help it," Enedina told me. "It's like I have to be creative every single day. It's like breathing to me."

Enedina opened her heart, and her emotions flew out in the form of paintings and sculptures. Nearly every inch of wall space in her home was covered with her art and writing. It was like a three-dimensional personal journal put on display for whoever dropped in to visit. And on the day that we dropped in, she was engrossed in her newest artistic outlet for all of her innermost thoughts and feelings, a simple craft called fused glass.

"Why glass?" I asked.

"Because it's very fragile," she told me, "and you have to be very careful with it, and I think that's life and a part of life and understanding life. You have to carry it carefully, and you have to handle it carefully because it will break. Like life."

Enedina said that another reason she loved glass is because it can be fused back together, but if you examine it closely you can see that it came from material much more basic than the finished product, and that, too, is like life.

Like the broken pieces of glass that she baked and melted together into a thing of beauty, Enedina was attempting to fuse together the broken pieces of her past, the disadvantages of growing up the daughter of migrant farm workers who could not read or write; the pain of the premature death of her husband, with whom she shared an artistic gift; and the lack of any tangible evidence of her childhood, which was all a distant, faded memory.

"My mother was a nice lady," Enedina said, "but I grew up feeling that I didn't want to be like her because she couldn't read or write, and that dictated her life. I knew I would make up for that with my life."

She told us that she had no pictures of her childhood because photographs were a luxury that migrant workers could not afford. And because she simply could not remember what friends and family members looked like, Enedina's home was covered with paintings of faceless people. When she grew up, she started buying old tintype photographs of children posing by a pony, on top of a wagon, playing with a ball, or waiting for a parade to pass. Those pictures became *her* childhood pictures, and she was leaving them to her son because, like her faceless paintings, those pictures could have been of her.

Scattered around Enedina's home were dozens of journals stacked among her art. A little bit sketch book, a little bit diary, they were poignant expressions of a woman who had done her best to cope with the hand that life had dealt her. Her strongest sentiments were painted on the doors and walls, works of art themselves. And it occurred to us that, just maybe, her *thoughts* were the real art she created.

"Everyone is free to come here, and we will chat like people do, and after we get to know each other, I invite you to sign my wall. It's like you're leaving your mark."

Enedina left *her* mark all around San Antonio. Her popular fused glass pieces were hot sellers at local galleries and art stores. They were creative, colorful, and full of life, a true reflection of the artist who created them.

"Change everything that you see, everything that you see changes you," she told us. "I will not be the same person I was yesterday because of my visit with you. I will see everything differently and that is good."

The French artist Émile Zola said, "If you ask me what I came into this world to do, I will tell you I came to live out loud."

Enedina Vasquez was an artist and philosopher who gently and softly poured her soul out for the world to see, but it was indeed loud. She was a quiet lady, but her art spoke at the highest volume.

"When I am gone," she told me, "I want people to know that I was a Mexican American who loved her culture and understood her culture and saw its beauty."

Before we left, I wrote the following on Enedina Vasquez's wall:

Live. Love. Laugh.
Truly one of the most inspirational people I have met.
Bob

AFTER PRODUCING A FEW HUNDRED STORIES ON ARTISTS and craftspeople of every shape, color, discipline, and calling, we have come to know that many of them do what they do to make a statement. Almost all of them will tell you that the message you take away from their art is strictly up to you, but we suspect the truth is that many of them wouldn't be upset if the message was their intended one.

Leon Collins is one of those artists. We met him one fine, clear day in Navasota, Texas. It was a long and winding road that led Leon to this particular place at this particular time, a makeshift studio in the corner of an uncelebrated antique store where he was giving form to the abstract motion of dreams and immortalizing the inescapable reality of heritage.

"My paintings are mostly about Black heritage because that's *my* heritage," Leon told me. "I don't believe there is such a thing as stereotyping. My art is intended to be art, and that's exactly what it is."

To understand Leon and his African American heritage, you have to know a little about him and the town he grew up in. Leon was a child when he moved from California to Texas, where he lived with his great-grandmother, who was born a slave. Her stories—coupled with his own experiences in Navasota and its rich history of Black people, cotton, and the blues—made him a bit of a self-taught historian.

I discovered Leon and his art one day when I was walking down a Navasota street and noticed some incredible scenes in the window of a store called Tejas Antiques. I would soon find out that they had been painted by Leon Collins.

He told me, "It was about 1975 when I wandered into an art studio and looked at the paintings and the colors and the subjects, and I came to realize that art is a part of life. I knew I wanted to be an artist."

But Leon soon found that the life of an artist is no easy row to hoe. He needed to make a living. Years later he met Duane Garner, the owner of Tejas Antiques, and he put away his paints and canvases to become an antique "picker," using the knowledge of all the old things he had grown up with.

"A picker is someone who has a lot of contacts with folks in the country," Duane said, "and they know how to work with those folks, and they know how to buy from them. Without Leon, I wouldn't be in this business."

If there is a gene for artistic ability, Leon Collins passed it on. When his daughter, Molly Bee, began to paint seriously, and when her paintings began to sell from the window of Duane's store, she encouraged her dad to pick up his brush again and paint with her. He agreed to do one painting with his daughter, and that painting was the one that put the word *artist* back on Leon's business card.

"I want my paintings to tell a story," he told me. "I want people to look at my work and know what I'm saying."

His paintings mostly chronicle the Black experience. They are artistic impressions and images of a way of life that, according to Leon, is not well understood, even by people of color.

"In California I didn't know anything about the ways of people who lived in the South," he said. "Coming to Texas to live with my great-grandmother was a blessing. Still, it's hard to believe how people in slavery lived."

It took his teenage daughter's encouragement to help Leon realize his dream of being a known and respected artist who could tell the stories of his people. Today this father and daughter team is making waves across the art world. Their work is in demand, and the stories of their ancestral past have flowed from a great-grandmother who was born a slave to a daughter who was born with a gift of creativity, and from there to hundreds of canvases in homes across the country. They paint with the colors of life, and live with the legacy of their heritage.

"Life is a journey," Leon said, "and all you've got to do is keep on living."

But for some people, going on living isn't an option—at least not *the life they love*. Some are forced to accept the reality of the times in which we live, like it or not.

IT WAS NEARLY NOON WHEN WE ARRIVED AT VIRGINIA Vaughan's farm just east of Austin. Nearly noon but no sign of the sun: one of those cold, grey days when the wind-driven mist puts a damper on almost any outdoor activity, especially landscape impressionist painting.

But Virginia wanted to remember *this* day: the way the sky looked, the way the damp air smelled, the way *this* day made an impression on her . . . and her canvas.

"I've painted out here in all kinds of weather," she told me, "in bitter cold, in hundred and five degree heat, in snow and sleet."

You might ask why this day on the farm was so special to Virginia that she wouldn't put off painting until nicer weather. Truth is, *every* day was special to Virginia then because her days there were numbered. Austin's explosive development had reached her family farm near Manor, Texas, where Virginia thought it never would. Rooftops peeked over the western horizon, and the bulldozers and concrete trucks idled at her gate, ready to chew up and pave over Virginia's family farm. She had been living out here since she was sixteen and always thought it was impossible that Austin would come this far, but it did.

So with paintbrush and canvas, Virginia Vaughan set out to paint her memories. For 365 days, one full year, she would complete a painting a day. The project would not only document her last year on the land but also represent a lifetime of impressions that live in the heart of an artist.

"My reasons for starting it were kind of selfish," she said, "so I could have a record for me and for my family to remember. And it became a symbol of time marching on."

"Right here where we're standing," I told Virginia, "will soon be someone's house, and another one right over there, and another one and another one and . . ."

"I won't come back then," she said. "I'll be done. I don't want to see that."

Seen together, Virginia's paintings read like a visual diary, a chronicle of the end of an era. Titles and images like *Blue Norther* and *Rainy Day Sunshine* reflect the first days of the project. *Why We Are Leaving* and *The Day the Cows Left* mark those near the end. But it was a diary that the author could no longer bear to read.

I said, "You have to stand out here, looking at your beloved farm, and wonder, 'Why do we have to leave?'"

"I don't like to dwell on that," she answered. "Nothing is for sure here on this Earth. We can't plan our way all the time. So I just want to be thankful. I regard this whole series as thanksgiving."

It is a story that has played out all across America countless times, family farms swallowed up and paved over in the name of progress. Soon driveways and well-watered lawns would cover the memories a family made here. And today the memories left to be made were counted in hours and captured in oils.

"We're not just losing our agricultural lifestyle," she said. "We're losing the meaning to our stories. The Bible says things about sowing and reaping, and saving for the lean times, and sharing when you have plenty, and what does all that mean if we don't have the farm as an example of that?"

When the final hour of the final day came, Virginia Vaughan's paintings fit in her truck, but her memories would have filled a boxcar. The best images were captured on canvas, and the rest would be a story for the grandchildren. She didn't know what was ahead, but, for certain, it would be a new adventure.

"I can't be anything but thankful," she said. "This whole life was just a gift, and I can't do anything but just say thanks."

So with a smile and a tear, Virginia looked back one last time . . . and drove away.

Thanks for sharing the memories, Virginia. Now they are part of our story too.

CHAPTER FORTY-NINE

PEOPLE ASK US ALMOST DAILY, "WHERE DO YOU GET your story ideas?" or "Where do you find all those stories?" The answer to that is lots of places. Some we hear about from our viewers. We get more than a hundred story ideas in email just about every day of the year. People who are, or have been, the subject of a story often say, "If you like me, you should check out this other person." And many times we just stumble onto them.

In all our years of traveling the back roads of Texas, we have *lost* very few stories. The number of people who turned us down when we asked them to let us spend time with them and tell their story on the show can probably be counted on one hand. At the moment I can't think of a single one, though I know it has happened.

We have missed a few stories or had a few, *very few*, just fall apart after we arrived on the scene.

One of the earliest ones that got away was a story about a guy I just call "the skunk man." Of course, there's a backstory that goes with this.

Frank X. Tolbert was a columnist for the *Dallas Morning News* for many years. He wrote a column called "Tolbert's Texas" that narrated his travels around the state and the people he met. Much of his column was historic in nature but included the characters and tales he stumbled upon along the way. Sound familiar? Well, it sounded familiar to Frank Tolbert, too, when we first started *4 Country Reporter* on KDFW-TV.

Frank and I had met a time or two but did not know one another well. By the time we started the show, he was trying to wind down his column, but he kept writing it until 1977, when he went to a once-a-week status. By then he was spending most of his time developing his chili parlor restaurants. Frank was, probably more than any other individual, responsible for the popularity of chili across Texas and beyond. His book *A Bowl of Red* chronicles the stories of the peppery dish, which some say was first made by cowboys on the trail who wanted to make "yesterday's meat" taste better. Frank and chili connoisseur Wick Fowler founded the Chili Appreciation Society International (CASI).

Frank also was the founder of the World Championship Chili Cookoff, held every November in Terlingua in Big Bend. If you don't know about Terlingua, or you don't know about Big Bend, I suggest you Google it, because if I get started on either one of those topics, my stories will take us down rabbit holes from which we may never emerge.

Early in the Terlingua Chili Cookoff years I let Frank talk me into joining a group of journalists there. He said it would be the best time I ever had. I wondered about that when we took off from Love Field in Dallas and headed for Alpine in an old, beat-up DC-3 tail dragger that belched smoke from both engines all the way from Big D to Little T. By the time we arrived, and that in itself was a miracle, most of the journalists on the old plane were three sheets to the wind. And the chili cookoff was more of the same . . . for two more days.

One day, in the early to mid-seventies, Frank called me and said he hoped to be fully retiring soon (as I recall, it took him a few more years to actually do that). He said he had a few ideas he thought I should look into for the show, and he thought some of his columns would be great TV pieces so he wanted to share them with me. He invited me to join him on Wednesday afternoon at the chili parlor on McKinney Avenue, Tolbert's, to share a bowl of red and chat. That meeting led to another, and our meetings turned into an almost weekly thing that lasted for quite a while. I never learned what the magic of Wednesday was, but I do know our meetings always took place around 2:30 P.M., after the lunch rush.

During one of those chili-eating meetings at Tolbert's, he said, "I thought of another good one for you last night. You gotta do a story on the skunk man."

"The skunk man? That sounds like an idea that stinks."

Frank missed my attempt at humor (that happens a lot) and kept on talking. He was a professional Texas humorist, and everyone knows Texas humorists are the best in the business, so trying to be funny with Frank was a mistake. He let it go.

He then told me about the skunk man, who made his living getting skunks out from under people's houses. If you live in the city, you've probably never heard of this and surely didn't know that people can actually make a living from it, but for people in the country, skunks can be a problem.

Frank said, "The guy is a real character. He went on that TV show *What's My Line?* one time, and they guessed it right away because they could smell him."

I could never confirm that tale, but lots of Frank's stories were just that . . . great stories.

But I liked this idea and said I'd call him up.

"Don't do that," Frank cautioned, "because he won't be the same if you let him know you're coming. Just drive up there."

As I walked out of the chili parlor, I turned back to Frank and asked where, exactly, the skunk man lived.

He said, "The skunk man lives in Uz."

I did not listen to Frank's advice. Oh, I intended to do the story, but Uz is west of and a little bit south of Gainesville, just south of the Red River, and I didn't see the sense in driving all that way on the chance that the skunk man would be there and be willing to allow our cameras to follow him around. So I gave him a call and told him Frank Tolbert with the *Dallas Morning News* gave me his number.

When we showed up in Uz a few days later, the skunk man was waiting on us. He was dressed like he was on his way to church. So were his wife, his kids, his grandkids, his neighbors, and just about everyone else the skunk man knew. They were all gathered there waiting . . . waiting to have their portrait taken so it could appear in the *Dallas Morning News*. Television be damned, these people thought they were going to be in print.

There would be no skunk-hunting that day.

I made a deal with the skunk man to call me on a day when he was going out to retrieve a skunk from under a house. It would take us about an hour and a half to get there, and we would do everything we could to race up to Uz and shoot the story.

In spite of my repeated calls over the next few years, I never talked to the skunk man again. Then he died. End of story.

ANOTHER ONE THAT GOT AWAY WAS A STORY WE WANTED to do about one of the last real cowboys. Funny thing about cowboys: the real ones will rarely call themselves that. They'll say they are cow punchers, or cattlemen, or ranch hands. The term *cowboy* seems to be reserved for the legendary giants among many other giants—the real deal.

For one story we did in the mid-eighties, we traveled to the Four Sixes Ranch near Guthrie, Texas, to meet a cowboy poet named Buster "Punch" McLaury. He was a young cowhand, but he also wrote some great poetry about his chosen field. The closest Buster would get to saying he was a cowboy was to say he "kinda likes workin' on these old ranches, just cowboyin'."

(Side note: Buster McLaury and his wife would later open a business to help people on the ranches in West Texas deal with problem horses. They were quite successful, and some people claim Buster is the best of the acclaimed horse whisperers.)

We spent a couple of days with Buster and the other cowhands on the Sixes as they rounded up cattle. Before we left, Buster asked if I'd ever done a story on the legendary cowboy Tom Blasingame, a "real" cowboy who had worked for the JA Ranch for more than seventy years.

I told him I had always wanted to do a story about the great Mr. Blasingame but couldn't figure out how to get in touch with him. The JA Ranch was one of the legendary Texas ranches that was started, in part, by the famous rancher Charles Goodnight. I had called the JA a couple of times, and they said they would give Tom a message, but I never got a call back. I suspect they didn't see him that much.

Tom managed a huge part of the JA, and during the week he lived in what is called a line house that had no phone or electricity. He spent most of his time on the back of his favorite horse, riding fence and checking on the cattle that were under his care. Pinning down a cowboy like Tom Blasingame to sit for a TV interview was probably not going to be easy, but oh, the stories he could tell if I could.

In 1989, Tom Blasingame made a rare appearance at an event in Lubbock held by the American Cowboy Symposium Association. By this time I had asked so many ranch people how I could go about setting up a visit with Tom that one of them called me with a tip. He told me he had talked to Tom at that gathering.

"Tom spends most weekends with his wife, Eleanor, at their home in Claude," the caller said. "Why don't you try calling Eleanor?"

Well, that's a no-brainer, I thought—and I apparently had no brain or I would have thought of it years earlier. I gave Eleanor a call.

"I expect to have Tom at home a few days around Christmas, though I never know which days those might be," she told me. "I'll talk to him while he's here, then you call me after the first of the year and we'll see if we can't make it happen."

I was excited that 1990 might be off to a good start with an interview with this legendary cowboy.

But on December 27, 1989, Tom Blasingame climbed down off his horse, Ruidosa; laid down on the grass on the edge of Palo Duro Canyon; folded his arms across his chest; and died. It's been said that when they found him,

Ruidosa was still standing over his body. (Even if the horse didn't do that, it still makes the story better.)

Tom was buried in the cemetery on the JA, where cowboys had been buried since 1870, following an "empty saddle" procession with Tom's horse leading the way to the grave site, with his *second-best* pair of boots turned backwards in the saddle's stirrups. Tom, of course, was buried in his best pair of boots . . . like all real cowboys.

So I never did meet Tom Blasingame, and to this day he is the one who got away that I think of the most.

THERE WERE OTHER STORIES OVER THE YEARS THAT NEVER came to fruition, but sometimes they led us down a path to another story— an even better story, when we got lucky.

For one story we traveled to the little wide spot in the road in Big Bend called Ruidosa. (Yes, it has the same name as Tom Blasingame's horse, spelled with an *a* at the end, not like the New Mexican town that has an *o* at the end.)

Set at the foot of the Chinati Mountains on the Texas-Mexico border, Ruidosa might have had as many as fifteen or twenty people living there at the time. Maybe. We had heard about a couple there who were restoring the old Sacred Heart Mission along FM 170.

Ruidosa is a long way to go for a story, but that's not something we steer away from—quite the opposite. For us, the more remote the better. But it *is* a long way to go for a story that doesn't turn out, so just like we did for the skunk man story, we called ahead and made arrangements with the folks who were working on the church.

And just like what happened when we showed up at the skunk man's house, when we arrived, we did not find people who looked like they were doing the back-breaking work of restoring an adobe building. Instead we found people who, in the words of producer and photographer Brian Hawkins, "looked like they were dressed to go to a George Strait concert."

We decided we had to say something, because it was either take a chance on offending these folks or letting them go on television looking like they weren't doing the work that they *were*, in fact, doing, which is what we wanted our viewers to see.

So we gently asked them if they would mind putting on their work clothes. They said okay, then left to go home and change . . . *and never returned.* Apparently our attempt at not offending them didn't work.

But what happened next was kind of cool.

We wandered next door to the church, where we met Celia Hill, the lady who runs a little store here in the Chihuahuan Desert in West Texas—a barren, empty place where the wind is the only voice, and rugged peaks stretch across the horizon. Perched on the banks of the Rio Grande, Celia's La Junta Store has to be the most remote shopping establishment anywhere.

"You'd be surprised at how many days we've gone without anybody coming into the store," Celia told us. "Nobody."

As the wind whistled through the scrub brush, Celia sat on her front porch and talked.

"I'm particularly amused at the number of people who come down here and ask questions like 'How far is it to the nearest mall? Or the nearest Walmart?'"

She said she tells them the nearest Walmart is in Chihuahua City, "165 miles away . . . in another country."

For those who didn't bother to look at the map before venturing this far into the desolate desert, Celia keeps a few snacks "to keep their stomachs off their backbones."

"We have Vienna Sausages and tuna and Beanee Weenees and peanut butter," she said. "Any time you have Vienna Sausages and peanut butter, why, what more could you want?"

But groceries cover only one small shelf in Celia's store. The rest she calls her little museum.

"I want to show you something," she said, as she opened an old trunk that sat by a window.

She pulled something out.

"This is the last blanket that was made from the hair of the goats we had on our ranch," she told us. "Every year when they sheared the goats, Daddy would send one sack of mohair over to Mexico, where they would make a blanket. I'm proud of this."

Celia's life and history belong to a rocky valley called Fresno Canyon Ranch. Her entire childhood was spent in the desert—away from towns, away from people.

"We had good times and we had hard times," she said. "And every afternoon I had to go find that cow and bring her back so we could have milk, and I resolved right then that I would go to school and one day make enough money to buy milk."

A few years ago Celia decided to put her memories on paper with the help of her friend Mariposa. As Celia recited her story, Mariposa wrote it all down. She was recalling a lifestyle that can never be recaptured.

"There are times now that I wish I could have those big pans of fresh milk with nice rich cream on it. We had some good Jersey cows."

We left Celia sitting there on the porch of her remote little store with her book, and her stories, and her memories, here where the mountains are guardians of the past. This simple grocery store and museum are backdrops to Celia's life story, a story that may never be told again. As we drove away, it was clear to us that this desert would never be the same without Celia.

<small>OVER THE YEARS, THERE HAVE BEEN MANY STORIES THAT</small> we thought we understood, but some of those simple stories sometimes took a sudden twist and a turn before exploding into something completely different from the story we came to tell.

Fred Beatty was one of those stories. We had been told about a man who lived on the edge of Palo Duro Canyon, a guy who could hand-feed the wild Aoudad sheep that run wild in the canyon. Those creatures have always been known as some of the most skittish animals around, so if this story was true, we had to see it for ourselves.

Pretty pictures are all we were after on this trip. We went there late one afternoon, in time to catch the sunset over Palo Duro. In case there were no Aoudad, and no man wandering among them, we could at least salvage our time with a beautiful sunset shot. You can never have too many of those.

Palo Duro is the second largest canyon in the United States after the Grand Canyon. Over the centuries this vast, broken landscape has offered the gift of inspiration to writers, poets, artists, and dreamers. But for Fred Beatty, it was something moving in the brush one morning before sunrise that caught his eye. There, backlit by a fiery red early-morning sky, were the silhouettes of dozens of horned creatures standing on the edge of the canyon in Fred's backyard.

As soon as we arrived at the home of Fred and Lanoma Beatty, Fred asked if I wanted to get up close and personal with a herd of Aoudad. I told him that's why we were there. We each grabbed a large plastic scoop, filled them with corn, and walked through a backdoor that opened onto the edge of the canyon.

There, patiently waiting, were at least fifty Aoudad sheep.

For the next few minutes Fred and I walked through the area sprinkling corn amongst those creatures, whose beautiful curved horns look like an adorning headdress. As we stood on the edge of the canyon, it occurred to me that this place—the canyon, the sheep, the view—would be like scenes from another planet for some people. But this was home to Fred. He told me that if he had to leave this place for some reason, it's definitely the animals he would remember.

But I soon found out that hanging on to those memories Fred cherished so much had become a frustrating struggle. Like a knife cutting deep into my heart, Fred's next words stopped me in my tracks.

"I have Alzheimer's."

This was not the cheerful, picturesque story we had come to Palo Duro Canyon to tell. What had brought us here was the lure of a man walking freely among a herd of wild animals like he was one of them. Now I knew there was yet another story to tell, one that would not have the happy ending we had planned for, but one that had to be told just the same.

I instinctively looked across to another promontory jutting out into the canyon fifty yards away, where Brian Hawkins was shooting tape of Fred and me walking and talking. Brian saw my look and gave me a thumbs-up, signaling that he had heard what Fred just told me, and that his camera had been rolling when Fred dropped that bomb in the midst of this moving scene.

"It's never going to be the same again," Lanoma told me later. "But I'm thankful that God has given him this. Us moving out here was totally a gift from God. These sheep are the one thing that he remembers day to day. He's a happy person, even with the disease."

"You gotta love it," Fred told us the next morning as the sheep once again roamed his backyard. "You get up in the morning and look out over this incredible scenery, and you can't help but thank the Lord every day."

"I'm glad You put me here?" I asked.

"Absolutely," Fred said with a big smile. "Absolutely."

THERE IS ONE MORE STORY, ONE MORE *KIND OF STORY*, that grabs us and won't let us go.

We often run across people who are facing incredible challenges, people who know the odds are stacked against them, yet they keep on going. These stories give us pause, and we wonder, time and time again, how they persevere despite the incredible obstacles they face. You probably think we would run toward these stories as fast as we can, but we have learned over the years that many of them are very difficult for us to tell because of the emotional toll they take on *us*. Still, they have to be told.

Stores about people like Diane Rose, the blind woman who pieced together incredible quilts from scraps of cloth she could not see. People like Orville Rogers, who was still running marathons at the age of ninety-nine . . . and eagerly awaiting his one-hundredth birthday, when he would advance into another age category. People like David Hartwig, the "dad" to the incredible Skidboot, who was the smartest dog in the world but also going blind. David vowed to carry him in his arms if need be, because "God gave me this dog to take care of, and I'm gonna do it no matter what."

People like Roxanne Roundtree, a nurse, wife, and mother who was diagnosed with ALS when she was in her late twenties. Amyotrophic lateral sclerosis, commonly known as Lou Gehrig's disease, has to be one of the cruelest of all afflictions. It eventually shuts off the signals to every muscle in the body, leaving the victim's healthy mind trapped in a motionless shell. There is no cure.

This was not an easy story for me to do. From the first time I heard about ALS, I have always feared it because, to me, it sounds like one of the worst fates a person could face.

Sitting in a wheelchair rigged with a computer screen, Roxy "talked" with me from the living room of her home in North Zulch, Texas, west of Madisonville. The computer screen was controlled by her eye movements, and a synthesized voice spoke the words and phrases that she spelled out one letter at a time. It took a lot of blinking to say the simplest thing, but Roxy seemed to have it down.

The most amazing thing was that Roxanne had written an entire book by blinking her eyes. *Roxy's Recipes* is a collection of recipes for the dishes she made for her husband and three boys, something to leave behind so her mother and sisters could still make the things her family loved after she was gone. It took two years, and a lot of eye blinking, for Roxy to write her book.

But Roxy was a super mom and was still the boss of her household, so she kept going, kept blinking, kept taking care of her family. Still, in the back of her mind, never leaving her thoughts for even, yes, the blink of an eye was the fact that she had ALS.

"I wish it was a bad dream," she told me through her computer voice. "The love I have for my husband and children helps get me through it."

Roxanne used to make big home-cooked meals for her house full of hungry men, and even though she could no longer lift a finger, she was still making sure that supper was hot on the table every night. All three of her sons and her husband, Don, made the evening meal a family affair, even though Roxy could not join them to eat what they'd made under her direction. She was fed through a feeding tube with nourishment and meds ground up by her family.

"I always watch every single thing that goes on," Roxy told me. "I am organized and require total structure in my house."

ALS had already taken so much from this family that they were holding tightly to whatever was left, like simple evening meals. Using her synthesized voice, she barked orders for cooking, setting the table, and doing homework. And even with three boys playing multiple sports, Roxanne never missed a game.

"I go to every one of my children's events," she said. "I have left hospitals, postponed treatments, so I wouldn't miss a thing. We can't let our children's lives change just because I am sick."

For a little while, when Don was busy doing chores and the kids were still at school, it was just Roxy and me sitting there. And for a few moments it felt as if we were the only two people in the universe, in spite of the fact that a TV crew hovered just a few feet away. Roxy opened up her heart, and it nearly broke mine.

"When I look in the mirror, I see a wretched cripple, but when they look at me, they see Mommy," she said. "They are the one and only reason I am still here."

In their late twenties, Don and Roxanne were living the classic American dream. Roxanne was doing it all: working as a nurse, preparing home-cooked meals, and serving as team mom for youth sports. Don had hit the jackpot. The mother of his three boys was also the girl he fell in love with back in first grade. And then ALS ripped out the pages of their storybook romance.

Don told me, "We had plans to be old people in rocking chairs."

"You were going to grow old together."

Don managed to nod his head as his chin shook and he wiped away his tears. It was clear that he was well aware that he would be losing the love of his life.

"I cry," Roxy said. "Not for myself but for them, because I am everything to my husband and children. And I know how much they will miss me. Every graduation, every wedding, every grandchild . . . they will wish I was there."

"You know what you call that?" I asked her. "That's called being a mom."

Roxanne and I cried together.

CHAPTER FIFTY

*T*HERE HAVE BEEN MANY STORIES LIKE THAT OF ROXANNE Roundtree over the years, but as our show grows older, and as we grow older with it, we find ourselves doing more stories with depth and meaning—stories of giving and caring, stories about people's passions—than we ever did before. Oh, we still do stories about great places in Texas to eat, like we have from the beginning, and we still do stories that just make you smile or sometimes laugh out loud, and we still do lots of stories about ordinary people doing extraordinary things, people living their lives in some meaningful way. Those have always been, and I suspect always will be, the lifeblood of *Texas Country Reporter.*

We set out to tell stories that would inspire people. Turns out, we are the ones who have been most inspired by the stories we tell.

Ours are stories about people you know, but not people you know from the headlines. You know them because they are the people who live down the block and next door, people like you—or maybe people you would like to be.

We love to do stories that remind all of us that things may seem like they are not going well . . . until we focus on an ordinary, everyday person who is doing something that reminds us that, above all else, there are still good people in this world.

We like to do stories about people who don't know there is anything special about them, about people who wonder why we are there. We love people who don't think they are anything special. We love showing them that they *are* special.

And, yes, we like doing stories that some people consider insignificant or irrelevant, stories that remind us that all is right with the world after all. We travel the back roads because it is our experience that this is where you find those special people: ordinary people doing extraordinary things that most people haven't even noticed. We like to talk to everybody by talking about one "nobody," and when they hear that person's story, they know that everybody is somebody, that everybody is important in some way.

And we like being different, being the ones that tell an alternate story. *Texas Country Reporter* has endured the not-so-friendly test of time on television partly due to our attitude about humans and what makes them tick. We travel with few preconceived ideas about what or who we will find, just the knowledge that they are out there, waiting—even though they're often not aware of it.

But the stories that reach deep down inside where you live—the ones that tug at you, the ones that leave you with a lump in your throat or a tear in your eye—those are the heart and soul of what we do. Those are the stories we hope to keep telling because we think those are the stories we all need to hear. There are lots more stories out there, and we'll keep telling them as long as people will listen.

For fifty seasons of *Texas Country Reporter*, it's been a good long drive.

And there is nothing we would rather be doing. Nothing.

Acknowledgments

N O TELEVISION SHOW CAN CONTINUE TO BE SUCCESS-
ful without finding a way to pay the bills. If you don't have
sponsors who believe in what you are doing, you will not last. It's simple
math.

We have been fortunate to have had wonderful people and organizations
stand behind us all of these years.

I already told you about Dairy Queen, the sponsor that helped us when
we started producing the show ourselves and syndicated it statewide. But
there have been others that have sponsored our show for even longer than
DQ.

Capital Farm Credit has been with us for twenty years and often enters
into multiyear sponsorship contracts to help ensure our show's stability.
They are the largest agricultural lending organization in Texas, and Tanya
Foerster and Jeff Moder get what *Texas Country Reporter* is all about and how
it ties in with what CFC does. We are blessed to have had them with us,
keeping us on the road.

Mueller, Inc., the company that's located in the little West Texas town
of Ballinger, makes the Cadillac version of metal roofs and buildings. They
have sponsored *TCR* for more than seventeen years, and Mike Fry and company owner Bryan Davenport have become much more than just advertisers.
We are friends and colleagues, and support one another in many ways. We
love our association with this company and its people.

The list of sponsors we have had over the years is fairly short and very
powerful. We like it that way. Hochheim Prairie Insurance has been with
us for twelve years; Southwest Airlines was an original sponsor dating back
to the *4 Country* days and continuing for more than forty years; the Texas
Ford Dealers, Farm Bureau Insurance, Golden Chick, Del Webb's Sun City,

Robson Ranch, and Kiolbassa Smoked Meats put their faith in the power of the *TCR* brand and the value of backing our show.

We appreciate each and every person and company that has believed in us over these many years. We could not have done this without you.

The TV stations that have decided to air our show over the years have been essential, of course, and we are so thankful to each and every one of them. KDFW-TV in Dallas was the one that gave our show its first chance, and the one that gave me a chance when I knew nothing and had nothing to offer. I will always be grateful for that. WFAA-TV was there when we needed to make a change, and they not only decided to air our show but also helped me start my production company so I could share *TCR* with the rest of Texas. And Patrick Gottsch and RFD-TV gave us the opportunity to share *TCR* with the rest of America. We are grateful to him for recognizing what we do and why it's important.

From the beginning, and for all of these years, *TCR* has been a team effort and continues to be that today. We love what we do. In television there is no such thing as a one-person success story because, more than most jobs, TV is a team effort. No one can be successful in this business without help from others. I am so grateful for the ones who helped me to get this show up and running, and for the ones who have helped me keep it going for almost fifty years, that I don't want to simply list their names. I want you to know something about them.

John MacLean, the original host, set the tone for the show, and today I can easily admit that had I been granted my wish to host the show when it first went on the air, the program probably wouldn't have made it. I wasn't mature enough or ready enough, and John was the initial draw that got people to tune in. His easy style and likeability established the early success of *4 Country*, and I thank him for that.

Jay Rydman was the first non-news photographer to work on the show. He was hired with a production film background and came to us from Ohio. He was the first person to say, "Let's kick this up a notch or two."

Jamie Aitken came to work with me in the early 1980s; I hired him from his "just out of college" job producing *PM Magazine* in Wichita Falls. He was the one who truly helped to establish who we are and what this show is all about. Jamie is the best TV writer I have ever known personally and is still number one in my book. He gave ten great years to the show.

Jason Anderson first approached me when I was twenty-nine years old and the youth director for the high school kids at a church in Waxahachie, Texas. He started volunteering to work with us when he was still in high school, and after college he came to work on *4 Country Reporter*. When I left

KDFW-TV to move the show to WFAA-TV, Jason was one of the guys I took with me, along with Jamie Aitken and Larry Ellis. Jason and I are very close friends, more like brothers. I would do anything for him and know he would do the same for me. He always has.

Michael Grant was an executive with Belo Corporation, the owners of WFAA-TV when I worked there. He left Belo to join our little company and spent the next fifteen years keeping us on track and on message. He retired a few years ago, but not before making an impact on our group and our product that will last forever.

Brian Hawkins has more than thirty years with the show and with me. From the moment I met him, I knew there was something special there, though I couldn't quite figure him out at first. Brian and I have traveled the world together doing both *TCR* and corporate work. We have laughed together and we have cried together, and we are senior members of the Texas Country Reporter Admiration Society. Our love for this show, what it's about and the people we meet, can't easily be defined or explained, but if you get *it*, you get *us*.

Our current crew is one of the best I have worked with in the history of *TCR*. Maybe *the* best. Besides Brian Hawkins, it includes:

Mike Snyder, our senior producer, who is a stickler for detail and for getting it right. While I care about the tiniest of things, I don't like to deal with them. Mike, however, is someone who loves the nuts and bolts and is a student of how they best go together. He's also an incredible writer and a wonderful teacher to our younger staff members.

Martin Perry, who has been with our group for more than thirty years and has devoted most of his adult life to *TCR* and the other productions our company does. He has been in love with the *art* of television since he was eight years old and even has childhood drawings he did of TV studios. Martin is an artist and a craftsman, and there is nothing in television he cannot do. He is my go-to guy for advice and counsel on so many things, and I love the man. He set the standard early on in our company for doing the right thing.

Christy Carnes, who, shortly after Martin Perry arrived, joined us to help keep the business part of our job straight. Our corporate business was exploding, and production people usually aren't very business savvy. Christy became an incredibly important part of our team and stayed with us for twenty-five years. Sadly, we lost her early in 2020 at the young age of fifty-four. She will be missed by everyone who knew her.

Dan Stricklin, who has personally shot and edited more than a thousand stories for *TCR*. For more than twenty years Dan has been there by my side, working diligently to make sure the product we air remains the quality show we are known for, and that we hold true to the reason I wanted to start it in the first place. Dan is a Texas treasure himself.

Quintin Blackwell, who shadowed Kelli while she was anchoring the news in Beaumont, Texas, at KFDM-TV and while he was still a student at Sam Houston State University in Huntsville. He constantly brings new ideas and creativity to our business. He is a great storyteller and has learned to do just about everything. He is an important part of our team.

Ben Hartmann, who is our newest employee and a Dallas-born and -bred boy like me. He knows things that went on before he was born, not a common quality for many of his generation, and he truly loves to connect life's dots and see how things came to be. We can throw anything Ben's way, and it will not only get done, it will get done well. We call him "the old soul."

Jo Caudle, who has worked for me for years, first as the general manager at our ranch in the Hill Country, where she ran the boutique hotel and spa. Some years later Jo wanted to move back to Dallas and "retire." She now works part-time keeping us organized and on track.

And probably the biggest improvement brought to *TCR* by just one person was when I finally convinced my wife, Kelli, to quit her job as a news anchor and join me as cohost of the show. Kelli's arrival seemed to spawn a renewed spirit among all of us, probably because she was coming directly from the negative day-to-day of most TV newsrooms into our world, where we only talk about good people and positive things. Kelli was so excited to be a part of *TCR* and to spread her undying will to see the good side of even the worst situations. She made what we thought of as our little Pollyanna world even better. And, for me, it made my life incredible. Now, every day of shooting stories is like being on vacation with my wife and best friends. I am blessed.

MANY COMPANIES REFER TO THEIR STAFFS AS MEMBERS OF their family, and many say "our employees are our most important asset," but at *TCR* we mean it when we say it. We are like brothers and sisters who don't always agree but who constantly work toward the same goal.

There was a time in the early days when the *4 Country Reporter* crew consisted of a photographer and me, just two guys putting together a weekly half-hour show the best way we knew how.

Today there are a few more people, but the goal is the same. And we are still having so much fun doing it, we cannot imagine *not* doing it.

TCR is in our hearts and souls.